SYMBOLISM AND BELIEF

Gifford Lectures

by the same author

HELLENISM AND CHRISTIANITY

SIBYLS AND SEERS

THOUGHTS ON INDIAN DISCONTENTS

THE HOPE OF A WORLD TO COME
(*George Allen & Unwin*)

CHRISTIANITY
(*Thornton Butterworth*)

HISTORY OF EGYPT
UNDER THE PTOLEMIC DYNASTY
(*Methuen & Co.*)

JERUSALEM UNDER HIGH PRIESTS
(*E. Arnold & Co.*)

LATER GREEK RELIGION
(*J. M. Dent & Sons*)

WORLD OF GREECE AND ROME
(*T. Nelson & Sons*)

STOICS AND SCEPTICS

THE POEMS OF LEONIDAS OF TARENTUM
(*Clarendon Press, Oxford*)

SYMBOLISM AND BELIEF

by

EDWYN BEVAN

New York
THE MACMILLAN COMPANY
1938

FIRST PUBLISHED IN 1938

TO MY FRIEND

ALFRED EDWARD TAYLOR

without whose prompting and
encouragement these lectures
would never have been written

PREFACE

THE lectures contained in this volume were given for the University of Edinburgh on Lord Gifford's foundation in the years 1933 and 1934. I have delayed their publication in the hope that with process of time I might, by further reading and thought, be able to expand and modify them, so as to make them more worthy of presentation to the public in the form of a book. This hope has been so meagrely realized that it now seems best to let them go forth, with all their imperfections on their head, hardly at all altered from the form in which they were delivered. Some changes in arrangement have been made in the order of lectures: the two on Time now follow immediately the two on the spatial symbol of Height. Four lectures have been omitted altogether from the present volume, those on image-worship and doctrines condemning the manufacture of images in antiquity and in the Christian Church. Since in the rest of the lectures the symbolism of material objects in worship was not the kind of symbolism under consideration, these four lectures seemed somewhat of a digression from the main line of argument. I hope later on to issue them as a small book by themselves.

As is generally known, Lord Gifford's Will prescribes that lecturers on his foundation are not to ask their audience to believe any statement on the ground of any special revelation, whether contained in Scripture or the dogma of a Church, but to rest what they affirm solely upon grounds of reason. That is to say, their basis must be the facts of the world so far as they are accessible to the reason common to mankind. I hope that I have nowhere transgressed this restriction imposed by the munificent benefactor to whom these lectures owe their existence. Of course beliefs entertained by the Christian Church, or by Theists, are, as psychological facts, among the indisputable facts of the world, and a Gifford lecturer is, I take it, permitted to point to them, as such, though he may not ask his hearers to accept them on the authority of Church or Scripture.

Since my two lectures on Time were written, a noteworthy contribution to the subject, from a Christian standpoint, has been made by Mr. F. H. Brabant in his Bampton Lectures, *Time and Eternity in Christian Thought* (delivered in 1936, published in 1937). It was unfortunate for me that I had not Mr. Brabant's book before me, when I wrote my two lectures.

Of one thing I am sure: that the questions I have raised regarding the element of symbolism in our religious conceptions take us to the very heart of the religious problem. How inadequate my attempts to answer them have been no one can be more conscious than I am. But if I have succeeded in putting the questions themselves in a somewhat clearer light, so that the thought of others may be directed upon them with richer result, that at any rate is something which I trust the University which honoured me by appointing me to this lectureship will accept as something worth doing.

January 1938

8

Contents

INTRODUCTORY

"SYMBOLISM and Belief" is the subject chosen for these lectures. In his little book on *Symbolism* Professor Whitehead gives a definition of that term with which we may start. "The human mind," he says, "is functioning symbolically when some components of its experience elicit consciousness, beliefs, emotions, and usages, respecting other components of its experience." That definition will perhaps have to be qualified for our purposes as we proceed. A symbol certainly, I think, means something presented to the senses or the imagination—usually to the senses—which stands for something else. Symbolism in that way runs through the whole of life. Every moment we are seeing objects or hearing sounds or smelling smells which bring to our minds a vast complex of things other than themselves—words, for instance, as spoken or written signs. And if symbolism thus runs through life as a whole, it is a factor of the first importance in religion.

But we have, for our purposes, to make a distinction at the outset between two different kinds of symbols. There are visible objects or sounds which stand for something of which we already have direct knowledge. Such symbols are not intended to give us any information about the nature of the thing or things symbolized, but to remind us of them, or tell us something about their action at the particular moment, or prompt us to act in a certain way at the particular moment because of them. The Union Jack does not give a patriotic Briton any information about his country or the part it has played in the world, but it reminds him of a whole world of things which he knows otherwise. The sound of a trumpet announcing the arrival of a king to inspect his army, or the tolling of a bell to announce his death do not tell those who hear the sound anything about the appearance or character of the king: nor would it give them any idea of what coming to inspect an army meant, or what dying meant, if they had not already the idea of those things in their minds: the sound tells them merely that the man they otherwise know is going to perform the action, or has suffered the experience, which they otherwise knew, at that particular moment of time. Or, thirdly, the trumpet which orders the troops to get up in the morning or begin their march, does not tell them anything about getting up in the morning or marching which they do not know already; it tells them only that these actions, of which they have already definite ideas, acquired otherwise, have to be performed now.

The other kind of symbols purport to give information about the things they symbolize, to convey knowledge of their nature, which those who see or hear the symbols have not had before or have not otherwise. There is the old story of someone born blind having explained to him what the colour scarlet was by his being told that it was like the sound of a trumpet. Whether that was a happy analogy or not, it is plain that the only possible way in which a person born blind could be given any information regarding colour is by the use of some things within his own experience, as symbols working by analogy.

This difference between the purpose of the two

different kinds of symbol implies a difference in their essential character. The symbols of the first kind, which remind, or signal, or command need have no resemblance at all to the thing symbolized. A Union Jack is not like our country: the word "lion" is not like a lion. Their connexion with the thing symbolized is either a matter of deliberate human arrangement, of convention, νόμῳ not φύσει in the Greek phrase, or has come about by a natural connexion in the actual events of our past experience which causes the presentation of certain objects to our senses now to call up a mass of other things which in the past we have experienced as accompanying or following the things we now see or hear or imagine. The connexion in either case is not one of similarity. The smell of a flower may now call up for us the days of our childhood, may in that way stand for them or symbolize them to us, though the smell does not resemble the other experiences connected with it in childhood.

But in the case of the second kind of symbols, those which purport to give information about the nature of something not otherwise known, resemblance is essential. The man born blind could not get any good from being told that scarlet was like the blowing of a trumpet unless there were a similitude of some kind between the two things—it may be the resemblance in the emotional reaction which each provokes. No doubt in the case of the other kind of symbols, resemblance may come in as well to reinforce the action of certain symbols upon the mind—many words, for instance, or phrases are onomatopoeic. "Quadrupedante pedum sonitu quatit ungula campum" does resemble in sound the galloping of a horse. The weeping-willow, taken by the Elizabethans as a symbol of unhappy love, does resemble in its lines the drooping head and hanging hands. But the resemblance in the case of symbols of the former kind—those

13

which remind or signal or command—is an extra thrown in: it is not essential. It would be possible to call up in the imagination the idea of a horse galloping in words that had no resemblance to the sound of galloping, or if convention had once made a holly-bush instead of a weeping-willow the symbol of unhappy love, an association would in time be created in the mind between them, so that the sight of holly would immediately suggest the other. But in the case of symbols which purport to give information about something not otherwise known the resemblance, as has just been said, is essential.

When we turn from these general considerations about symbols to the field of religion, we see at once that symbols of both kinds have an important place there. Visible objects in great variety, sounds in words and music and bells, smells in incense, are used to remind men effectively of great complexes of things they know or believe otherwise, or signal some special moment in the *cultus*, or prompt to some immediate religious act. But also in religion things are presented to the senses, or ideas presented to the mind, which purport, not to call to mind other things within the experience of the worshipper, but to convey to him knowledge of things beyond the range of any human experience. They are like the blowing of a trumpet to the man born blind, something chosen within the worshipper's experience to tell him about something lying outside his experience. We see now how Professor Whitehead's definition of symbolism, if we applied it to the religious field we are studying, would be inadequate, unless we took the view that human experience covers all the Reality there is and there is nothing outside it. I do not think that Professor Whitehead meant to affirm that: he was only thinking of symbolism as applied to the field of human experience which it was the task of his little book to consider.

14

In these lectures we shall not have to do with symbols of the former class. We shall not go into the history of religious ritual, the vast mass of symbolical actions by which different peoples have expressed their devotion according to their different conceptions of the deity or the peculiar suggestions of their natural environment. But our time will be given to a consideration of the other kind of symbols, those which purport to give information about the unseen world, those in which resemblance of some sort between the symbol and the thing symbolized is essential.

That all the conceptions we can have of God or of the spiritual world are inadequate symbols is now a religious commonplace. But it is odd to think that this belief which we to-day take for granted has not always been held by men. Milton, indeed, represents it as having been told to the first man by the sociable archangel during a pleasant conversation one sunshiny day in the bowers of Eden.

> High matter thou injoinst me, O prime of men,
>
> .   .   .   .   .
>
> The secrets of another world, perhaps
> Not lawful to reveal. Yet for thy good
> This is dispenc't, and what surmounts the reach
> Of human sense, I shall delineate so,
> By lik'ning spiritual to corporeal forms,
> As may express them best, though what if Earth
> Be but the shadow of Heav'n, and things therein
> Each to other like, more than on earth is thought ?[1]

It is Milton rather than Raphael who speaks in that last phrase, for by general opinion on earth the archangel could hardly have meant what was thought by a single human couple, or perhaps by Adam alone. But it is odd to look back in the real history of men and see how far from having been general in antiquity the idea was that there was a world to which our conceptions of material

---

[1] *Paradise Lost*, v. 563–576.

form and time did not apply. I do not know that you find it earlier than Plato among the Greeks. You no doubt find many expressions in the fragments of earlier Greek literature, dwelling on the limitations of human knowledge, like the well-known fragment of Xenophanes "That man has never yet been born, nor ever shall be, who knoweth the certain truth about the gods and about the things I utter concerning the universe; for even though he should hit the mark most perfectly in his speech, he himself knoweth not when he doth so: everything is a matter of opinion." Or a fragment of Pindar: "What conceit hast thou of wisdom, wherein one man is but a little stronger than another? Yea, by no manner of means shall a man search with his human mind into the thoughts of the gods: surely of a mortal mother was he born." No doubt the idea that the universe was very big and the part of it a man knew very little, the idea that the life of supernatural beings was something more splendid and glorious than any life lived by men, such ideas were quite common. But that is something different from recognizing the existence of a world to which our categories of space and time do not apply. The world in which disembodied souls were thought of as living was invisible, but it was thought still to be spatial and the disembodied souls to be material, like a breath or a vapour. Perhaps one may see an approach to the idea of a mode of existence, wholly different from man's existence in space and time, in the teaching of Parmenides and the Eleatics that the variety and motion which man's senses seem to show him are illusions and that the world is really uniform and stationary. But with Plato you get clearly laid down that the world of eternal ideas, the world which alone is truly real, is non-material and timeless. You get the recognition that men can speak of that world only in language which is groping and inadequate.

Supreme Reality [τὸ πρῶτον, "the First"] the Good in itself, the Good to which no predicate can be applied; we are obliged to use such a form of speech, because we have no other way of expressing it. . . . What! Is that which *Is* by its own nature not good? Yes, it is good, but not good in the way in which the Supreme Reality is good. It [the Supreme Reality] does not have goodness as a quality belonging to it: it *is* good in itself (VI. 2. 17).

Shall we say that Necessity made itself into a Reality [in order to explain the existence of the Supreme Reality]? Nay, we cannot even say that it ever became a Reality, since everything real has come into existence only subsequently to It, and through It. How then could we say of that which is antecedent to all realization that it was made real by something else—or even by Itself? This then which cannot be said to have become real—what is it? Nay, all we can do is to depart in silence. We must leave the matter as something which brings our mind to a standstill and search no further. . . . When we have bethought us of the absurdity involved in the very way our minds work, we no longer set any outline about Him, no longer draw, as it were, a circle round Him, describing Him as just so big. We recognize that bigness is not any property attaching to Him. Quality, as such, does not attach to Him. No form belongs to Him, not even one for the Intellect. No relation to anything else. For He subsists by Himself, before there *is* any other. What meaning can there be any longer in saying: "This and this property belongs to Him?" How can we use such an utterance, when everything else said about Him is only a negation? So that instead of saying: "This and this property belongs to Him," it would be truer to say: "Not even this or this property belongs to Him." The belonging to Him of property of any kind is impossible (VI. 8. 11).

Plotinus indicates his own procedure. Since no phrase you can use about the Supreme is adequate to the Reality, all you can do is to throw out your phrase at It and then deny that the phrase is true. This leaves a kind of impression or idea in the hearer's mind, but at the same time prevents him from committing himself to it too fast and fixedly. In the later Neo-Platonists the practice comes up which went on in the later mystical tradition, of calling the higher apprehension of the Supreme Reality *nescience* because it is a knowledge which transcends knowledge in the ordinary sense, transcends knowledge consisting in a relation between intellectual concepts, expressible in language. The philosopher Isidorus (5th century A.D.), we are told in the fragments of the life of him written by Damascius, "did not care to offer homage to images: he went to the gods themselves direct, the gods who are hidden, not in the holy places of temples, but hidden within the soul, in the inexpressible region, whatever it may be, of nescience (ἀγνωσία). How then did he go to gods such as these? He went by a kind of mighty love, itself inexpressible. What we mean by this love those who have experience of it know, but to say what it is in words is impossible, even to conceive it in thought is not any easier" (*Vita Isidori* § 38).

This conviction that ultimate Reality was indescribable in human language was the result amongst the Greeks of a process of intellectual activity, a thinking about the universe and about the way in which the human mind worked in its attempt to understand the universe. When we turn to the other great tradition which has gone to make up our European culture, the Hebrew, we cannot expect to find there the same philosophical interest. The apprehension of Reality which we see in the Old Testament prophets was of quite a different kind. Yet here too we find the conviction that God is, to use Rudolf Otto's phrase, the *Ganz Andere*, the wholly different from man, speaking with a power of command from an invisible world. If we leave out of account the peculiar development of pantheistic mysticism in India, seen already in the Upanishads, which are perhaps older than Amos and Hosea (8th century B.C.), it cannot be denied that the idea of God in the Old Testament, as we have it, is less anthropomorphic than the idea of God in any other religion of the ancient world, till we come to the philosophical transformation of the religious tradition in Greece.

It was not, of course, philosophy, but a religious sense

20

of what was appropriate—whether you regard that as due to the action of the Divine Spirit in the minds of men or not—which made the Hebrew prophets remove from Jehovah all those mythological accessories—a visible form, a consort, a family—which other peoples attached to their gods. We find the idea insisted upon that Jehovah cannot be seen. This may well at the outset have been such an idea as was common to Israelites and other peoples—that it was dangerous to see a divine being. Indeed, that is clearly the idea in some Old Testament passages. "We shall surely die," Manoah says (Judges xiii. 22) "because we have seen God." "And Jacob called the name of the place Peniel: for, said he, I have seen God face to face and my life is preserved!" (Genesis xxxii. 30). But such a primitive idea might pass gradually, as men's minds became more mature, into the idea that man could not see God because man's faculties were incapable of apprehending the Divine Reality. When Deuteronomy forbids the making of any image of Jehovah "for ye saw no form on the day that Jehovah spoke unto you in Horeb out of the midst of the fire" (iv. 15), it is implied that Jehovah actually has no form of a visible kind. How important it was felt to insist upon this characteristic of Jehovah is shown by the prominence given in Judaism after the Exile to the law which forbade the making of images. How careful Ezekiel is, when he does, in the chariot vision, represent Jehovah by the figure of a man, to insist that it was an appearance only, by an odd reiteration of words to guard against the supposition that he was describing the reality as it was! "Above the firmament was"—not a throne but—"the likeness of a throne . . . and upon the likeness of the throne was the likeness as the appearance of a man above upon it. And I saw as the colour of amber, as the appearance of fire round about within it, from the appearance of his loins even upward, and from the appearance of his loins even downward, I saw as it were the appearance of fire" (i. 26, 27).

All this is not, of course, equivalent to a philosophical belief that God and the spiritual world are essentially indescribable by any categories drawn from human earthly experience, but it certainly points that way. When a Jew, with his inherited belief in the impossibility of seeing God and the impiety of attributing to God any material form like that of a human body, came into contact with the Platonic philosophy which taught the essential incomprehensibility of God by human thought, the two lines of tradition were congenial and easily fused. We see this in Philo.

Of the Reality ($\tau\grave{o}$ $\check{o}\nu$) above the particular Divine Powers nothing is apprehended save that it *is*. The Divine ($\tau\grave{o}$ $\theta\epsilon\hat{\iota}o\nu$) visible and apprehensible and appearing everywhere is in truth invisible and inapprehensible and in no place, even as the oracle says: "Here am I standing before thee" [$\pi\rho\grave{o}$ $\tauo\hat{v}$ $\sigma\epsilon$ (Exodus xvii. 6), which Philo elsewhere explained as meaning "before thou wast," that is, God has steadfast being before any part of the transient world exists], seeming indeed to be shown and to be apprehended, though transcending created things before all showing and before all appearance."[1]

Philo explains the passage in Exodus, in which Moses is allowed to see the back, but not the face, of God, as meaning:

Everything which is subsequent to God the virtuous man may apprehend: God alone is inapprehensible. That is to say, God is inapprehensible by direct frontal approach—for such approach would imply God's being disclosed such as He is: but He is apprehensible through the Powers which are consequent upon His being; for those Powers do not present His being, nature, essence ($o\check{v}\sigma\acute{\iota}a$) but only His existence ($\check{v}\pi\alpha\rho\xi\iota s$) from the resultant effects (II. p. 37).

And what wonder [Philo asks] if the Supreme Reality ($\tau\grave{o}$ $\check{o}\nu$) is inapprehensible to men, when even the mind in each one of us is something we cannot know? For who knows the nature, essence ($o\check{v}\sigma\acute{\iota}a$) of

[1] II. p. 255 (in Cohn and Wendland's Edition), as emended by Wendland.

the Soul? (III. p. 158). When even the Logos is unspeakable, so must the Supreme Reality be, and therefore inconceivable and inapprehensible, so that when Scripture says: "The Lord appeared unto Abraham" we are not to suppose that the Ground of the Universe Himself shone forth to Abraham and was manifested to him—what human mind would be capable of containing the greatness of such an appearance?—but only that one of God's subordinate Powers, His Royalty, was caused to appear (III. p. 159).

What comes to the same thing is Philo's application of the term ἄποιος ("without qualities") to God. Ἄποιος γὰρ ὁ θεός, οὐ μόνον οὐκ ἀνθρωπόμορφος, "God is not only not human in form; He is without qualities at all" (I. p. 70). In one place indeed, even to say that God is ἄποιος seems to Philo to make a statement about God which man has no right to make. The expression attributed in Genesis to God, "I have sworn by myself," means, Philo says:

None of the things which serve as warrants can be a firm warrant concerning God; for God has not shown His nature to any of them; He has made it invisible to the whole race. Who would have power to affirm positively that the Ground of the Universe is bodiless or that He is body, that He is of a certain quality *or that He is without qualities*, in a word to make any statement about His essence or character or mode of relations or movement? God alone can make an affirmation about Himself, seeing that He alone knows His own nature infallibly and exactly (I. 159).

By calling God ἄποιος Philo does not mean that He is without positive character. He only means that no human expression which attributes a particular quality to God can be adequate to the Reality. Every such statement is in some degree a mis-statement. The same thing some thinkers of our own time have expressed by saying that the only true mode of speech in regard to God is in the second person, 'Thou';[1] God is the supreme 'Thou'; in addressing himself directly to God man can come into

[1] This has been said, probably quite independently, by the Protestant professor of philosophy at Tübingen, Karl Heim, and by the French philosopher, Gabriel Marcel, now a Catholic.

contact with the Ground of the Universe and have a sense of the Reality which touches him; but the moment he makes a statement about God in the third person—even though it is that God is good—he is more or less disfiguring the truth. To say indeed that God may properly be addressed as 'Thou' is in a way to state that He is personal, since you cannot with any meaning address an impersonal thing as 'Thou': you give it fictitious personality, if you do. Nevertheless, the thinkers we refer to would no doubt say that though your action in addressing God as 'Thou' was wholly right, nevertheless, if in your justification of it you bring in such a term as 'personal,' if you make a statement about God in which by the copula 'is' personality, or anything else is attached to Him as something other than Himself, as an idea which can be applied to Him, then your form of words can be no more than a futile attempt to express the inexpressible. That, no doubt, is what Philo meant by calling God ἄποιος. We have seen that Plotinus later on declared that the Supreme Reality was without properties, and there is a precise parallel in Vedantic Hinduism, according to which the supreme *brahma* is *nirguna*, without *gunas*, the Sanskrit word for qualities or properties.

In Christian theology it became a fixed dogma that God is incomprehensible, that all human language applied to Him tries by figures and parables to state truth about a Reality which infinitely exceeds all man's powers of understanding or imagination. It would be a waste of time to prove by a series of quotations something which runs through all Christian literature. The classical expression of this conviction was already given in the great phrase of St. Paul. "For now we see through a glass darkly," "through a mirror in a riddle." Later on, no doubt, formulations of the belief in God's being essentially incomprehensible owed a good deal to the Neo-Platonic

24

tradition, which infiltrated into the Church mainly through the Pseudo-Dionysius Areopagites. The belief, of course, as formulated by that writer, finds its most extreme expression in the doctrine of the *via negativa*, that God can be reached only by stripping off every quality which the human mind has attributed to Him, so that the ultimate and perfect apprehension of God can be described as nescience (ἀγνωσία, "unknowing").[1] Similarly, some Christian mystics have felt it appropriate to describe God as "Nothing."[2] Even ordinary Christian theology, which may shrink from this extreme of paradox, insists that God is essentially incomprehensible.

But if that were all that Christianity had to say of the Ground of the Universe, Christianity would be indistinguishable from the most complete Agnosticism. The difficulty is that while Christian theology asserts that God is unknowable, it simultaneously asserts that God can be known. And not Christianity only, but any form of belief which can be called theistic is bound to assert that in some sense God can be known.

We must expect to hear ever afresh some hostile critic of Christianity look round with triumph after uttering, as if it were a new penetrating thrust, the word "anthropomorphic." There are no doubt views of God which are *called* impersonal and which have had wide prevalence among men—those embodied in religions which are pantheist or tending to pantheism. But it is a mistake to call such ideas of God impersonal in the same sense in which a material force like electricity or gravity is impersonal. For although all these religions deny that God is an individual person in the way a man is, they form their

---

[1] καὶ ἔστιν αὖθις ἡ θειοτάτη τοῦ θεοῦ γνῶσις ἡ δι᾽ ἀγνωσίας γινωσκομένη. Pseudo-Dionys. *De Divin. Nomin.* Ch. vii, p. 872 (Migne).

[2] καὶ ἐν πᾶσι πάντα ἐστί, καὶ ἐν οὐδένι οὐδέν. Pseudo-Dionys., loc. cit. "Dum vero (divina bonitas) incomprehensibilis intelligitur, per excellentiam non immerito nihilum vocatur." John Scotus Erigena.

25

idea of God out of elements which we know only as constituents of a human personality, and can imagine only as belonging to a personality analogous to man's.

Thus, Vedantic Hinduism ascribes to its Supreme Reality the characteristic of joy (*ananda*); the Stoics ascribed to their Divine Fire which interpenetrated the kosmos the characteristics of infallible wisdom and reason; Mr. Wells, in one of the phases of his speculation, asked us to believe that behind all the movement of the world was a Purpose which might be written with a capital letter, even if it must not be taken to imply any individual Person. A criticism urged against all such views of the Ground of the Universe is that to speak of a joy which is not the joy of someone who rejoices or a wisdom which is not the wisdom of someone who is wise or a purpose which is not the purpose of someone who purposes is a form of words without meaning. If that criticism is just, such views make the distinction in human personality, between that which is merely human (or at any rate belongs only to finite individuality) and that which is analogous to God, in the wrong place; in taking away from God personal individuality they make it meaningless to attach to Him the ideas of joy or wisdom or purpose. Whether the criticism is just or there is some sense in which joy or wisdom or purpose can be conceived to exist in a diffused manner, like the ether, without any individual centre, we need not now inquire. What is plain is that even if personal individuality can be taken away from God, and joy or wisdom or purpose left Him, such a view is still anthropomorphic.

Not to get rid of anthropomorphism, which is impossible if man is going to have any idea of God at all, but to make the division between right and wrong anthropomorphism where it ought to be made—that is the main problem for all philosophy of religion.

Such questions as these regarding the relation of man's symbolical conceptions to Reality we shall have in our course of lectures to consider. In the present course we shall consider first three mental images drawn from men's earthly experience, which have had a very wide use in religion, as presenting something which is believed to characterize the Divine life—images which at the outset were no doubt understood by men as literal descriptions of God or of the Divine world, and which, although we no longer understand them literally, we cannot discard, we cannot eliminate from discourse about God, so inextricably are they woven into the fabric of our religious thought and language. The first we shall take is the symbol of spatial height—the tendency of men everywhere to regard the chief Divine Power as living in the sky, to place Him as high up as is imaginable, which goes with the odd, but universal, association of distance from the earth's surface with spiritual or moral worth, seen in such words as "superior," "sublime." We shall next in Lectures IV and V consider the application to God of expressions taken from men's experience of Time, the idea of endless duration. Then we pass to a symbol of almost equal extension, that of light, in its double reference to knowledge and to glory. This will be the subject of the VIth lecture. The fourth symbol we shall consider will be that of Spirit, breath, air in motion; this will take up the VIIth and VIIIth lectures. After this we shall come to a symbol taken, not from material nature, but from the inner life of man, the "Wrath" of God (Lectures IX and X). The remaining six Lectures will deal no longer with any particular symbol, but with the general relation of symbolism to truth and belief.

HEIGHT

THE Divine Being whom the prophet Isaiah says that he saw in a vision he describes as "sitting on a throne high and lifted up." Another prophet whose writings are incorporated with those of Isaiah describes the same Divine Being as "the High and Lofty One that inhabiteth eternity." The idea which Hebrew prophets in these words apply to the Supreme Being of the Universe, as they conceive Him, was far from being peculiar to them. If there are two characteristics upon which men all over the world from the earliest stages of human thought traceable, have agreed in attributing to the Chief Being of the Universe, they are height and length of life. So much is this the case that when man reached a stage of thought in which he came to understand clearly that height was not to be attributed to God in a literal spatial sense, the idea of height, as an essential characteristic of supreme worth, was so interwoven in the very texture of all human languages that it is impossible for us even to-day to give in words a rendering of what was meant by the metaphor. We are inevitably forced, if we try to explain the metaphor, to bring in the very metaphor to be explained. Supposing we say that what it means is that God is superior to all other beings, the word "superior" is simply a Latin word meaning "higher." If we say that it means that God "excels," "celsus" again is a Latin word for "high." If we say that it emphasizes God as "transcendent," transcendence embodies the metaphor and suggests a visual image of God occupying an otherwise empty space above the space occupied by all the created Universe. The Sanskrit word, *brahman* (neuter), Rudolf Otto tells us in his book on the Aryan deities[1]— the word which is specially used to denote the divine, or, as Otto expresses it in his terminology, "numinous" power—is explained in the Indian tradition as derived from a word meaning "height." *Brahman* was used with noticeable frequency for a hymn of praise to a deity. But also the word for "height" (*brih*) was similarly used. The singer summons men to sing a "*high* song" to the god. "Here," Otto comments, "the word for 'high' is clearly used to signify what is sublime, wonderful, worthy of admiration."

Language does not, of course, apply the metaphor of height to God alone, but generally equates height with value, or with a kind of value—the value which makes something deserve admiration or reverence. The word "superior" is commonly used as connoting the possession of more of this value. We contrast "higher" with "lower" pleasures, "high" thoughts with base thoughts, and so on. To call God the Most High means that this value belongs to God in a supreme degree. I cannot say that, observe, without bringing in the word "supreme" and the word "degree"; a degree is in its literal meaning a step by which we may move up and down in space.

Our survey of symbols in religion showed that the symbols by which man has tried to express his idea of the Divine are taken partly from the material world accessible to his senses, partly from constituents of conscious life as he knows it in himself from within and in others, that

[1] *Gottheit und Gottheiten der Arier* (1932), p. 47.

is to say from human emotions, acts of will, values. Of those symbols which are taken from the outside material world the significance of height seems to have come to men everywhere immediately and instinctively. We may feel it to-day so obvious as not to call for any explanation. And yet if one fixes the attention on what height literally is, the reason of this universal instinct may seem problematic. For height literally is nothing but distance from the earth's surface or extension of something on the earth's surface in a direction at right angles outwards. The proposition: Moral and spiritual worth is greater or less in ratio to the distance outwards from the earth's surface, would certainly seem to be, if stated nakedly like that, an odd proposition. And yet that is the premiss which seems implied in this universal association of height with worth and with the divine.

To survey in detail the imaginations connected in the multitudinous religions of mankind with the belief that the gods—or the chief of the gods—live in the sky would take a volume by itself, and would perhaps in the end be for our purposes only a proving of the obvious. Sir James Frazer, a Gifford Lecturer in this place nine years ago, gave from the immense store of his knowledge in the anthropological field an invaluable presentation of facts, and he himself refers those who desire fuller data to the work of Professor Pettazzoni of Rome (published in 1922) on primitive beliefs in the Sky-God.[1] We shall, however, note that some recent researches, especially those of Father Wilhelm Schmidt, who has a chair of anthropology in Vienna, have made certain views regarding the primitive belief in the Sky-God which seemed a little while ago to be taken as proved appear exceedingly questionable.

The belief in the Sky-God may have, of course, two

[1] Sir J. G. Frazer, *The Worship of Nature*, Vol. I (1926).

forms according as the sky itself is personified, is identified with the Person up there, or as the Person is conceived more anthropomorphically, as a being with a form more or less like that of a man, and the sky is regarded simply as the place in which he lives. In the ancient civilizations which have advanced beyond the primitive stage—the Babylonian, Persian, Greek—the Sky-God is definitely a Person like a man who lives in the sky, not identical with the sky. "The Babylonian Sky-God Anu," Sir James Frazer writes, "was naturally conceived as dwelling in the radiant heaven; there was the throne on which he sat, and from which, as occasion served, he also stood up" (p. 67). Ahura Mazda, as he is conceived in Zoroastrianism, is certainly not identical with the sky. In one passage of the Avesta, quoted by Frazer, he is represented as saying, "I maintain the sky, there above, shining and seen afar, and encompassing this earth all around." . . . "It is like a garment inlaid with stars, made of a heavenly substance, which Mazda puts on" (p. 34).

The theory, however, has been largely held in recent times that this belief in a Divine Person living in the sky is the modification of a more primitive belief according to which the sky itself was believed to be animate, to be a god. Primitive man, we are told, did not regard consciousness as belonging only to men and animals, but supposed all kinds of natural objects—rocks and trees and rivers—to be endowed with conscious life. It was a later advance in rationalism which made men realize that consciousness went only with human or animal form. Thus, the primitive idea that the sky itself was a god gave place to the idea that someone of form like the human lived in the sky. You may find such a view put forward especially in regard to the Sky-God, who, we are told, was the deity of the prehistoric Indo-Europeans, Dyaûs in Sanskrit, Father Dyaus, Dyauspitar, and who is seen changed into

31

an anthropomorphic deity in the Greek Zeus and the Roman Jupiter. Look, for instance, at the opening of Professor A. B. Cook's monumental and immensely erudite work on Zeus. There arguments are put forward for accepting this view as the true one. But notice, Professor Cook quite frankly admits that there is no actual document showing us this prehistoric god identified with the sky. It is a conjectural reconstruction of what the belief of primitive Indo-Europeans must have been in days before Dyaûs or Zeus had changed from being the sky itself to being the man-like deity living in the sky. The arguments are linguistic. Even in historical times you have phrases imbedded in Greek, such as *endios*, "at midday," or the Latin *dies*, and so on, which still, Professor Cook urges, reflect the old belief for which Dyaûs meant the shining sky itself. You must suppose that such a phase of thought had existed, in order to account for such forms of speech, although you have no direct proof of it. The process by which the change took place to the anthropomorphic idea of Zeus is one, Professor Cook says, wholly hidden from us in the past, something of a mystery.

But now we have Rudolf Otto, in his book on the deities of the Aryans, declaring outright that there is no reason to suppose that the Indo-Europeans ever had this supposed Sky-God. The apparent analogy between the Sanskrit Dyauspitar and the Roman Jupiter is, Otto holds, misleading. And it must be remembered that Otto is a specialist in the field of Sanskrit studies, so that, if the arguments for believing in the primitive Aryan Sky-God are linguistic, as A. B. Cook allows, Otto's judgment on such a matter must have singular weight. Otto's theory is that, although *dyau* in the Rigveda is a common word for "sky," another word *naka* is the older word for sky; *dyau* originally meant simply "shining," and *dyaus*, "shining one," came to be equivalent to *deva*, a god, apart from any particular reference to the sky. *Dyau*, "shining," was at first applied to the sky simply as a kind of ornamental epithet, just as a word meaning "broad" was commonly applied to the earth. After the idea of marriage between Heaven and Earth became current (Otto does not seem to think that this belongs to the earliest phase of Indo-European belief), the two epithets, contrasting the two members of the pair, "the shining one" and the "broad one," came to have the value of actual names for the sky and the earth, as you find to be the case in the Vedas. The Greek Zeus is, of course, linguistically equivalent to the Sanskrit Dyaûs, but it originally described Zeus simply as a shining one, a god, and did not connote any special connexion with the sky.

The Latin phrase *"sub Jove,"* meaning "under the open sky," has been used to show that Jupiter was originally the sky, but the phrase, Otto maintains, meant, at the outset, "under the god" literally. A god was believed to live in the sky and it gave ancient man a feeling of discomfort that he had nothing between him and this awe-inspiring *numen*, but this does not mean that the word for the god originally meant the sky. And as for the supposed parallel of Dyauspitar and Jupiter, "father," Otto says, means something quite different in the two cases. Dyaûs becomes "father" only after the idea of his marriage with Mother Earth is current: and in regard to that you may notice that the idea of a marriage with Earth is not specially connected with Zeus: Hera is not the earth. In Jupiter, on the other hand, the term "father" is simply a mode of address which might be used in Latin religion for any male deity in the cult: Jupiter is originally a vocative.

Otto recognizes that later on the sky becomes the special abode of the Supreme God or the gods generally.

They are represented, he says, as conquering the sky: he uses the term "Cölisierung" for this process in thought about the gods—"Caelization," "En-sky-ment." If the gods do not belong to the sky, to start with, sooner or later they become dwellers in the sky.

But to all such arguments it may be objected that an important consideration has been left out. Granting that there is no direct proof of a primitive Indo-European god identical with the sky, it is not enough simply to analyse the data of Sanskrit and other Indo-European languages. You must consider the beliefs of other peoples outside the Indo-European sphere: if you find evidence elsewhere that at the most primitive level of human culture the sky was regarded as itself a god, if you find such a belief amongst the races on the most primitive level to-day, then it is reasonable to suppose that a similar belief preceded the belief in anthropomorphic deities living in the sky which we know in Indian and classical mythology. Yes: but do you, as a matter of fact, find the belief in question among very primitive people? Professor Foucart, when he wrote the article on "Sky Gods" in Hastings's *Encyclopedia of Religion and Ethics*, thought that you did. But he recognized—rightly—that it was a doubtful business to reduce the childish thoughts of primitive man, so far from our own, to clear, logical expression in terms of our own thought. On the question how far primitive man thought of the sky-deity as someone living in the sky, how far as the sky itself, Professor Foucart tried in that article to describe what he imagined the thought of primitive man to be. This is how he did it:

Personification, in its fundamental *processus*, starts from the idea that under the appearance and within or behind the material exterior there exists a being, or rather a personal force (of course, it cannot yet be conceived as immaterial) closely bound to the substance of which it is the energy and the life, unable to exist without this substance, but distinct from it and, if necessary, separable from it—at least momentarily. The sky-god is therefore radically different from the substance which forms the material sky. He lives in it; he lives by it; he is mingled with it; the physical sky is not merely his habitat—it is his very substance; but the personification of a substance is distinct and separable from the substance which it animates; it is superior to it, and yet the substance is indispensable to its existence, for without it, it would return to the vortex of the impersonal forces of chaos.

This careful and subtle statement, which its delicate avoidance of making the union between God and material sky too close on the one hand, and of minimizing its closeness on the other hand, is certainly thought expressed by a highly cultured modern French scholar, expressed as no primitive man could ever have expressed it. In spite of this it might still be true that Professor Foucart was giving accurately what primitive man would have said about his ideas in our language, if he had been able to think them out clearly. But one cannot help fearing that Professor Foucart's description, like some other descriptions of the mind of primitive man, was an able exertion of the imagination, constructing a primitive man to correspond with what a present-day scholar supposes that primitive man ought to be like. For here comes along Father Wilhelm Schmidt with his substantial volumes on the *Origin of the Idea of God*,[1] and has a very different story to tell.

It should be explained that Father Schmidt begins by pointing out how misleading it is to talk at all about primitive man in the general. Amongst the primitive men still surviving to-day there are marked differences of cultural level, with corresponding differences of religious belief and practice. He accordingly devotes his attention specially to the most primitive of the primitive, those most backward in the arts of life—that means, to some, not all, of the Australian aborigines, some of the American

[1] P. W. Schmidt, *Der Ursprung der Gottesidee*, Vols. I.–VI. 1926–1935.

Indians, some of the Andaman Islanders, the African Pygmies. With regard to these races, Father Schmidt claims to have established the astonishing result that you find a purer form of religious belief than among the more advanced races—a Supreme God of ethical characteristics, who is really worshipped, and practically no magic. Of course, this result is very like that arrived at a generation ago by a distinguished Scot, Andrew Lang. When Andrew Lang called attention in some of his later books to belief in the High God among very primitive men, he was not taken very seriously by anthropologists, partly, no doubt, as Professor Rose says in the introduction to his translation of a book by Father Schmidt, because Lang was a brilliant man of letters and it seemed incredible that anyone who wrote capital light verse could be much good in anthropology. Father Schmidt tells us openly that he regards Andrew Lang as a predecessor whose conclusions have been confirmed by his own very much more extensive inquiries. They seem to show that the belief of the most primitive people surviving to-day does not at all support the theory that behind the idea of a god living in the sky was the earlier idea of a god actually identical with the sky.

Father Schmidt says in his *Origin of Religion* (translated by Professor Rose):

The Supreme Being of the Primitive culture is not nearly so indissolubly connected with the sky as he is in later cultures, especially that of the pastoral nomads. Among most peoples it is said that he used formerly to live on earth with men, whom he taught all manner of good and instructed in their social and moral laws. (Southern Andaman Islanders, South-East Australians, North Central Californians, Indians of the North-West, many Algonkin tribes.) However, another story is often told among North American primitives, namely that he came down to this earth from the sky, while among practically all peoples of primitive culture, the important doctrine is propounded that he left the earth, generally because of some sin of mankind, and went up to heaven where he now lives. . . . While the connexion of the primitive Supreme Being with the sky is

36

undoubtedly clear, it is equally manifest that he is an independent and separate personality; there can be no possible identification of him with the material sky itself (*Origin and Growth of Religion*, pp. 264, 265).

In many cases the conception of him is anthropomorphic: in the Andaman Islands he is imagined as very old with a long white beard. In a whole list of cases his form, if thought of as like that of men, is distinguished by a supernatural radiance: he is described as "shining white" or as "like fire." "Among the Maidu of North Central California we are assured that the whole form of the Supreme Being shines like the light of the sun, but that his face is always covered and no one has ever seen it, except the Evil Spirit, who did so once." But there are a number of cases amongst the most primitive people— including the people of Terra del Fuego, the Boni Negrillos of East Africa, and some of the Andamanese —who have a conception much more spiritual. The Supreme Being cannot be seen, but can only be heard or felt: he is like the wind, inapprehensible; he is without shape like the sky. The last description is that given by the Samoyeds: it does not apparently identify the Supreme Being with the sky, but only uses the sky as a figure of his freedom from spatial limitation.

Father Schmidt uses the result of his inquiries to tilt quite outspokenly against the theory of evolution in religion, the theory that all higher religions come by a gradual process of change from savage superstitions and magic. If it is found that the beliefs of the most primitive existing races show a relatively high ethical belief in a Supreme God, that fact may no doubt be pointed to as supporting the belief in a primitive revelation. And since Father Schmidt is a Roman Catholic, some other anthropologists have naturally suggested that he may have been led to his conclusions by a subconscious desire to establish the traditional belief of the Catholic Church. Still, there the facts are which Father Schmidt has put forward with elaborate documentary attestation; his competence as an anthropologist has not, I think, been questioned; and some other anthropologists who are not Roman Catholics have accepted his results as generally true. The suggestion put forward by some anthropologists, when attention was first drawn by Andrew Lang to these primitive beliefs in a High God, that they were derived from the influence of Christian missionaries, seems to be disproved by the facts and is now, I gather, no longer offered by the anthropologists of recognized authority as an explanation. Now, while it is perfectly true that a man who holds the Christian belief may be influenced by that presupposition in estimating facts, it is absurd to suppose that the Christian is the only person who comes to the study of anthropological material with a presupposition. The theory of evolution may equally be a presupposition which leads an anthropologist to pick and choose amongst facts in such a way as to establish the conclusion at which he wants to arrive.

I think in the present state of knowledge we can at any rate say that the theory of this supposed primitive identification of the Supreme God with the sky rests on very weak evidence. But it remains true that the Supreme God is regularly associated with the sky. The sky, according to the primitive belief as Father Schmidt describes it, is where he now lives. And Rudolf Otto, who denies that the Aryans had a Sky-God to start with, admits that sooner or later the process of *Cölisierung* took place, by which the gods were regarded as having the sky for their home. Father Schmidt in one passage which I read out, indicated that in the pastoral nomad phase of primitive culture the connexion between the deity and the sky became closer than it had been on the more primitive level. Wherever the myth of a marriage between Sky and Earth came into currency, the Sky itself was necessarily regarded as itself a person.

38

In Egyptian religion the Sky-deity seems, as represented pictorially, to be the sky itself. It may be impossible to say how far Egyptians in the historical period took such imagery literally. The Sky-deity, feminine in Egypt, is represented as arched over the body of her husband the Earth-god, as the real sky is arched over the earth. Her whole body and limbs are bespangled with stars and her son, the Sun-god, is sometimes spoken of as entering her mouth when he sets, and traversing her whole body till he reappears at the opposite extremity of it the next morning. The identification of the Sky-deity with the sky itself seems here to be close.

You cannot, of course, say that it is utterly impossible, even on Professor Wilhelm Schmidt's theory, that the anthropomorphical conception of the Person up in the sky which you get in Babylonian, Persian and Greek religion, was preceded by a phase of thought in which the sky itself was personified. Only on Professor Schmidt's theory this personification of the sky would not be the most primitive human view. It would itself be the degradation of a view which had thought of the Supreme Being more anthropomorphically, as the Person in the sky. The view of the Babylonians, Persians and Greeks would then be a return to anthropomorphism, not an advance to something quite new. But the anthropomorphism of the Babylonians and Greeks at any rate would be, on this view, much more gross than the primitive anthropomorphism inasmuch as it attributed to the gods human characteristics, bodily shape, passions, appetites, of which the primitive conception of the great God in the sky had been free. (The Zoroastrian conception of Ahura Mazda is much more spiritual.)

If it is true that the anthropomorphic conception of those ancient peoples was preceded by a phase in which the sky itself was personified, then it is curious to observe

39

that Greek thought in some of its later forms returned to the view which identified God with the sky. This was the case in Stoicism, the most popular and widespread of philosophies in the centuries immediately preceding and immediately following the rise of Christianity. Stoicism was, of course, Pantheist in so far as it asserted that everything was made out of God and that everything periodically returned into God, into the one Divine Fire. But in such a state of the world as that in which we are now living, a state in which there is a manifold of elements and things, only one region of the world retains its Divine quality, the outer envelope of the spherical universe which consists still of the Divine Fire in its proper state. And it is to that outer envelope which we look up whenever we look up into the sky. There plain before our eyes is God. Stoicism was of course unlike modern materialism in endowing this Fire, although a material element, with some of the characteristics of personality. The Fire was itself supremely wise, the fashioner of the world according to the best pattern, the director of all movement in the world to the ends of greatest worth. It was of one being with the spark of reason in each individual man. Yet it also had spatial extension as matter and formed, in fact, the sky. It had its purest individual embodiment in the fiery stars, all gods supremely intelligent, the highest kindred of man, to whom he could look up with his corporeal eyes any cloudless night.

Before Stoicism, the identification of the sky with Zeus had been made a current idea in the Greek world by the fifth-century sophists. It is put forward in the much-quoted verses of Euripides (Fragment, 935):[1]

[1] Ὁρᾷς τὸν ὑψοῦ τόνδ' ἄπειρον αἰθέρα
καὶ γῆν πέριξ ἔχονθ' ὑγραῖς ἐν ἀγκάλαις;
τοῦτον νόμιζε Ζῆνα, τόνδ' ἡγοῦ θεόν.

For other passages in Euripides, see Paley's edition, Vol. I. p. xxviii.

> Thou seest yon infinite Aether high above,
> Engirdling Earth with soft intangible arms:
> Hold this for Zeus; give this the name of God.

Herodotus had explained Persian religion to the Greeks by finding this idea in it: "The Persians," he had said, "call the whole round of the sky Zeus" (I. 131). Ennius, familiar as he was with the philosophic notions current amongst the Greeks, introduced this idea to the Romans. A line is quoted from one of his plays:

> Yon high, shining vast above us which men pray to, and call Jove.[1]

But the idea as given by Euripides and Ennius was probably different from the idea in Stoicism. Euripides and the sophists he drew from may have meant that men, by a mere imaginative fiction, attributed personality to something which was in truth impersonal, the airy expanse overhead: these verses may be just an expression of philosophical scepticism. The Stoics, on the other hand, believed quite seriously that the sky (the outmost aether, that is to say, which one could see through the region of air) was really and literally God, was Divine Reason.

The Stoic view which identified God with the outer fiery envelope of the kosmos, the highest heaven from the point of view of an inhabitant of the earth, was, of course, prepared for by the philosophy of Aristotle, which taught that the outer envelope of the world was composed of a fifth element, aether, finer than any of the old four elements. Since the doctrine of a fifth element appears in the *Epinomis*, and Professor A. E. Taylor has shown that there is no good reason for doubting that the *Epinomis* is a work of Plato himself in his old age, Aristotle was in this respect following the master of his youth. The fifth element, as Aristotle conceived it, was not indeed itself

[1] Adspice hoc sublime candens, quem invocant omnes Jovem (Ennius, quoted by Cicero, *De Natura Deorum*, II. § 65).

God: Aristotle's God was not in space at all; the *primum mobile* whence all movement in the universe was derived was itself moved by love of the transcendent God: the aether was only a material substance. Yet it was of all material substances the finest, the nearest, if we may say so, to soul. The bodies of the stars, which were for Aristotle, in his earlier phases at any rate, as for Plato, conscious divine beings, were made of aether. The *pneuma*, by which the life of a rational being was transmitted from human parent to human child—the *pneuma*, not "spirit" in our sense, but a fine air-like substance concealed in the semen—was, Aristotle says in one place,[1] "analogous to the element of which the bodies of the stars were made." The sphere of ether, therefore, up there, was for Plato and Aristotle, a diviner world than earth, the home of visible gods, the region of perfect regularity. The Stoics only took the step of bringing God into the world from outside it, of identifying him with the element composing the outermost sphere. They did not commonly distinguish this element as a fifth from the ordinary four; they called it fire; but they explained that it was a fire of a finer sort than the earthly fire we know, which burns; so that their view practically differed little from that which called it a fifth element, ether.

Thus, all the three great schools of philosophy which shaped the thoughts of men in the ancient world from Alexander to the last days of paganism, Platonic, Peripatetic, Stoic, co-operated to make them think that the sky into which they looked up was divine—was God Himself in the Stoic view, was the home of gods made of the matter nearest to soul in the Platonic and Aristotelian view. In the last century before the Christian era the epithet ὕψιστος "Highest," "Most High," had come to be attached in popular cults to various gods to express

[1] *De gen. anim.*, II. 3, p. 736.

their pre-eminent dignity. But it was specially attached to Zeus. It may well be, as Cumont supposes, that if Zeus Hypsistos or Theos Hypsistos came to be a name under which the chief god was worshipped, that was in part due to the influence of Hellenized Syrians and Babylonians, who represented their own Baal Shamîn, "Lord of the Sky," by such a Greek phrase. It is unquestionable that Jews of the Dispersion sometimes presented Jehovah to pagans as Theos Hypsistos, and that cults sprang up of mixed Jewish and pagan character addressed to the Supreme God under this name.[1] We may see in the extensive use of such a name evidence of a general feeling in the Graeco-Roman world that it was particularly important to emphasize *height* in connexion with the Divine Being. In Latin inscriptions sometimes language is strained by a new compound superlative form. Jupiter is not merely high, he is *"Exsuperantissimus."* The same term is applied by Apuleius to the Supreme God: *'Summus atque exsuperantissimus divom"* (*De Mundo*, 27). *'"Summi exsuperantissimi deorum omnium"* (*De Platone*, I. 12.)

One psychological motive behind the general belief in a system of concentric spheres surrounding the earth may have been the desire always to push God still higher beyond the highest heaven so far reached in imagination. This seems clear in Gnosticism, for whom the world of the Supreme is the Abyss, the Silence, in the utmost beyond. Sometimes the actual identification of God with the sky is found not merely in philosophical thought, but actually in popular *worships*: there are dedications in Latin to the personified sky, to *Caelus*.[2] We need not doubt that the dedicator did think of the material sky as

---

[1] See the passages in F. Cumont's *Les Religious Orientales* given under "Hypsistos" in the Index; also the atricle in the *Harvard Theological Review*, xxix, No. 1 (January 1936), by C. Roberts, T. C. Skeat and A. D. Nock.

[2] *Caelus aeternus Jupiter.* CIL. vi. 81. Kroll, *D. Lehr. d. Herm. Trism.*, p. 99.

a person, since in Stoicism qualities of personality were, as we have seen, seriously attributed to the material sky, and the ideas of ordinary men were in various degrees affected by the teachings of the philosophic schools.

The influence of Plato would, of course, tell against the identification of God with a material expanse. So we find the Platonist Macrobius commending Cicero because he called the universe the *temple* of God: this, Macrobius says, definitely corrected the view of those who recognized no other god than the sky itself with the visible heavenly bodies it contained. Cicero wanted to show that the supreme God was not a God who could be seen by human eyes: He was the Invisible Being for whom the whole visible universe was only the temple.[1] In the Hermetic tract entitled "Asclepius" there is a curious combination of the Stoic with the Platonic view. The visible sky is indeed a god, *caelum, sensibilis deus*; but it is not the Supreme God, who, as Platonism teaches, is invisible and νοητός, apprehended by the mind.[2] No doubt this conception could find some support in the *Timaeus*. The world is there called an αἰσθητὸς θεός, a *sensibilis deus*, the image of the God who is apprehended only by mind, and Plato describes the world in that passage as εἷς οὐρανὸς ὅδε, "this one heaven," οὐρανός here meaning not the sphere of heaven exclusively, but the outer sphere together with everything it contains.[3]

Amongst the ancient Hebrews, so far as their ideas are preserved in the Old Testament, there is no trace of an identification of Jehovah with the sky. Jehovah is a Person who sits enthroned in the sky. It is impossible to trace the process by which the cruder anthropological conception gave place to a more spiritual conception in the Hebrew writers, because the old anthropomorphic

---

[1] *Comm. in Somn Scip.*, i. 14. 2.   [2] Asclepius, I. 3c.
[3] W. Scott, *Hermetica*, iii. p. 19.

language continued to be used as symbolical imagery long after the belief in its literal truth had disappeared, and the change in idea took place invisibly below the apparent uniformity of the language. Christians and Jews to-day habitually speak of the Hand and Eyes of God, of God's throne in the heavens, and so on. No doubt the process by which what was once understood literally came to be understood symbolically was a gradual one, with many confused intermediate stages in which the idea hovered between the literal and symbolical. It is hard to say how far the Psalmist meant it literally when he spoke of God looking down from heaven on the children of men, when the writer of another Psalm wrote: "He that sitteth in the heavens shall laugh, the Lord shall have them in derision." We can be pretty sure that the Hebrew who first put into writing the story of Babel, how Jehovah came down from heaven to see the city and the tower which the children of man had builded, or the story of Sodom, how Jehovah said: "I will go down now, and see whether they have done altogether according to the cry of it, which is come unto me; and if not, I will know," understood it quite literally, and that the later Hebrew who incorporated these old documents in the book of Genesis understood them as figures. In the matter of the Sodom story we have a curiously close parallel in Greek mythology as given by Ovid. Jupiter, before the Deluge, sets before the gods the wickedness of men, and says: "The evil report of the present days had come to my ears. Hoping that it might be false, I glided down from heaven and travelled through the earth disguised in human form. It would take too long a time to describe all the evil which I found everywhere: it is enough to say that the reality was even worse than the report."[1]

We may say at any rate that by the time that the

[1] *Metamorphoses*, i. 211-215.

constituent of the book of Genesis, which modern critics call the "Priestly Code," and which they believe to belong to a time near that of Ezra, was composed, a conception of God as locally circumscribed by His sitting in the sky had given place to a more worthy one. The first chapter of Genesis is assigned to the Priestly Code and in its first verse it demolishes in a single phrase any idea of God as coinciding with the idea of the sky. "In the beginning God created the heavens." If God created the heavens, He must have existed in almighty power before there was any heaven there at all. Perhaps one does not easily realize in the case of a verse so familiar what a breach it meant with the conception hitherto almost universal in the religious traditions of mankind.

To the Jews at the beginning of the Christian era the belief that God had a being independent of any material thing had become a matter of course. They no doubt still believed, as the early Christians did, that heaven was literally a place up there overhead, in which the glory of God was manifested to the multitude of heavenly beings, the angels, as it was not manifested to men. When St. Paul speaks of his having been carried up to the third heaven, he was, as we know, going upon a current idea, traceable back into Babylonian conceptions of universe, according to which there was a series of heavens one above the other. The hero Etana in the old Babylonian story is carried up by the eagle as far as the third heaven, but fails to get any higher. At the beginning of the Christian era, as we have just seen, an idea of the universe had come to be widely accepted, according to which the earth was a globe at the centre of things, surrounded by a series of concentric spheres, the outermost region being held to be the divinest. This Greek astronomical scheme fitted in with the old Babylonian mythology in so far as anyone proceeding to the highest heaven, that is the heaven furthest away from the earth, would have to travel through the intermediate spheres or heavens, in order to get there.

It is odd to find that amongst the Jews of the early Christian centuries, amongst people for whom any identification in idea of God with the sky, as we have seen, was out of the question, an identification of God with the sky in language became customary. Now that it had come to be felt as reverent to avoid speaking of God directly as God, allusive or symbolical ways of referring to Him were often adopted in common speech, "the Holy One, blessed be He"—"Our Father in heaven"—and other such expressions. It is curious to note that among such verbal substitutes for the name of Jehovah or the word "God," the word "heaven," *shamayyim*, was used. The usage has been prolonged into modern speech, in such phrases as "Heaven knows," "It is the will of heaven." The usage arose amongst the Jews probably after the Exile. In the first book of Maccabees, whose Semitic original belongs, it is generally believed, to the second century B.C., we read, according to the best-supported text: "With heaven it is all one to save by many or by few" (iii. 18), where "heaven" is simply a substitute for the word "God." The phrase "kingdom of heaven" in St. Matthew is, of course, simply an equivalent for the phrase "kingdom of God" found in the other two Synoptists. It is a question whether Jesus himself used the more direct mode of speaking of "God," and the Aramaic-speaking disciples who reported his words in St. Matthew's form substituted, according to the Jewish scruple, "heaven" for "God," as is generally supposed, or whether Jesus himself followed Jewish practice in this case, speaking of "the kingdom of heaven," and "heaven" was afterwards translated by the term God for the benefit of Greek-speaking Gentiles, as Dalman holds.

A still odder way of identifying God verbally with

47

heaven was another substitute term: in Rabbinical Hebrew, God is often spoken of as "the Place," *hamma-quom*,[1] and that this usage too goes back to the very beginning of the Christian era is shown by the equivalent word in Greek, *ho topos*, being known to Philo of Alexandria, as a mode of designating God. There can be no question that when Jews spoke of "Heaven" or "the Place," and meant "God," they were as far as any people could be from really identifying God with the material sky: the identification was purely verbal. It was just accidental that it happened to coincide in verbal expression with the primitive belief.

In view of the great body of facts, in the field of human thought and language, which we have glanced at in this rapid look backwards, it is surely not too much to say that the idea which regards the sky as the abode of the Supreme Being, or as identical with Him, is as universal amongst mankind as any religious belief can be, and is traceable back to the most primitive stages of culture known to us. With the belief as it existed among our savage ancestors the belief in God held by philosophical Theists to-day is connected with a continuous process of intellectual modification. Each of the two alternative forms which we have noted among the civilized peoples of antiquity could be maintained against the other on grounds of Rationalism. The common mythological form was due, we have seen, to the rational induction which concluded that personality goes only with the human form: this mythological view, holding fast to the primitive belief that there is a person, or a company of persons, up there, conceived these persons as like men in form, action and individuality. Such a conception, however, while it satisfied Rationalism in retaining the association between personality and the human form, offended Rationalism in another way: the

---

[1] Rabbinic parallels. Schürer, *Jahrb. f. prot. Theol.*, 1876, pp. 166 ff.

supposition of persons in human form living up in the air did not correspond with what Rationalism inferred regarding the nature of the universe. If that supposition was rejected and yet the belief in a Person up there was retained, it could only be by going back upon the inference which had made the human form an invariable accompaniment of personality. Rationalism thus yielded the other form of belief, found in Greek Stoicism, that the fiery aether which constituted the outer sky was itself, although a widely extended material substance, nevertheless personal. The highest kinds of persons, it was insisted, had not human form, but the form of globes—the sphere of the universe as a whole, the fiery globular stars, human souls when they quitted the body and rose upwards in the shape of balls. There was thus a clash between Rationalism and Rationalism: one side insisting that personality could not be divorced from the human shape, and the other insisting that beings of human shape could not live in the sky.

And it was, of course, not only the early tentative efforts of Rationalism embodied in the traditional mythology which placed persons of human shape somewhere up there. In the full tide of Greek philosophical thought the rival school to Stoicism, the Epicurean, which always boasted that it delivered man from the terrors of religion, still did not give up the belief that there were persons up there. Epicurus thought that gods existed in the spaces between the worlds, and on purely rationalist grounds, he argued that if they were persons they must be like men in shape, not balls, as the Stoics foolishly supposed, and if they were persons like men they must converse with each other, and if they conversed with each other they must talk a language not so very unlike Greek, the most perfect of human languages.

No doubt in separating the idea of God from the

human form, in applying it to the spherical world as a whole, and in especial to its envelope of fiery aether, the Stoics inevitably to some extent blurred the idea of personality in God. This Divine Being could not be personal quite in the same way a human individual was. Nevertheless the attributes of consciousness, rational providence and benevolence, which the Stoics continued to emphasize as belonging to Him are inconceivable otherwise than as belonging to personality. The dilemma of either attributing personality to an expanse of inorganic matter or of supposing the existence of beings in human form somewhere in the sky the Platonists escaped, by denying this association of the Divine Personality with matter in any form. By them it was first clearly asserted that God had no local position in any part of our three-dimensional space: the most real Reality was not spatial at all; the spiritual world was not the sky or any region in space above the sky. Of the three elements of primitive belief—the Person, in human form, up there in the sky— they had discarded the human form; they had discarded "up there in the sky"; they still held fast to the third element, the Person. At the time of the Christian era this Platonic belief had spread to the Alexandrine Jews— Philo emphasizes the immateriality of God and explains that all the Old Testament language which spoke of His hand, or of His eyes, was purely figurative. That was commonly repeated by Christian Fathers when they had to put forth a philosophy of Christian beliefs.

To present this process as a fact is felt by some dis-believers in Theism to be in itself sufficient refutation of a belief in God. The belief in a Personal God, or a God with some of the constituents of personality, is shown to be a mere attenuated relic of a primitive delusion, all the rest of which has been corroded and dissipated by the action of Rationalism in the course of the centuries. It seems natural to conclude that the sooner this relic goes too, the better. We shall then clearly recognize that, not only was there no man-like Person in the sky, but there is no Reality corresponding to the idea of God at all.

We can call the attempt to refute Theism by displaying the continuity of the belief in God with primitive delusion the method of anthropological intimidation. If we look squarely at it, we shall see that it has no cogency at all. It has no cogency because the process described is equally compatible with the hypothesis that the belief in God is true and with the hypothesis that the belief in God is false. The fact that there is a process is by itself no evidence for either. If the belief in God is a delusion then, it is true, we can by knowledge of the process understand how it is that such a delusion survives amongst civilized men to-day: the existence of the belief is accounted for as we see one bit after another of a universal primitive delusion dissipated by Rationalism, till nothing remains but the form of theistic belief prevalent to-day. But, equally, if the belief in God is true, and if it was the Divine plan that man should apprehend the truth in successive stages, more and more clearly, that involves just such a process as we have traced, in which the conception of God becomes gradually freed from the fancies of man's childhood.

We may think of a man looking at a human figure through shifting mists. His idea of the figure he sees may at first be largely falsified by the wreaths of mist: he may not distinguish it from neighbouring trees or rocks: as the mists thin, he will gradually correct his first impressions by seeing bits of the figure more truly: some of his first illusions may remain longer than others: in the end the reality may come through clearly and he may recognize the human face. His ultimate recognition, "That is a face," will be the end of a continuous process going back to his first supposition, that it is a strange-looking tree. If you gave an account of the process simply as a series of changes in his mind, you could show how each new supposition arose by modification out of the one which went before. But the mere fact that such a process has taken place would not prove that his present belief "That is a face" is a delusion. It would be compatible indeed with the hypothesis that his present idea was just as much a delusion as the preceding ones which he had rejected: there might really be no person there at all: his whole series of suppositions might be mere fancies suggested by the various play of light in the mists; but it would be also compatible with the hypothesis that the changes in his mind had been in part caused by a real face showing through clearer and clearer. We could only determine which hypothesis was right by examining the circumstances as they are now, ascertaining whether he has good ground now for believing "That is a face." According to the result of that inquiry the previous process will take on a different character. If we find that there really is somebody there facing him, we explain the process as one in which a real person became increasingly clear: if we find that now there is nobody there, we explain the process as a series of fancies. Just so the fact that a Theist's belief in God to-day is connected with the primitive belief about someone up in the sky does not yield any evidence whether the belief is true or false. Theism has to be examined on its own merits as a view of the universe. If our consideration of the universe as a whole up to to-day, including, of course, the spirit manifested in man, leads us to the conviction that the belief in God is a delusion, then we interpret the process of belief in the past in one way; if we come to the conviction that the belief in God is justified, then we interpret that process in another way. But there is no reason why we should be intimidated by the process being simply pointed to.

In the case of the person looking at a human figure through the mist, if he looks back from his ultimate discovery of the figure over the series of suppositions which preceded it, he sees that even from the beginning there was something true in all his suppositions. It was not a series of completely different ideas, each of which was wholly rejected when he adopted another one; it was a series which had running through it something that remained, the true element mixed at first with a great volume of false imaginations but persisting and gradually increasing as the proportion of true perception to false imagination became greater. Similarly, if we have come now to the conviction that the belief in God is true, then, when we look back at primitive man's belief of someone like a man up in the sky, we do not see it as wholly false: we see it as a rudimentary apprehension of the Reality, mixed with a volume of childish imaginations. It is of course solely from the ground of the ultimate conviction that we can determine what was true and what was false in the earlier suppositions. Rashdall used to remind us that the mathematical conceptions of the most advanced mathematicians at the present day were connected with the most rudimentary ideas of primitive men about numbers by a process of gradual correction and expansion. That does not cause us to regard the conceptions of mathematicians to-day as a survival of primitive fancy.

Once upon a time it was common to suppose a spring of occult wisdom in the earlier generations of mankind: it was supposed that they deliberately hid that wisdom in symbols which were handed down in the various religious traditions. Such a supposition was connected with the belief in a primitive revelation which the fathers of mankind had received, a revelation which the polytheistic religions, it was supposed by Christians, had distorted and corrupted out of recognition. Modern knowledge of the past of mankind has made it impossible for most people to retain such a view. We are sure that if a primitive man told his children that there was a Great Person up in the sky he was not enshrining any occult knowledge in a symbol, but meant what he said in the most literal *naïf* way. And yet any belief in God is inseparable from belief in some kind of revelation. The figure I used just now, of the face gradually showing through mists, failed in one point to correspond with the actuality, as all Theists must believe it to be. The face was spoken of as if it were passive throughout the process, simply there to be seen and nothing more. But no Theist can think of God as simply passive in the process by which men come to fuller apprehension of Him. An impersonal system of law behind phenomena, or an impersonal pattern of the universe, might be thought of as progressively discovered by the human spirit without any activity of will on its part towards man. But if the Reality is itself spirit, it cannot be merely passive. God must be active upon and in man, as man is active in his movement towards God. The process by which man discovers God must be throughout a process in which God reveals Himself.

The idea of a primitive revelation is not altogether incompatible with the modern Darwinian view of human origins. It has only to be supposed that at some point of time, after the creature whose body came by descent from lower animal ancestors had become man, ideas of a certain kind arose in some one man or some set of men, through the operation within the human mind of the Divine Spirit, and that these ideas were passed on with various corruptions or distortions to later generations. And this would, I take it, be the view of Father Wilhelm Schmidt. He would regard the belief in the High God found to-day amongst the most primitive peoples as a relic, preserved comparatively pure, of such an early revelation, and the wild superstitions rife everywhere in savage religion as the outcome of a declension. No doubt, to-day, few anthropologists outside the Roman Church would subscribe to such a hypothesis; and the facts actually ascertained (so far as my knowledge goes) may be presented in a way compatible with the ordinary view that the races which to-day exhibit a rank growth of magic and superstition show what the most primitive religion was, rather than the Pygmies and Bushmen with their comparatively pure belief in a great Sky-God of ethical character. Yet there is perhaps one consideration which goes to support Professor Schmidt's view. The idea that religion advances by a process of gradual evolution does not seem true of the period of which we have historical knowledge. Advances can almost always be traced to the irruptive action of great personalities, for whom the field may indeed have been prepared by a gradual process before their coming, but whose coming means a stormy crisis, whereby some portion of mankind is impelled along a new path in religion; and it is common to see their teaching disfigured and mixed with more primitive elements in subsequent generations. The view then that at some moment in the past of mankind before the purview of history begins, certain individuals came forward with ideas about God, which, from the modern theistic standpoint, were higher and purer than those which constitute primitive religion as pictured by the generality of present-day anthropologists is a view not out of accord with what one finds in the historical period.

Rudolf Otto in his book on the Aryan deities already referred to insists that advances in religion in prehistoric times, just as advances in art, are not to be thought of as due simply to a sense—a religious sense or an artistic sense—diffused equally through the whole community.[1] They were due to an initiation on the part of certain peculiarly endowed individuals, to intuitions which at the outset they had, and other men did not have. If such intuitions, as Theists believe, came from the action of a divine Reality upon the mind of these men, they may not inappropriately be described as revelation.

But the belief in revelation does not stand or fall with the belief in a primitive monotheism. Even if it is true that the earliest stage of religious belief was a mere mass of savage superstitions and that the view of modern Theists was evolved from that by a process of successive purifications, it is still unthinkable, from the theistic standpoint, that each advance to clearer truth was made without the active operation of the Reality upon the mind of man. There is indeed a conception of revelation which it is hard for a modern man to accept. We cannot think of any apprehension of the truth which primitive man had as a miraculous putting into his mind of a belief about the universe framed in the logical and metaphysical conceptions at which man in his later progress arrived. Such a bit of advanced thought thrust into the midst of primitive mentality would be a monstrosity not at all corresponding with the mode of God's working which human history leads us to expect. If primitive man had an apprehension of God in essence true, it must still have been a thought of God like the thought of a child, mixed up with much *naïve* imagination. For primitive man himself the High God's location in the sky was not a symbol: it was literal fact.

Some of the imaginative accessories which primitive man attached to the idea of the Divine have ceased to have any significance for us at all, except as characterizing primitive psychology. They are just fancies which the

[1] *Gottheit und Gottheiten der Arier*, p. 18.

advance of knowledge has discarded, ideas blown away for good into limbo. On the other hand some imaginations of primitive man, while to us absurd in the literal sense, may seem to be primitive man's translation into sensuous imagery of something that his heart told him truly about God. Into which category can we put the association of the Divine with spatial height, the location of God in the sky?

The universality of this idea amongst mankind may, I think, give us pause if we are inclined to say that it is nothing but fancy.

HEIGHT

(continued)

Although it is, perhaps, not impossible that all races of mankind everywhere might by an accident have lighted upon one and the same fancy which was wholly baseless, it would certainly be very odd. And if one believes that man's thought about God was in any way guided by God Himself, it is all the more difficult to suppose that an imagination as universal as that which connects the Divine with height was not in some sense veridical. As I said in my last lecture, it is not conceivable that such a feeling meant an intellectual apprehension of truth as we should express it to-day, but it does seem possible that it was something we may call a feeling of appropriateness which outran intellectual understanding. It seemed somehow appropriate to primitive man to think of the chief Being as very high, as living up there in the sky. That kind of instinctive feeling of appropriateness seems to me to constitute on the side of human psychology —of primitive human psychology—what may be revelation looked at from the Divine side. There seems nothing monstrous in supposing such a feeling of appropriateness in minds still very backward in knowledge of the universe and in logical thought. For even in the psychology of modern man a feeling of appropriateness, a sense, a *flair*, often outruns clear established knowledge, often even the possibility of rational justification. Yet it may turn out—in poets especially—when clear established knowledge comes, to have been veridical. No doubt such feelings may also turn out to have been false lights, *ignes fatui*: it is only when looked back upon from the standpoint of larger knowledge, from the ultimate practical result, that true and false feelings of appropriateness can be distinguished. Yet we certainly believe that some truths, before they are grasped by the intellect, do throw by anticipation a veridical image of themselves upon the feelings—whatever the psychological or philosophical explanation of that may be—and we pronounce afterwards that the men who followed such feelings did right.

In regard then to this particular imagination of primitive man, that the Divine is the Most High, that His abode is up there, can we find things in our own conception of God, which made those images really appropriate, which continue to give them value for us, as symbols? We are here brought on to a field of speculative conjecture. I can only put forward with a query what seem to me the constituents of the feeling attached to the idea of height.

In the first place, that feeling does not seem to me to be derived from one aspect or implication of spatial height only but to be a focusing in one compound feeling of different aspects and implications. We noted in the last lecture that it is not with the Divine only that the idea of height is conjoined, but with value generally—as in our word "superior." We have to ask, How is it that "more distant from the ground" comes to mean "better"?

One constituent, I think, is the greater power which a blow delivered from a height has because it is reinforced by gravity. The taller man would have the advantage over the shorter in primitive warfare. A man lying on the ground is comparatively helpless against a man standing over him. The symbolism thus instinctively chosen by inferiors to express their recognition of the greater power of their superiors—a recognition which is often used by suppliants or captives to mollify and conciliate the stronger—is an actual lying on the ground in prostration, or a shortening of the stature in kneeling. But there is another advantage which distance from the ground gives —a larger range of vision. The commander who needs to see what the multitude of those under his command are doing has to be placed high. The idea of high position comes then to be associated with command. The throne of the king must be high. In Homer the two adverbs associated with κρείων, "ruling," "commanding," are one, εὐρύ, "wide"—the range of command—and the other ὑπατῇ, "lofty," the high position of the commander. "High on a throne of royal state" in Milton's hell, Satan exalted sat. In the common use, extending, I suppose, to all languages, of the prepositions meaning "over" and "under" to signify authority or power on the one side and subjection on the other—someone is "set *over* a kingdom," "I would never work *under* such and such a man," and so on—it is difficult, I think, to say whether the metaphor is derived from the advantage which height gives in striking a blow or the advantage which it gives in increasing the range of vision. Perhaps both associations have coalesced in the idea of authority.

But into the feeling with regard to height there enters something not derived from any differences between man and man but from the difference between the human individual and natural objects very much higher than himself. Possibly the awe which a man feels in looking up a huge mountain wall is not based on any explicable ground, but is something primary and unanalysable. All the same the feeling must, I think, depend in part upon man's experience of gravity. His subconsciousness suggests the question what would happen to him if that immense wall of rock leant outwards and fell upon him: it is that which gives him his feeling of utter smallness and helplessness. If he saw an equal expanse of rock on the level in front of him, he would not feel emotionally the disproportion in size between that and his own body: it is because the rock towering upwards might fall upon him.

But perhaps there is another element in it. For it is looking up into the sky which gives man most chiefly awe in regard to height, and, although the Celts who presented themselves to Alexander the Great are said to have told him that the only thing they were afraid of was that the sky might some day fall upon them, there is, so far as I know, no evidence that the possibility of the sky falling was a common obsession of primitive man. It is in regard to the sky especially that man has the feeling of the sublime, and that sense we have some warrant for thinking as unanalysable as the sense of beauty. To describe the object which affects us in that way as sublime, of course, tells nothing, since "sublime" is simply one of the Latin words for high. We are, apparently, just confronted with the fact that great height above him gives man a peculiar feeling which can be known only by having it. Yet it may be possible to discern certain qualities of the sky which give man the feeling in question.

One, I think, is its difference from the terrestrial world. Nature offers the eyes of man, from the outset, two different worlds. There is the earth's surface, in which the two dimensions constituting a plane surface predominate, all a world more or less accessible to man. Even the mountains with some trouble he can climb, and he can cross the water in his canoe. And there is the wholly separate world he sees overhead in the direction of a third dimension. He can see it there as plainly as he sees the rocks and trees around him; but it is a world utterly inaccessible. In it some of the natural phenomena which have the most terrifying resemblance to the expressions of human anger—the roaring winds, the lightning, the thunder—occur. And, especially on starry nights, it gives, as nothing else can give, the vision of overarching immensity. And there are two other characteristics of the world overhead. (1) It is the world of light, in the daytime all shining with the light of the sun, in the night-time covered with the luminous dust of innumerable stars. (In another lecture we shall consider the connexion of light with the Divine.) (2) It, that is to say, its higher region above the clouds, is the world of order. While the terrestrial world offered primitive man a region in which regular law seemed to prevail only in particular strands (fire always burnt, and so on) amongst promiscuous irregularity, the movements of the shining bodies seen in the world overhead repeated themselves with invariable regularity.

Henri Poincaré has remarked somewhere that this spectacle of law in the sky gave the first impulse to systematic science among mankind: if, he says, the sky had always from the time man was on the earth been covered with clouds so densely that men never saw the heavenly bodies, scientific speculation would probably have started very much later. It is no doubt not accidental that the man who is regarded as the initiator of scientific philosophy amongst the Greeks, Thales of Miletus, was noted primarily as an astronomer. Primitive man, when he looked at the moving heavens, may have had small interest in scientific speculation, but he must even so have been impressed, as Meredith's sonnet tells us that Lucifer once was, by that regularity undeflected by any of the chances and changes of the terrestrial world.

> Around the ancient track marched, rank on rank,
> The army of unalterable law.[1]

Yet one other constituent perhaps entered into the association of height with the divine or with worth generally. The law of gravity, we have seen, gave additional force to a blow from above, but the same law of gravity operating on a man's own body, made the ascent of an altitude seem like a conquest of difficulty, an attainment. Probably this is more pronounced in our use of the metaphor of "height" in ethical connexions—"higher interests," "lofty thoughts," and so on. There is, I think, in such phrases the suggestion of climbing a mountain, or achieving something by a deliberate direction of the will against the pull of the "lower" nature. "Vice," some well-known verses of Hesiod say, "it is easy to acquire in abundance: the road thereto is smooth and the thing sought is near: but between men and virtue the immortal gods ordained much sweat: the track is long and steep upwards, rough at the outset, though when a man has arrived at the summit, then it becomes easy."[2] This figure no doubt describes a quality in moral goodness which men have instinctively felt everywhere. It is a movement of will against gravity: to follow the worser impulses is the line of letting yourself go, like being carried by gravity down a slope. If the Christian doctrine of original sin is found by many people difficult of acceptance in our day, if it has been maintained on the other side that man is naturally good, or at any rate that his good impulses and bad impulses are pretty equally matched, it certainly requires some explanation how it is that all over the world to follow the good impulses has seemed like going uphill, and to follow the evil ones like going downhill.

To climb a mountain is a continued achievement of will

[1] George Meredith, the sonnet entitled "Lucifer in Starlight."
[2] Hesiod, *Works and Days*, pp. 287–292.

against gravity, and at the same time the range of vision increases with the altitude. There is something in intellectual, artistic, moral, spiritual achievement which gives a feeling that man instinctively recognizes as analogous. The higher summits of a mountain were for primitive man, if not utterly inaccessible as the sky was, at any rate very difficult of access, and those upper mountain regions were, if not quite unknown, at any rate a world very rarely seen, very little known, a world apart from the familiar places through which primitive man roamed. Thus the great gods were sometimes thought of in the mythology of many different peoples as enthroned on the top of a mountain. Here again it would be waste of time for me to go through material which anyone can find in the article on Mountains and Mountain-Gods in Hastings's *Encyclopedia of Religion and Ethics*, though the data there seem tumbled out without much discoverable arrangement according either to chronology or ethnological affinity. It would, I think, be a mistake to suppose that the idea which located the seat of the Supreme God upon a mountain-top was more primitive than the idea which placed his seat in the sky. Some wit has said that the ancient Greeks believed that the gods had their dwelling on the top of Mount Olympus till one day someone climbed the mountain and found it untenanted: then, and not till then, the Greeks began to say that the high gods lived in the sky. Against such a theory is the fact, if Professor Wilhelm Schmidt's researches are sound, that the belief which puts the chief god in the sky goes back to the most primitive stage of human culture we know. It seems better to suppose that the location of the seat of the gods in the sky and the location of it on a mountain-top were not really two alternative beliefs, but the same belief differently expressed. When the distance of the heavenly bodies was not known, and when men seldom or never ascended to the highest mountain regions, it was possible for them to think of a mountain summit as actually reaching the sky.

It is a proof how strange the higher mountain summits were to the peoples of Greek or Roman antiquity, that a popular belief from Homer onwards supposed the highest peaks actually to reach beyond the region of clouds and meteoric disturbances. We find it laid down by the early Peripatetics, and accepted generally as a truth, that when a sacrifice was offered on a high mountain-top and the place was visited a year later, the ashes might be seen quite undisturbed by any wind. When Dante says, in regard to the earthly paradise at the top of the mountain of Purgatory, that the only movement of air there was the unchanging circular movement round the earth which corresponded with the movement of the spheres, he was merely repeating established Aristotelian doctrine about high mountains.[1] To the earthly paradise Dante could perfectly logically apply a description such as Homer had given of the Elysian plain. In the upper parts of the mountain of Purgatory there was no rain nor hail nor snow nor dew nor hoar frost, no clouds either dense or rare, no lightning, no rainbow (*Purg.* xxi. 46–50). Homer had said of the Elysian plain: "There is no snow there and hardly any storm or rain; only the uniform blowing of a soft west wind" (*Od.* iv. 565). There could, of course, be no snow or rain in a region above the clouds. How the ancients accounted for the fact that the higher peaks of mountains could be seen from below covered with snow I do not know. The fact that such a belief as I have just indicated can have gone on for all the centuries of the ancient civilization uncorrected is a curious proof how weak that civilization was in regard to scientific

[1] Philoponus on Arist., *Meteor*, i. 3. p. 33, 3 ff. (Hayduck), quoted in W. Capelle, *Berges und Wolkenhöhen bei griechischen Physikern* (1916), p. 35.

verification, for all its intellectual and logical nimbleness. The ancients seem to have made mountain ascents only for the purposes of occasional sacrifices, and the higher regions continued to be for them largely an unknown world.

But before we leave the subject of mountains it may be worth while noticing an odd belief which sometimes crops up in Rabbinical Jewish literature and which illustrates the close association in the human mind between material height and spiritual dignity. It was maintained, in defiance of ascertainable fact, that the land of Israel was higher above sea-level than any other land, the Temple-hill being the highest point in the land of Israel.[1] Philo has to admit that the site of the Temple is relatively low, but he asserts that, in spite of that, the Temple itself rises to a height which does not come short of the loftiest mountains.[2] The germ of the belief goes back to the Old Testament. "A glorious throne set on high from the beginning is the place of our sanctuary" (Jeremiah xvii. 12). Ezekiel represents Jehovah as calling the Temple Hill "mine holy mountain, the mountain of the height of Israel" (xvii. 23, xx. 40). If these phrases do not go as far as to assert that the Temple Hill is actually higher than any other hill, Isaiah, or whoever wrote the opening verses of chapter ii in our book of Isaiah, does not indeed claim that the Temple Hill is, at the present time, higher than all other hills, but he looks forward to this being brought about in the glorious future. "It shall come to pass in the latter days that the mountain of the Lord's House shall be established in the top of the mountains, and shall be exalted above the hills" (Isaiah ii. 2).

That unknown world at the top of the mountains and

---

[1] Heinemann, *Philos griechische und jüdische Bildung*, 1932, p. 30.
[2] *De Special. Leg.*, i. § 73.

the inaccessible sky-world were all one world up there in which the gods dwelt, or the Chief Being dwelt. But so far as the mountain was thought of as a kind of staircase leading thither, men, if they never reached the top of the staircase, could scale its lower steps and experience, as they did so, the effort of conquering gravity. This gave to the idea of height, even as applied to the inaccessible sky, the idea of something which it would be a supreme attainment for man to reach, if any human effort could so far triumph over the downward pull. But it was felt also that any attempt of man to emancipate himself from the limitation of his condition was a sin against the law of the universe, an attempt which the gods rightly resented: "Lo, man would become as one of us." The mythological heroes who made the attempt came to a bad end. Μήτις ἀνθρώπων ἐς ὠρανὸν ποτήσθω. "Let no man fly up to heaven," says the old poet Alcman, and Horace gives the attempt of Daedalus to fly as a stock instance of human presumption, sin, *scelus*, which could only call forth Jove's thunderbolt.[1]

If the constituents I have suggested really do in combination give the idea of height its peculiar significance in religion and ethics, the further question, what aspects of God height may still properly symbolize for modern men, is one which can obviously be answered only according to the particular idea of God each modern man has. For there is, of course, not one modern idea of God, but various contradictory modern ideas. Some of them represent God as immanent, some as transcendent, some as both immanent *and* transcendent, in different ways. One can say, of course, immediately, that it is the idea of God as transcendent with which the symbol of spatial

---

[1] Caelum ipsum petimus stultitia neque
per nostrum patimur scelus
iracunda Iovem ponere fulmina. (*Odes*, i. 3. 38–40.)

height corresponds. The very term transcendent, as was observed at the beginning of our last lecture, brings in the image of an otherwise empty space which God occupies above all the created universe, and it may be impossible to state what we mean by God's transcendence without the use of spatial metaphors. It is the *difference* of God from man, the essential infinite unannullable difference, which the term transcendence proclaims. That, of course, is an idea which has been very repugnant to some forms of religion—those of a Monist cast. In the *advaita* forms of Hinduism, it is expressly denied. The idea of God as different, as transcendent, that doctrine teaches, is merely an illusory image of still immature religious apprehension: the sage penetrates the illusion and makes the supreme discovery of his fundamental identity with God—"That art thou." In Stoicism the identity of God and the ruling principle in man was asserted in a cruder way: the reason in man was a little bit of the fiery aether which surrounded and penetrated the universe and was God. In the ideal wise man it was of precisely the same quality as it was in the rest of God: so that when the Stoic teachers declared that the wise man was in no way inferior to Zeus—shocking as it might seem to Hebrew and Christian ears—it was simply a logical consequence of the Stoic theory of the universe.

If we survey the religious beliefs of mankind at the point now reached by human history, and if we rule out of consideration the beliefs of the people on a savage or primitive level, the remaining religions, the religions, that is to say, of the relatively civilized peoples in Europe, Asia, and the other hemisphere, do not present a multitude of wholly different and unconnected forms of belief, as is sometimes supposed. Anyone, to-day, who has to decide for himself to what religion he is going to give his adherence has had his choice made simpler for him by

68

the operation of time. For time has eliminated for good a number of the religions which once commanded the allegiance of great, and relatively civilized, peoples. No sane person now could contemplate becoming a worshipper of the Egyptian Isis or the Babylonian Marduk or the Greek Apollo or the Roman Mars. If, indeed, a man were going to found a wholly new religion for himself, not continuous with any religion which has hitherto existed amongst mankind, the universe might offer him a bewildering number of possibilities. But any such religion would labour under the improbability of its initial supposition. It would profess to be a relatively true apprehension of the Reality behind phenomena, the Reality which has always been there from the beginning impinging upon the minds of men, and yet it would have to declare that the Reality had never, throughout the ages in which man has contemplated the universe, ever till now shown through the veil. That would seem improbable if the Reality were believed to be impersonal: if the Reality has any kind of personal character, it would be unthinkable that all the attempts of man to apprehend it hitherto had been uniformly futile.

But if the idea of a wholly new religion, unconnected with anything in the religious traditions of mankind, is once ruled out, one of the paths now being followed by man must be taken to be the line which, more than any other, has led to apprehension of the Reality. Now, if one line among these actually being followed has to be taken —it may not be as giving absolute truth, but as going further along the way to truth than the rest—the choice of a man to-day is limited by the fact that the actual religions of civilized mankind are divided into two great groups, and two only, according to the basic belief about God. Within each group there are, no doubt, great differences; but the first question is: Inasmuch as the one group is divided from the other by a different idea of God, which idea is the truer?

The religions of one of the groups are based upon the idea of God which was affirmed by the ancient Hebrews. These religions are Christianity, Judaism and Islam. One may also include in the group Zoroastrianism, since Zarathushtra's doctrine, although not in the Hebraic tradition, shows a parallel line of remarkable affinity to the Hebraic tradition. Zoroastrianism, however, can hardly to-day come into consideration as a religion for anybody outside the small Parsee community. The religions of the other group are those based on an Indian idea of God, the various forms of Hinduism and Buddhism. It is as if at a point in the pilgrim's progress of the human family, they had come to a forking of the ways; part went to the right and part to the left. After the two groups had separated, there came further divergences within each group; but the initial question is: At that great forking of the ways which divided the two main groups, which group took the right direction?

It is that division, the division between the Hebraic and the non-Hebraic religions, which is the real division, not, as people sometimes fondly suppose, the division between Western and Oriental. Christianity has sometimes been commended to Indians on the ground that Christianity too is an "Oriental" religion: Jesus, it is said, was an "Oriental." The question whether a religion arose in a country nearer to, or further from, the longitude of Greenwich is completely irrelevant in this connexion. No doubt Palestine, nineteen centuries ago, and ancient India had certain features in common in so far as both were still untouched by modern Western civilization; but these resemblances were as nothing compared with the immense difference between the Hebraic view of God, which was the view of Jesus, and which underlies the present religion of Europe, and the Indian view of God. East and West has nothing to do with it. As a matter of fact, the view of the universe prevalent in old Europe, before it was conquered by a Hebraic religion, was much more like the Indian view. Greek thought, too, ran into Monism, as Indian thought has done. "Ah! The Aryan view then against the Semitic!" someone may exclaim. But no, that will not do either, since the Zoroastrian Persians, who have to be classed with the Hebrews, were Aryans.

The truth is that these labels which purport to indicate an illuminating scientific generalization in the background are mostly vain pretence. If one were obliged to stamp a geographical or ethnological mark upon the Hebraic-Zoroastrian group of religions, one could not label them either eastern or western, either Aryan or Semite. One could only say that they all arose in some country of the Nearer East, west of India and east of Europe. From the fact that Zoroastrianism was one of the group and that Zoroastrianism is in some rather problematic way connected with the people called Magi, Otto Spengler, in his book, *The Decline of the West*, gives the whole group the label of "Magian" religions. Even if that book is a mass of pretentious pseudo-scientific generalizations and the name "Magian" in this connexion most unhappy and misleading, Spengler was right in seeing that those four great religions formed a group with certain common presuppositions which distinguished them alike from Graeco-Roman religion on the one side and Indian religion on the other. But I question whether any valuable conclusion regarding their character can be drawn from the fact that they all arose within a particular geographical area.

The common ground upon which the Hebraic religions and Zoroastrianism all stand is a conception of God which emphasizes His infinite transcendence, His eternal difference from any created being. Primitive man had expressed his feeling that the chief Being was transcendent and eternally different by thinking of Him as in the sky. In the stage of *naïf* polytheism represented by the older phase of Indian and Greek religion (which continued in popular religion after the rise of philosophic thought in the leading class) the elements which point to the difference of the Divine from man and the elements which point to identification are there side by side. The gods are thought of as living in the sky and as living endlessly: that points to the difference. But the gods have come to be thought of as exceedingly human in their appearance and passions and characters: that points to identification. There is no great gulf between men and gods. In an instructive passage of Pindar the two sides are presented in combination:

There is one self-same race of men and gods; and from one mother have we both the breath of life; only faculties altogether diverse distinguish us; since man is a thing of nought, and those have brazen heaven for a sure abiding home. And yet we have some likeness, either by greatness of soul or by fashion of body, to the Deathless Ones (*Nem.*, vi. 1–6).

One might say that such a *naïf* polytheism had in it the potentiality of development either in the direction taken by Hebraic religion, if the difference between the Divine and the human is emphasized, or in the direction of Indian and Stoic thought if the resemblance is emphasized. Supposing it is true that Hebrew religion arose by a process of purification out of an earlier *naïf* polytheism, both Hebraic religion and Indian-Greek thought will have branched apart from the road which Hebrews and Indians and Greeks had once alike trod, and the figure used just now of a forking of the ways will not be far from the historical truth. Indian thought emphasized the resemblance, not the difference, between men and gods. As appearances, the differences might still be there for popular Hindu religion; Indian Monism was quite compatible with polytheism understood in a certain way; there were gods and there were men, but below the differences there was one Divine Something, the same in gods and in men, and to deeper thought the differences vanished: "That art thou."

If the road taken by the Hebrews at the forking of the ways was the right one, then the movement of mind in the other group which led to this conclusion—the ultimate identity of God and man—was not a movement to deeper truth, but a disastrous aberration, a darkening of the mind to the essential difference which it was the beginning of true religion to recognize. When Ezekiel sees the glory of the Lord, he falls upon his face (Ezekiel i. 28). "The Lord is in his holy temple: let all the earth keep silence before him" (Habakkuk ii. 20). "I have heard of thee by the hearing of the ear; but now mine eye seeth thee. Wherefore I abhor myself and repent in dust and ashes." (Job xlii. 5, 6). "The beginning of wisdom is the fear of the Lord."

I believe that the two attitudes are in truth incompatible, that, as the human family had to choose one of two alternative ways, when the division came, so always the individual man has to choose between regarding the infinite difference of God as ultimate truth and Monism as profoundly wrong, and regarding man as himself essentially divine and the Hebraic attitude of adoration as unworthy. There are numerous people to-day in Europe who find the Hindu-Stoic view the only satisfactory one. Some have tried to combine it with Christianity: the mystical tradition in Christendom, largely derived, as it ultimately is, from Neo-Platonism through Augustine and the Pseudo-Dionysius, has always been liable to incline

c* 73

in that direction, though Catholic theology has made a dogmatic fence to save Christian mysticism from tumbling over into the Monistic abyss, and has condemned would-be Catholic teachers who went, in its judgment, too near the edge, such as Meister Eckhardt.

In Hinduism itself not all religion is Monistic in the full sense: there are the sects which denounce an *advaita* view of the universe as definitely wrong and assert the eternal difference between God and any human soul. The great religious teacher of the eleventh century, Ramanuja, whose followers in South India to-day number millions, attacked the absolute Monism of Sankara with an outfit of philosophical learning and a dialectical ability as great as any exponents of that view. His writings have been recently made more accessible in the German translations by Rudolf Otto, who has devoted especial attention to this remarkable development in Hinduism and done much to make it better known.[1] Ramanuja's opposition to absolute Monism made his view of the universe so far accord with the Christian view, and since there had been a Christian church in South India for at least three centuries before the time of Ramanuja, it has been suggested that this form of Hinduism was due to Christian influence.[2] This, however, the best authorities seem to think unlikely: the doctrine of Ramanuja can be explained, they think, as a spontaneous development in Hinduism, and there is no sign in it of any impulse from outside.

Again, not all Greek thought was Monistic. It would perhaps be a question how far Neo-Platonism implied an ultimate identification of the human soul with God,

---

[1] R. Otto, *Vischna-Nārāyana* (1923), *Siddhānta des Ramanuja* (2nd ed., 1923), *India's Religion of Grace and Christianity* (1930).

[2] G. A. Grierson, in his article on "Bhakti-Marga" in Hastings, *Encyclopedia of Religion and Ethics*, thinks Christian influence probable; A. Berriedale Keith, article "Ramanuja" in the same Encyclopedia, thinks the supposition unnecessary.

because it is hard to say exactly what in the Neo-Platonic system can properly be called "God" in any sense like that which the Hebraic religions attach to the name. But Plato himself was decidedly not a Monist. In his theology, as set forth in his latest work, the *Laws*, God is the supreme Soul, an individual Soul definitely distinct from any human soul. Nor was Aristotle a Monist, though his God, without concern for the world and occupied solely in thinking about thinking, has much less resemblance than Plato's to what the Hebraic religions have understood by "God." It is a strange irony of history that in Europe the most impressive Monistic view of the universe should have been put forward by a Hebrew, Spinoza. The Synagogue which banned him may have been too narrow-minded to understand the reach and significance of his thought, but the Synagogue may nevertheless have been right in holding that his view of the world was an abandonment of the essential ground of the Jewish faith.

The attempt to amalgamate Christianity with a Monist view—to suppose that one can hold a Christian view of the universe and go on talking about the human soul as a portion of God, a little pool of the one Divine ocean, and so on—surely shows an undiscriminating woolliness of thought which blurs the real alternatives in religion. What may obscure the absoluteness of the division is that, though Christianity asserts the otherness and transcendence of God, it also teaches that God is always active in the souls of men and that He "came down" Himself—it is impossible to avoid using the spatial metaphors of height and descent—in the Person of a particular Man. That is to say, while Christianity regards it as an evil aberration for any man but that one to say, "That art thou," when he explores the inner core of his own being, it teaches that this is precisely what that One Man could say—He alone. No doubt, modern versions of Christianity have denied this uniqueness of Jesus and asserted that his difference from other men was only in degree, not in kind: all men at the core of their being are God, but Jesus realized that more clearly than other men. We are not discussing now which view is right: at present it is only a matter of recognizing the difference of such a view from what has in the history of men been Christianity. The Christian doctrine of the Incarnation is not another way of saying what the Indian means when he asserts the essential identity of man and God. The doctrine of the Incarnation has its point solely on the Hebraic presupposition of the otherness, the transcendence of God. It is because God is infinitely above the world that His coming down into the world is wonderful. What gives its whole meaning to the Christian recognition of God in Christ is that this is the same God before whom man's proper attitude is that of Job—adoration and confession of his own utter unworthiness.

In our own day we have seen a strong movement among Christian thinkers for asserting with new emphasis the difference, the transcendence, of God, and repudiating the tendencies shown by certain Christian groups in the nineteenth century to regard God as immanent in a way which came near the actual identification of the Divine and the human spirit. The movement, reasserting God's transcendence, has not been in one Christian communion only. It was manifested as signally by the Roman Catholic philosopher, Baron Friedrich von Hügel, as it is in some later developments of German Protestantism. Baron von Hügel was, as everyone knows, closely associated with the group in the Roman Church called Modernist, the group charged by a Papal Encyclical with going astray in the direction of Immanentism. Possibly, it was precisely because he had been in close touch with those who had such tendencies, persons with whom on questions of Biblical criticism he was mainly in agreement, that Baron von Hügel recoiled all the more vehemently from an immanental philosophy which went against his profoundest religious instincts. It may be remembered how the very word "Immanentism" came to be charged, when he used it, with sinister meaning. No one could attribute to the Baron a lack of sympathy for mysticism or a lack of interest in it: it was the subject to which his largest book was devoted; but a mysticism which went the length of identifying the worshipper with the God worshipped it would be impossible to repudiate more strongly than he did.[1]

In German Protestantism the Otherness of God is asserted to-day as the central thing in his message by Karl Barth. But before Barth was heard of it had been asserted by another German Protestant thinker, to whom Barth is on many points opposed, Rudolf Otto. It was Otto who brought into currency as a mode of describing God the phrase *"das ganz Andere"*—"the altogether Other." In his widely read book, *Das Heilige* (called "The Idea of the Holy" in the English translation) Otto gave an account of what he believed to be the essential quality of religion. He found it in a feeling of awe *sui generis*, a feeling for which Otto coined the now current term "numinous." It was the feeling of awe which man felt in the presence of an unknown something charged with dread mystery, *mysterium tremendum*. The element in religion therefore which expressed itself in such ideas as the fear of God, inward prostration before a Being felt as incom-

---

[1] "I have had for years, increasingly, a double sense: of the large, spacious range of our ethical, etc., capacities, and of the necessity and value of an ideal and indefinite exercise for them; *and* of all this not being God, not one bit, not one bit. Until a man feels this, sees this, till it pierces his soul . . . he has not, I think, waked up to the *specifically* religious consciousness . . . God is emphatically *not* simply our Highest Selves" (*Selected Letters*, p. 124.)

prehensibly great, was not a lower element which religion, as it becomes purified and rationalized in civilized man, could throw off: without it religion lost its essential character, although, no doubt, religion in its higher forms expressed that element in a different way from primitive man.

The symbol of diverse dimensions is now a favourite one with German religious thinkers to express this difference of God's being from our own. "*Senkrecht von oben,*" "Vertically down from above," is a phrase in which Karl Barth likes to describe the Divine action on the plane of human life. It does not belong to this plane at all: nothing we do can lead up to it: it cannot be explained by a process which has gone on in human experience or will: it smites upon this plane sheer down from a wholly different dimension; from the point of view of our life the Divine action must necessarily be something paradoxical, impossible.

Nothing in God that is given fact, nothing that can be contemplated, nothing that constitutes an object. If there were, God would not be God! There is no intrusion of man into that realm, nor projection of that realm into this world. We are precisely the men for whom God is, definitively and along the whole range of our knowledge, the Other, the Stranger. And our world is precisely that world within which God is, definitively and in the whole of its compass—outside it![1]

It is sentimental, Liberal self-deception to suppose that there is any direct way leading from Nature and History, from Art, from Morals, from Science, from Religion itself, to God's impossible possibility.[2]

No doubt it would be unfair to Barth to take some few of his violent paradoxes apart from the whole body of his writing in which they will be found counterbalanced in many cases by apparently contradictory assertions. But, even if his philosophy as a whole, so far as any consistent system can be drawn from his rhetorical self-contradictions

[1] *Der Römerbrief* (1929), p. 301.   [2] Ibid., p. 321.

is unsatisfactory, we may perhaps agree that the strong assertion of the Otherness of God, the distinction of the Divine from human life as something in a different dimension, does emphasize an element in religion of which too little account had been taken.

Another Christian thinker in Germany, Karl Heim, who holds a chair of philosophy in Tübingen, has put forward in his book, *Glaube und Denken*, a philosophy of religion, in which the symbol of diverse dimensions is worked out further than in Barth. So far as he insists that God acts upon the life of this world from a wholly different dimension, that God can never be rightly regarded as an object of which man can speak, Heim represents the same tendency of the day which we see in Barth, though Heim's criticisms of Barth are largely adverse and severe. For Heim, too, as for Otto and for Barth, God is *"das ganz Andere."*

When once we have recognized that the Hebraic-Christian view and the Indian-Greek Monist view are incompatible alternatives, that any attempt to amalgamate them means hopeless mental confusion, we are in a better position to make our choice between them.

There are, as I said, people to whom this whole Hebraic way of looking at things is repugnant. They prefer to think of God—whatever they may mean in this case by "God"—as only immanent in the world-process; or they are attracted by the Vedantic view that if a man, any man, can push his introspection to the very core of his own being, he discovers that he is identical with God.

In such a case the judgment of value is so fundamental that it is impossible to prove its rightness by any deducing of it from value-judgments still more fundamental or more generally recognized: a man's choice is the expression of his own personal reaction, of which he can only say: "I have a conviction that this is right," just as he can only

79

say, in justification of his thinking something beautiful, "I see it so." No doubt each of the alternative attitudes to the universe is rightly judged only as giving its character to a whole mode of life and way of thinking about things. A man's self-abasement before a goodness, a holiness, a wisdom, a beauty, infinitely above him and yet stooping down to him in a strange love, so far as it is genuine, must give a particular kind of note to his life and personality. The life and personality of another man, whose view of the universe leaves no place for such self-abasement before anything higher than himself, higher, at any rate, than his own best self, will have a difference in it which those associating with both will probably be able to feel.

We may, I think, say so much: if there are people to whom the view which identifies the human soul with God is attractive, there are others to whom it is just this view which is repulsive. There is in them a religious exigence which cannot be satisfied except by the adoration of a Being not themselves, reaching to heights above them beyond all power of thought, to an infinite height which rules out for ever for any finite being what would be a sad attainment, the arrival at an end, a limit, at which it might be said: "There is no more in Reality than this, than my own being." Worship, adoration, prostration of spirit, confession of unworthiness, is ignoble and servile only when it is prostration before the unworthy— prostration of the mean-spirited, for instance, before arbitrary power. To normal men the natural reaction to the revelation of some supreme beauty in man or nature is the impulse to bow down before it. No one thinks such adoration of the beautiful an unworthy self-abasement: it is the right recognition of consummate worth. It is not accidental that in early expressions of Christian worship this note is prominent. "Thou art *worthy*, O Lord, to receive glory and honour and power" (Revelation iv.

11). "*Vere dignum et justum est, aequum et salutare te quidem, Domine, omni tempore . . . praedicare . . . et ideo cum angelis et archangelis . . . cumque omni militia caelestis exercitus, hymnum gloriae tuae canimus.*"

If such a view of the Divine transcendence is the right view, then, when we look back upon the primitive tendency to regard the sky as the special domain of the Chief Being, we see it as a singularly apt anticipation of the truth. It expressed in a vivid way the feeling of the otherness of God: the sky was the other world removed from the accessible world round about man by distance in a third dimension; its distance when he looked upwards gave him a feeling of the sublime which we can recognize as analogous to the feeling which, for us, is the ground-tone of worship, the recognition of God's incomparable worth; in the phenomena of wind and lightning and thunder primitive man saw a revelation of overwhelming power, and, if Otto is right, no religion even to-day can dispense with an element akin to fear: in the higher starry region primitive man saw the revelation of perfect order, unvarying law, and Christians to-day face the spiritual disorders of the world about them with the belief that there is a sphere of being in which there is no disharmony and no evil: "Thy will be done on earth as it is done in heaven."

TIME

In our last lecture we were considering the use of a spatial figure, that of height, to express beliefs about the Divine Reality. We must now consider the application of the idea of endless duration in time to God. The Divine Being was described by the old Hebrew writer not only as the "High and Lofty One," but as the Being who "inhabiteth eternity." "I will remember the years of the right hand of the Most High," says a Psalmist (lxxvii. 10). Amongst all peoples the attribute of "deathlessness," "immortality," is the chief characteristic of the gods. When we use the spatial metaphor of "height" in regard to God, no one to-day would doubt for a moment that this was just a figure of speech. God, it is recognized, does not occupy any particular position in space and no spatial measurements can be applied to Him. Can we say the same thing about ideas of time applied to God? The old Hebrews spoke of the life of God as going on through an indefinite number of ages or generations—endless temporal duration. Must such a mode of speaking be for us a mere metaphor just as when God is spoken of as the "Most High"? Yes, we are told. It is generally agreed to-day that God is no more in time than He is in space. The application of temporal measures to His life—even though infinite temporal measures—is declared to be just as inappropriate as spatial measures. God's mode of being is Eternity, and Eternity is not time prolonged to infinity: it is the negation of time, something without duration, without successiveness; a *Nunc Stans*, a Now that remains unchanging, with no past and with no future. We shall have to consider this view.

Time is regarded as a problem not only for religious philosophies but for practically all metaphysics. The question raised is whether time is *real*. If you are, both in religion a Theist, and in philosophy an upholder of the view that time is not real, you, of course, must hold that all temporal language applied to God is a purely symbolical way of referring to a mode of being which is altogether timeless. The religious interest in the question is not precisely the same as the metaphysical. Even an atheist may have the metaphysical interest, the desire to ascertain whether it is only our human (or animal) mode of apprehending reality which causes our experience to appear as a sequence in time, the reality which the mind apprehends in this way being itself timeless. The religious interest, on the other hand, is first and foremost the desire to apprehend God, and one may say, I think, that there are three main questions to which the religious interest in the problem of time is directed: (1) Ought we to think of God as above time in the sense that for Him there is no movement from past to present, no after or before? (2) The time process of which we experience a little bit, what are we to think of it as a whole? Is it ordained and guided by God to realize a Purpose whose full meaning can be understood only when the Purpose reaches its completion? (3) We are concerned to know how far finite human spirits, if the life of God Himself is timeless, ought to, and can, transcend time, and experience timeless eternity, and this question would have two applications: it may be asked with regard to men still in this life, how far men can rise in spirit into the sphere of the timeless, or it may be asked with regard to the existence of men beyond death, how far it is to be thought of as timeless.

To attempt, in the time at our disposal, to grapple with all the problems raised for metaphysics by our experience of time in general would be absurd. All I can hope to do is to throw out a few observations which may bear more directly on our special problem, how far we are to regard all temporal language applied to the being of God or the life of finite beings in the spiritual world as symbols of a Reality which is timeless. The problem of Time, we are told, is both the most central problem of metaphysics and also one of the most baffling. My impression is that the attempt to define Time, or explain Time, or understand Time, is one doomed necessarily to eternal frustration. Time can only be known and pointed to, but never defined or explained or understood. And the reason of this is that time is something wholly unique, unlike anything else we know. For immediate experience time is no problem at all. When St. Augustine said: "If nobody asks me what Time is, I know; if I want to explain it to anyone who asks me, I am at a loss," he was stating what is an elementary truth. When we actually witness any event, we know quite well the difference between "before" and "after," and everyone to whom we speak of something happening before or after something else knows quite well what we mean. But if we try to define or explain time we have to do so in terms of other things, and because time is something unique, unlike anything else, every such attempt must misrepresent the reality. If you keep terms of temporal significance out of your explanation, it is wide of the mark: if you admit them, your definition, or explanation, is circular, presupposing a knowledge of the very thing to be defined or explained.

The view, for instance, which I believe has been expressed at some time by Lord Russell, that the difference between past, present and future can be resolved simply into differences in our cognitive relations to different events, seems to me to take us nowhere, because the moment you try to describe what the difference in our cognitive relation to the past and our cognitive relation to the future is you have to bring in the differences of past and future as something already known to explain it. There are some sentences in Professor Taylor's Gifford lectures which, taken by themselves, might seem to imply an intention to define time. "The past *means* that from which *we* are turning away, the future that to which *we* are turning,"[1] or again: "If we were asked to say what a present or 'now' *is*, as it is actually lived and experienced we should not be far wrong in saying that whatever we experience as *one* satisfaction of endeavour is experienced by us as one 'now.'" If we took these words as purporting to define what time *is* or *means* in terms of conation, I think the definition would be circular. Conation implies time, is inconceivable apart from time, is the way in which time most comes home to us, but time is not, and does not mean, conation. I do not even think that time is inconceivable apart from conation.

There are, no doubt, certain obvious analogies between time and some spatial objects and this has led to the description of time in spatial figures. It is represented as a line infinitely prolonged both ways with the present occupying some point in it between the past and the future. But, except for the fact that both a period of time and a line in space can be measured and one bit of it pronounced to be equal or unequal to another bit, time

[1] *The Faith of a Moralist*, I. p. 88.

is not at all like a line in space, and any language used about time as if it were like a line in space inevitably leads at once to self-contradictions. Another figure, which naturally suggests itself and is used for time in all languages, is that of a stream flowing. But sometimes it is the series of events which is said to flow through Time, as if Time were a stable medium and the events only which flowed. In truth, of course, neither does Time, nor do events, flow. Events follow each other in temporal succession, but there is no way you can express what that means more lucidly or precisely than by saying that they happen before and after, no way in which you could explain to anyone what "before" and "after" meant, who did not already know. Sometimes, the standpoint of the observer is regarded as stationary, and the events are thought of as moving past him like a pageant, sometimes it is the temporal order which is represented as existing already there, stationary, and it is the observer who moves along it, like a boat, in a figure used by Professor Gunn,[1] gliding past a row of houses on the bank, or like a policeman who goes along a row of houses at night, in Professor Broad's figure, lighting them successively with his bull's-eye lantern.

However you describe the unique fact of Time in terms drawn from other things, you fall into self-contradictions, and it has mainly been these inevitable contradictions, I think, which have led some modern philosophers to declare that Time must be unreal. Our idea of it is, they say, self-contradictory. The contradiction is not in Time but in the inappropriate conceptions, drawn from other fields of experience, applied to Time. McTaggart's argument, for instance, that to the same event the terms "past," "present" and "future" could be applied, and these terms were incompatible in reason,[2] overlooks the

[1] J. A. Gunn, *The Problem of Time* (George Allen & Unwin Ltd).
[2] "The Unreality of Time." *Mind*, October 1908.

fact that it is in the time-process, and in the time-process alone, that this odd thing happens, that a present event becomes a past event, and you cannot say what is compatible or incompatible in the time-process by arguing from what is compatible or incompatible in things apart from time.

Again, in regard to the controversy whether the present is an instant of no duration between the past and the future or a bit of time of a definite length, the question, it seems to me, is raised because the inappropriate figure of the line in space haunts men's minds when they think of Time. It is certain that in order that we may apprehend in perception a bit of Time, it must have a certain length, and that our "specious present," in the phrase made now familiar by psychologists, is of more or less measurable duration. In the stock instance of someone listening to a bar of music, he does not, we are told, so much remember the earlier notes when he hears the last one, as apprehend the whole bar together in one immediate perception. The length of time which can be apprehended in this way as a whole differs apparently very much from one individual to another. Professor Gunn tells us that the most recent experiments, when he wrote, had established its length as varying from half a second to four seconds. I question, however, whether any exact measure is possible, because the series of recent sense impressions fades gradually in vividness, as they are further from the last one, and I do not see how it is possible to draw a hard and fast line between the specious present within which you have immediate perception and the past in regard to which you have only memory.

If anyone goes out of the room in which we are sitting and shuts the door behind him, our knowledge that he has gone out and shut the door remains for more than four seconds, I think, not a mere memory but a kind of perception. The sound of the door shutting abides in our consciousness for a while as the ghost of a sound or a perceived resonance after the actual sound has ceased, and fades away by degrees. Our thoughts may have been engaged in reading when the person went out and we may have taken no conscious note of the fact, yet if anyone else in the room with us who could not see whether the person in question was still in the room or not were to ask us a minute or two after we had heard the door shut whether so-and-so had left the room, we *should* attend to the sound we had just heard of the door shutting, as to a direct perception we could still recover before it passed into a mere memory.

The question, however, of the "specious present" and its length, does not appear to me one of consequence for the metaphysical problem of time: it is of psychological interest only, concerned with the manner in which we apprehend the passage of events and the minimum bit of time we can detect: it is quite separate from the question whether there is an actual objective instantaneous present of no duration at all. I think we must say that there is, if Professor Broad is right, as I think he is, in describing the future as non-existent and giving, as the characteristic of the present, that it precedes literally nothing at all.[1] That is to say, the time-process at each moment has a definite end, though an end always moving forward and adding new reality to the reality which exists and has existed. If we have to make a spatial symbol of time, in regard to this characteristic, it would not be that of a line in which the future was represented as continuous with the past, but that of a comet or a rocket shooting through the void, the luminous head symbolizing the present, and the trail of light behind it the past. In front of it, there is nothing but emptiness and blackness,

[1] *Scientific Thought*, p. 66.

though, as it moves onward, more and more of that emptiness is changed into its line of light. Of course, like all spatial figures of Time, it misrepresents; but it illustrates the character of the present as an end, the end of something which is continuous behind it. But the actual end of anything, whether a line, or the point of a spear, or a temporal process must be without any thickness at all, just the end and nothing more.

Thus, it seems to me that when Professor Taylor gave it as his conviction in his third Gifford lecture (p. 73) that the purely instantaneous present, the knife-edge, is a product of theory, not an experienced actuality, he was right in holding it not to be experienced actuality, if you lay stress on "experienced," but hardly right in thinking it was only a product of theory, not something which actually exists. Of course, you cannot see the point of a spear apart from the rest of the spearhead to which the point is the end, and you cannot perceive the instantaneous present apart from a bit of past time with which it is continuous. Yet you can distinguish the point of the spear, as the end, from all the rest of the spearhead, and within the specious present, you can distinguish a before and after. You may apprehend the notes of the bar as a whole, yet it is a whole within which there is clearly marked temporal succession; the notes are not perceived as simultaneous. Thus the specious present itself has an end, the real present, though you can never take note of the real present, because the act of perceiving allows no time for simultaneously thinking about it. When you begin to think about it, it is already no longer present but past, and you think about it only as you remember it or apprehend it as a past bit of the specious present. This is certainly true of any momentary sensation: you can in a way think about the present in regard to a sensation still continuing. If you think about a toothache,

89

while you still have it, you are no doubt thinking mainly about the sensation of pain you have had in the preceding seconds or preceding minutes, but you are conscious in doing so that the sensation is still going on in the real present. If your toothache suddenly stops and you think about it a fraction of a second later, your thought is different from what it would be if the pain were still there. You can thus think about the present as included in a little bit of time all the rest of which is past, but you cannot think about the present otherwise than so included.

The question has been discussed whether you can properly attribute existence to the future and to the past. Professor Broad pronounces, as we have seen, the future to be non-existent, to be nothing, but he regards the past as existing. Some people have maintained that the future already exists, only that we have not got to it yet. This would correspond with the view which symbolizes the conscious self as a man in a boat gliding past the row of houses on the bank and seeing them one after another, or the policeman lighting them up successively with his bull's-eye lantern. It is supposed that the succession of events in time is the translation into a temporal order of an order which exists already complete, though not a temporal one. The figure on which this theory proceeds seems to be that of a gramophone record. On the record there is an arrangement of minute prominences all there together, a definite order *totum simul*: when the record is run off on the gramophone, this order is translated into a temporal order, a succession of sounds.

The trouble, I think, about such a theory is that it leaves the fact of time as inexplicable as before. The gramophone record does not make the temporal order: because Time is there already, you can produce a temporal succession of sounds which corresponds with a previously existing spatial order. Supposing that there

90

does exist somewhere, in the mind of God, or anywhere else, a fixed scheme already complete of the events in the universe throughout the whole time-process, you might in that case, no doubt say with St. Augustine, "futura iam facta sunt," yet it would remain true that the realization of the part of the scheme not yet realized lay in a future which so far does not exist. The running off of the scheme as a temporal succession would imply the reality of Time as something different from the scheme.

It is important not to confound the proposition that the future is already determined with the proposition that the future already exists. The two propositions are not identical in meaning. The gramophone view might be true, and Professor Broad nevertheless be right in saying that the future does not exist. If, for instance, it is already a fixed event in the world-plan that I am going to have a toothache the day after to-morrow, my actually having the toothache is an event which has not yet occurred. Only the time-process has been transferred by this view from the series of events to the subject who experiences them, and the subject at the present moment has not yet got to the toothache of the day after to-morrow. It remains as true as ever that if the toothache is already in some sense a part of reality, I have not yet had it.

Of course, the belief in such a complete scheme of events to the end of time (if time has an end) already existing would be incompatible with belief in the reality of any volitional choices. We seem by our free choices so to determine each successive present that if we decide in one way the future will be different from what it would have been if we had decided in a different way. If the whole series of events is already fixed, this appearance of freedom of choice must be an illusion. We should have to say that the gramophone record was always being run off in our inner life as well as in the events round about us. That brings us again to the eternal controversy about Free Will. And this much is plain— that any such view of the time-process as the running off of a gramophone record is utterly abhorrent to those who feel the reality of volitional choices to be essential to belief in moral values, and thus to any view of God which regards God as caring for righteousness. Certainly when St. Augustine said, "futura iam facta sunt" he was far from meaning to state the gramophone view: his phrase was deliberately rhetorical. Christians have always believed that the history of the universe in its main lines follows a Divine plan, there from the beginning, though it is essential to the Christian or Hebrew view to believe that within those main lines, bad volitions, at any rate, are choices which are not pre-ordained by God. What St. Augustine no doubt meant was that many things in the future would correspond with an already existing Divine Plan, and that, in that sense, they were already a part of reality, though in the literal sense they were not yet facts.

If there were some overwhelmingly strong reason for taking the gramophone record view of the time-process, we might not be able to reject it simply on the ground that it conflicted with our moral feeling. But there seems no reason at all for taking it. It is an arbitrary fancy. There are no facts of the universe which it is required to explain. This may be disputed by some people who have been impressed by instances of apparent foreknowledge of the future alleged, for instance, in the recent book by Mr. Dunne, *An Experiment in Time*. Yet if when you have allowed for a certain play of coincidence and distortion in reporting, some cases remain established in which future events are foreseen, this does not prove that the events were real before they happened. So far as men have made out the pattern of the universe, they can predict a large number of events which actually occur— we may remember stories of how Europeans have dominated the minds of savages by predicting eclipses. An experienced physician can often predict accurately the future course of a disease perhaps by minute signs he could not completely set out in words. If, therefore, it has been proved by Mr. Dunne, or by anyone else, that in certain abnormal psychic conditions particular people have foreseen future events, the hypothesis that the future already exists is quite unnecessary. People in abnormal psychic conditions may be affected by a number of things in the present, ordinarily imperceptible, which may indicate the course which things are likely to take, just as a number of subtle symptoms do to a physician. Or, rather than suppose anything so irrational as that the future already exists, one could believe that there are discarnate intelligences cognizant of a multitude of present facts which no man in the flesh can know, so that they can forecast future events just as an astronomer forecasts an eclipse, and that the medium or the dreamer comes somehow into *rapport* with these intelligences. We may then be impressed by the fulfilment of the prevision, just as savages are impressed when they see the darkness foretold by the white man really come over the sun. But probably before anyone can be required to believe in such hypotheses far more thoroughly proved cases of prevision have got to be established than we have at present.

The question whether God foreknows what choices will be made by those of His creatures endowed with volitional freedom is somewhat different from the question whether the whole series of events exists already as a Divine Plan. On the gramophone hypothesis, every event, including all our volitional choices, is already fixed on the record, but it has been believed by many people to be possible to reconcile the view that future choices are not yet determined, that bad choices at any rate are not willed by God, with the view that God nevertheless knows what all future choices are going to be. This is the view, of course, maintained in the philosophy officially approved by the Roman Church. Dante tries to make it intelligible by a figure. The image of a ship going down a river is reflected in the eye of a distant observer; the observer does not cause the movement of the ship, he only mirrors it. So in the case of future contingent events, events, that is, which may or may not occur, they are not necessitated by God; He only sees them as present.[1] St. Thomas himself has a slightly more elaborate figure: if a number of men are going, one after another, at intervals, down a road, the foremost man cannot see the men behind him, but an observer on a distant hill may see the whole series of men in one inclusive purview.[2] So each of us cannot see following events, but to God, the whole series of events is present as a *totum simul*.

The theory, indeed, that for God there is no after and no before, but that everything which for us is past or future is for God one eternal present implies that God knows the future in the same way in which He knows the present and the past. This view, as was said just now, is concerned to secure both God's complete knowledge of everything that is going to happen and the complete freedom of rational beings to choose between alternative lines of action. The two things *appear* incompatible; to affirm both together *seems* a plain self-contradiction. Some thinkers have pronounced them to be really incompatible and have declared that God does *not* know what the voluntary choices of rational beings will be. Till the choice has been made it does not exist, and God cannot know the non-existent as if it did exist. God's general

[1] *Paradiso*, xvii. 40. [2] *Summa*, Pars. I. Qu. xiv. Art. 13.

94

plan for the universe, we are told, will be carried out, whatever individual rational agents decide to do, but their freedom of choice makes it impossible for God to know at present in detail how His plan will be carried out. Most of you probably will remember William James's figure of the supreme chess-player playing against a poor opponent: he does not know precisely what moves his opponent is going to make, but he knows, whatever the moves may be, he will win in the way he intends. A similar view was maintained by James Ward in his *Realm of Ends* (p. 478). God's "purpose or creative ideal," Ward wrote, "is perfectly definite, unchangeable and assured. But the world's future history, the course by which that purpose is to be attained, depends not on Him alone, but also on the free agents, whom He sustains, but never constrains. This course then is *not* part of His creation; nor is it, we seem entitled to conclude also, part of His knowledge."

Of course, if you take this view, the teaching of Dr. Inge's *philosophia perennis*—that all time, what to us is past, present, and future, is equally present to God without any "after" or "before"—must be definitely wrong. There is a view which essays a kind of middle way between the Thomist doctrine that there is no temporal successiveness in God's knowledge and the view of William James and James Ward, which supposes that God does not know the future so far as it will depend on the voluntary choices of His rational creatures. This is the view maintained by two previous Gifford Lecturers, Royce in his *World and the Individual*, and Professor Sorley in his *Moral Values and the Idea of God* (p. 465). It brings in the idea of the "specious present," or, as Professor Sorley calls it, the "time-span." You have to suppose that, just as there is for us a little bit of time, alleged, as we saw, to be from half a second to four seconds, which we apprehend by a single perception, so the whole time-process is apprehended by God in one act of cognition. There would then be successiveness indeed in time for God, as for us—it would not be true to say, as the Thomist philosophy says, that there is for God no after or before, but God would know the whole series of events, as Professor Sorley puts it, "in a single or immediate intuition." Professor Sorley thinks that this saves the reality of choice by free agents. The future, so far as it will depend on my volitions, is not at the present moment known by God, but for God that future, when it becomes present, is separated from the present moment by an interval so brief, that God apprehends both moments of time in a single act; God's ignorance, at present, of what I am going to do is so instantaneously for Him succeeded by knowledge, that we can hardly make any distinction between the present moment, when He does not yet know, and the future moment, when He will know. This theory is an admirably ingenious mode of effecting the reconciliation between God's omniscience and human freedom of choice; but I cannot say that it gives me personally peace. It does not seem really to get rid of the supposition that at the present moment God does not know what the future volitions of rational creatures will be. This surely is inevitably implied if there is a real successiveness in Time for God. I do not see why you may not as well say frankly, with James and Ward and others, that God does not know the future so far as it depends on these free volitions. It seems to me also to theorize about the psychology of God in a way which it is absurd for human beings to do. This is also true, I think, of the doctrine of the *philosophia perennis*—that all events are present to God in a *Nunc Stans*, without any successiveness at all. How do we know? What ground have we for making any such statement?

It is, I think, apparent at the outset that the language commonly used in Christian theology, to the effect that the eternity attributed to God is not Time infinitely prolonged, but something wholly different from Time, different not in quantity, but in quality—it is apparent that all this language has come into Christian theology from the Greek Neo-Platonic infiltration. There is nothing in the Jewish or Christian scriptures to support it. So far as the language of the Bible goes, there is nothing to show that the eternity of God is understood in any other sense than that of unending Time. When St. Paul says: "The things that are seen are temporal, but the things that are not seen are eternal," there is no reason to suppose that he meant anything else than that the things which are seen come to an end in time, but that the things which are unseen do not. Where God is called, as He is in the book of Revelation, "He which was and which is and which is to come," that suggests rather an existence going on through infinite Time than a timeless existence. The theory, made popular in theological circles by Frederick Denison Maurice, that αἰώνιος in the New Testament means something different from endless time, is not, I believe, confirmed by a study of the use of the term in the Hellenistic Greek spoken and written by contemporary Jews.[1] When, later on, Christian theologians began to say that all these terms in their scripture were to be understood only figuratively, of a mode of existence in which there was no distinction of past, present, and future, but only an eternal Now, a *Nunc*

[1] There are, it is true, some passages in Hellenistic Jewish literature in which αἰώνιος is applied to limited periods of time. But I think that here a term strictly meaning "everlasting" is used with a kind of poetical exaggeration, as when we speak of "the everlasting hills." Mr. Brabant, in his Bampton Lectures (*Time and Eternity in Christian Thought*, 1937), examines the question in detail, and his conclusion is that though "αἰώνιος could at a pinch always (except perhaps where it is used of God) be translated 'age-long,' the context generally inclines the balance towards the sense of 'everlasting'" (p. 258).

Stans, that was definitely due to suggestion got from the pagan Platonic schools.

It is curious to note that, after this theory has become a commonplace of Christian theology, other views have been still maintained quite incompatible with it. For instance, the doctrine of God's eternity being timeless, without distinction of past, present and future, is clearly laid down by St. Thomas, on Neo-Platonic lines: but in another section of his great work, he discusses the old question whether God can change the past, can make what has happened not to have happened, and he pronounces decisively in the same sense as the ancient Greek poet Agathon, who said:

> One power there is that God Himself hath not—
> The things which have been done to make undone.[1]

God's omnipotence, according to the Scholastic philosophy, means only that He can do whatever is "possible" —possible being explained to mean "not involving a self-contradiction." To make something which has happened not to have happened would involve a self-contradiction, and therefore that is something which God cannot do. But consider what such a doctrine implies— that the distinction between past and future does hold good for God. If events in time are divided for God into two main parts—on the one side the past which is fixed beyond His power to alter it, on the other side the future which He can still fashion as He will, how can one say that temporal differences do not enter into His mode of existence? It might be said in answer that the past was fashioned precisely to correspond with His will, as the future will be, and that, since His will cannot change,

---

[1] μόνον γὰρ αὐτοῦ καὶ θεὸς στερίσκεται
ἀγένητα ποιεῖν ἅσσ' ἂν ᾖ πεπραγμένα.

(Quoted by Aristotle, *Ethics*, 1139 *b*.)

the whole series past, present and future equally corresponds with it. But if the series is thus determined as a single block by God, why lay stress, as St. Thomas does, on God's inability to change the *past*? This implies that for God there is no similar inability in regard to the future. Or why should not St. Thomas have said that God cannot make the present different from what it is, or the future different from what it is going to be?

Probably, so far as people dimly picture what a *Nunc Stans* would be, they picture it as a state of things enduring perpetually without change. But that must be quite wrong. Duration is essentially temporal. Of the objects round about us some change much less than others with the passage of time. If there were absolutely no change at all in ourselves or in surrounding things, Time would either not exist or be imperceptible. We could hardly be conscious, since we should not be able to think, thought being essentially a play or movement of mind. When we apprehend anything as enduring or changeless we do so only because we measure its duration by something else which is changing. Should change cease in the universe round about us, the universe would still endure in Time if we, looking on, could measure Time by the succession of our heart-beats or the play of our thought. There would still be past, present and future, not, for us at any rate, a *Nunc Stans*. A *Nunc Stans*, if it can be pictured at all, would be much more like an instantaneous flash, only a flash after which nothing more came.

It is conceivable that a particular individual might be removed from the passage of Time, his state at the present moment continuing without change, without any new perception, while change went on in the universe round about him. This is what is supposed to have happened in those stories we all know, about a monk, or someone, listening to a mysterious bird and then finding, when he

99

returned home, that a hundred years had gone by, in what had seemed to him only a few minutes. If this can be imagined in regard to a hundred years, it can be imagined in regard to a million years, or an infinite number of years. In the latter case, the experience which an individual has at a particular moment would be for him his final experience. For those looking on at him from the outside, in his ecstasy, his unchanging experience would seem to be spread out through Time, but for the individual himself there would be no duration, because no further event would come for him in contrast with which his present moment would become past. There would thus seem, so far as the individual experience goes, no difference between time ending for me to-morrow in a *Nunc Stans*, and my being annihilated to-morrow. Supposing my last experience were to see the flash and hear the report of a rifle, and I were annihilated immediately afterwards, that last experience would have for me no perceptible duration because there would be no more any I to perceive a next event: similarly, if I myself did not come to an end but that last experience were not succeeded by any other, then even if time continued for others who were looking on, I should know nothing but the flash and report, and that momentary experience would be the last I should have.

These considerations suggest incidentally that the controversy which has gone on between those who have maintained that the ultimate fate of lost souls is to be annihilated and those who have maintained that their punishment is eternal, may be a controversy about expressions which stand for no essential difference. If a painful experience becomes a *Nunc Stans*, which is never followed by a re-beginning of time, that is for the sufferer precisely the same as if, after his last moment of experience, he were annihilated. The difference would be only for others, whose experience was still successive in time. Any other spirit who could enter into the experience of the lost soul at intervals, say, of a thousand years, would always find the experience there the same as it had been a thousand years before, but for the lost soul itself there would be no protraction of its experience through periods of time; it would all be shrunk up into one moment with nothing afterwards. I do not at all mean to imply that there seems to me any good ground for believing that this will actually be the case with any human soul. I merely point out that when we argue about the state of persons beyond death, there may be possibilities in a different apprehension of time which we cannot know, and which may make all our arguments wide of the mark. But if this is the best conception we can get of what a *Nunc Stans* would be, it would seem an inappropriate conception for the eternal life of the blessed and an even less happy symbol for the unimaginable life of God than Royce's idea of a specious present.

TIME

(*continued*)

IN our last lecture we were considering the problem of Time in connexion with the question: How far are temporal modes of expression, when applied to God, symbolic of a Divine Life which is wholly timeless? It is obvious that if Time, as some philosophers have held, is not real, if it belongs merely to the way in which the human mind apprehends a timeless Reality, then it certainly follows that there can be no Time in the life of God. But I have suggested that the Scholastic theology, in adopting from Neo-Platonism the doctrine of God's life being a *Nunc Stans*, a *totum simul* in which there is nothing like temporal succession, claims to know more about God's life than man without absurdity can do.

Idealist philosophy has often been moved to deny the reality of Time just as it denies the reality of Space, and make both merely phantoms of the human mind. But I should follow those who hold that this coupling together of Time and Space has been the cause of a good deal of confusion in thinking. Time and Space are not analogous, except in respect to a few of their characteristics—such as that of being measurable. We saw in our last lecture how people entangled themselves in contradictions by applying spatial figures of speech to Time. Time is unique. Time also, it is plain, belongs much more intimately to the life of the spirit than space. Spatial objects are around us, outside us; our feelings and thoughts have no spatial dimensions but they have temporal succession. We can, I think, imagine a universe in which there was no space, but only a succession of feelings and emotions: we cannot imagine a universe in which there was no Time, that is to say, no events. Bishop Berkeley, who first clearly asserted that all spatial objects were merely ideas produced in the human mind by God, still believed that there was a real temporal succession in each individual's experience. And we can see, I think, that even if we not only went with Berkeley in denying that the spatial world had any existence outside the mind recipient of sensations, but went further than Berkeley in denying that there was any temporal process outside conscious minds, those minds' experience of Time would still not be subjective in the same sense as their ideas of space were subjective. It would be an absolute truth that the experiencing individual did have that series of sensations and feelings in that temporal order. You might deny that there was any temporal order outside to which the order in his mind corresponded, that his idea of Time was an illusion in so far as he regarded his sensations and feelings as indicative of a reality outside; the fact would remain that a particular being in the universe had those feelings and sensations one after the other in a succession through Time. That psychological fact would be a fact not only for him but for any other intelligence who could be cognizant of what was going on in his mind. And the fact that only one individual in the universe had a temporal experience would constitute in regard to him, the reality of Time, for even if it was only in regard to him that the series of events occurred, it would not be only in his supposition. It would be an absolute truth that they occurred, and in experiencing the succession the individual would apprehend a bit of reality.

But if one may believe that Time is real, one must, I think, make a distinction between Time as an order of succession and the sense of duration. It seems easier to believe that the order of succession belongs to ultimate reality than that the sense of duration corresponds to any absolute measure of Time. The sense of duration, the pace at which Time seems to go, differs from person to person, and in the same person differs according to his mood and circumstances.

There is nothing illogical, or even inconceivable, in the supposition that the same series of events as experienced by one sentient being might move much more quickly than as experienced by another. The medieval story about the monk who, when out walking, listened to the song of a peculiar bird and found when he returned to the monastery that a whole century had gone by, which was referred to in our last lecture, does not contain anything which we cannot imagine as true for some kind of being not living under human conditions. The relativity of temporal duration is suggested by our own every-day experience. But it is quite a different matter with the order of succession. That is something irreversible. And the order of succession has especial significance for the spirit. Ezekiel describes two supposed cases, one that of a man who lived a righteous life almost up to the end, but at the end turned to wickedness, and the other that of a man who lived a wicked life almost up to the end, but at the end repented and turned to God, and, speaking in the name of the Lord, he declares that God's way of treating one man will be the opposite to His way of treating the other.[1] It is the order of temporal succession which makes one spiritual process to have an altogether different value

[1] Ezekiel xviii. 21–28.

from the other. Whether I feel hostility to someone *before* he has shown me kindness or *after*, makes all the difference to the spiritual quality of my attitude.

Is there any public time, an order in which events actually happen apart from the perception of the events by different individuals? Your answer to this question is surely Yes or No, according as you believe, or do not believe, in the real existence of things apart from the sensations of individual minds. If you are sufficiently a Realist to believe in any objective existence of the external world, you must believe in the objective reality of the time in which events of the external world happen. The Now which is now for me is the same now for the whole universe to the furthest star.

I am afraid that in saying this I go against the opinion of someone whose judgment is based on a far larger philosophical knowledge than mine, Professor A. E. Taylor. "I should frankly concede that a 'universal' Time is an impossibility and a 'common Time' a makeshift, derived for specific necessary purposes, like a common creed, or a common party programme. The 'lived' Time of each of us is a 'perspective' peculiar to himself."[1] I am, however, bound to put things as they appear to me. If we are going to deny any public Time on the ground that we perceive events from an individual standpoint which makes our perspective different from that of anyone else, we ought on the same ground to deny any real external world at all. If there is any process in the universe which realizes a Divine Purpose the events of that process must happen in a Time which belongs to the process as a whole. Professor Gunn, in speaking of the theory that God apprehends the whole of Time as a process indeed, but one comprised in a single "specious present," observes that God must in that case at least know at any moment

[1] *The Faith of a Moralist*, i. p. 117.

D*

105

"where in the time-order His world has got to" (p. 140).
I think that is so, and this implies a public Time, not
indeed a common sense of duration, but an order of
succession in which events, apart from variations in the
perception of them, actually happen.

To some people it may appear that such a belief has
been shaken by Einstein and the doctrine of Relativity.
But the doctrine of Relativity, so far as I can gather,
leaves the public Time in which events happen quite
untouched. What that doctrine is concerned with is the
measurement of periods of time and the different times
at which the same event is perceived by observers with
different standpoints. It may no doubt be true that it is
impossible to get any absolute unchanging standard by
which to measure one bit of duration in respect of another.
It is certainly true that what to some observers might seem
a single flash of light may seem to others a series of flashes.
It would even be possible, if an observer could travel away
from the earth through space at a speed greater than that
of light, and catch up successively the rays which had left
the earth in a series of moments before, he might see the
events on earth in the reverse order to that in which they
happened. But that leaves the time in which they *happened*
quite unaffected, just as unaffected as the time in which a
man takes off his clothes is unaffected by the process being
shown afterwards in reverse order on the cinematograph.
We may have seen such a film, in which the coat the man
had really taken off and thrown on to a chair seemed to
rise spontaneously from the chair and fly on to his back.

Einstein says: "I call two events *simultaneous* for a
given observer when they are perceived or seen at the
same time by that observer while he is equidistant from
both."[1] But why should the recognition of simultaneity
be made by Einstein to depend on the observer being

[1] *The Theory of Relativity.*

equidistant from both events, except on the supposition that there is a real time, apart from the observer, in which light travels from the two events? The very word "simultaneous," in such a proposition, has no sense except in reference to an objective public time. When an astronomer tells us that the light of a fixed star visible to us left the star 400,000 years ago, the immense distance of Time between our perception of an event in that star and the perception of the same event by an observer on the star itself (if one existed) does not invalidate belief in an objective Time common to that star and to the earth: it implies it. It means that the event on the star which we see to-day was really simultaneous with events on the earth 400,000 years ago. Relativity shows how widely the order in which a series of events are perceived by observers elsewhere may differ from the order in which we perceive them. In that sense it is possible for an event to be still future for us which is past for another observer. If an event occurred 200,000 years ago on the fixed star just referred to it would, for an observer to-day on the star, belong to a past as remote as that; we on earth could not perceive that event till the year A.D. 201,934. But all this has only to do with the order of perception, not the order in which the perceived events happen. And it is to be noted that however wildly the order of perception may differ for different observers after the event has happened, no exponent of the theory of Relativity has shown that any event can be perceived before it has happened. The actual moment of happening in objective public Time sets a limit behind which variation in perception cannot go. But this is so because all perception is perception (more or less true) of an order of events in objective public Time.

One phrase made current by recent theories in Physics is, I believe, unhappy, and, to the general public, misleading: that Time is a "fourth dimension." The phrase seems nonsense, and, although it may no doubt be understood by physicists in a sense which gives it value, it is, I think, as it stands, really nonsense. Each of the three dimensions we know of old is a direction in space at right angles with either of the other two dimensions. I do not think that anyone has claimed that Time is at right angles to each of the other three, but, unless it is, it cannot properly be called a dimension. What I believe the phrase means might be expressed more intelligibly by saying that for the existence of things in space, Time is a fourth factor which has to be taken account of in addition to the three spatial dimensions. And I do not question that that is true. That, however, does not seem to me to establish an essential difference between the time of physicists and time as we experience it. If it is true that their time has no present, but only an after and before, this is also true of our time when it is past.

The philosophy of Bergson has lost some of the prestige it had when it was new, twenty or thirty years ago, but it appears to me that his protest against the coupling together of Space and Time as two things of the same order will remain as the assertion of a valuable truth. Professor Alexander no doubt would dissent from such a statement, connecting the two things as he actually does by a hyphen. And I might feel it presumptuous of me to assert the contrary view in the face of an authority so eminent, were it not that I am in the company of others who find Professor Alexander's philosophy in this respect inacceptable. It may be true that there could be no measurement of objects in space apart from the factor of Time, but it does not seem to me true, as I said at the beginning of this lecture, that spatial perceptions or sensations are necessary to the experience of Time, even if in the actual experience of men on earth the two things go together.

108

No spiritual life—surely so far, at any rate, Bergson is right—can be imagined apart from Time, not only in its volitional activity (it is admitted that for the will and for all the moral values connected with the will Time is essential) but even for the exercise of the intellect. Thought is movement, play about some object. Perfectly unmoving thought is a contradiction in terms: you could not even contemplate such a truth as that the inner angles of a triangle are equivalent to two right angles without a movement of thought bringing general concepts to bear upon perception. It may be objected that in the mystical ecstasy you can have unmoving contemplation in which there is no flicker of thought round the object, but, if so, the contemplation would consist in feeling without intellectual content. We cannot imagine any worthy spiritual life which would consist entirely in such unmoving contemplation. No doubt the Christian doctrine of the beatific vision enjoyed by the redeemed in heaven may be believed to point to some kind of experience to which the unmoving contemplation of the mystic has a certain resemblance; yet a life in which the movement of thought and will was not in any way represented would be a poor life as compared with what the movement of thought and will, as we know it here in man's earthly life, leads us to hope for hereafter. In what way such a beatific vision could involve something analogous to thought and will we cannot, of course, now imagine. We can say so much: if there will be anything in it analogous to thought and will, then there must be something in it analogous to Time. The unmoving contemplation of the mystic cannot be taken to represent all that it will be.

It may, of course, be fully admitted that the doctrine of God's existence as timeless came into Christian theology from the pagan Greeks and is not found in the Scriptures written by men of Hebrew race, and at the same time be maintained that the doctrine is true. But if it was not the authority of their Scriptures which led Christian thinkers to adopt so largely the Neo-Platonic view of eternity as timeless, what was it that commended the doctrine to them? There must have been something which moved them to adopt it.

I think we can see the enormous difficulty to thought if we suppose God to experience Time *as we experience it* —always supposing that there is really a Being who fulfils the requirements which must be fulfilled, if the exigences of the spirit in man are to be satisfied. What has driven on Christian thought is the underlying assumption that a Being must exist to whom nothing can attach that would present itself to thought as an imperfection: no other Being can properly, for Christian or Theist feeling, be called "God." This is why we find Christian theology affirm with such confidence that the existence of God, the life of God, must be of such and such a character. In contrast with the Hebrew writers who had regarded man's life as imperfect simply because it did have an end and such a speedy one, the Christian theologians who adopted the view that God's eternity was timeless felt that the imperfection of human life went further than this— they felt not merely that threescore years and ten was such a short bit of time, but that all experience in Time, however long, must be imperfect.

Partly, perhaps, we must allow for the psychological effect of prolonged time being for men associated with fatigue. We cannot think of any kind of activity as indefinitely prolonged without our having a sensation of physical fatigue or mental tedium. From the imagination of a series of changes going on and on the spirit recoils, and cries out for a cessation of the process, for a stationary rest—the cry expressed in an ancient Collect, "that we who are wearied by the labour and the changes of this transitory world may repose upon thy eternal change-lessness." But it seems to me a *naïveté* to use this fact against the supposition of a prolonged activity in heaven, since plainly it is possible to suppose that only the conditions of physical life on earth make fatigue the necessary consequence of prolonged activity. So far as our recoil from the idea of endless Time is determined by this accidental association (it may be without our realizing it) the recoil is hardly reasonable. If we are to show that there is something in temporal experience which makes it impossible to attribute it to God, we must show that it is beset, not merely with an unpleasant accompaniment in consequence of the laws of animal physiology, but by an essential imperfection. This, I think, can be done. In the first place, any temporal experience, if its character is reflected upon, must disclose our state as one of helplessness, of subjection, to an irresistible power not ourselves. We cannot arrest the process which carries us inexorably on. "*O lente, lente, currite, noctis equi*"—the line of Ovid in his mistress's arms which is quoted grimly by Marlowe's Faustus when his moment to be carried off by Mephistopheles is almost come. But no one can make those horses stay in their course. There is nothing that anyone can do to prevent the present living moment turning instantly into the dead past. To think of God's experience as Time prolonged is to think of Time as stronger than God.

Secondly, Time, as we experience it, means continual loss and deficiency—loss in so far as all the successive moments which were each ourselves, our being, in the past, are gone and non-existent for ever, deficiency in so far as all the moments which will be ourselves, our being, do not yet exist at all. Only the moment in which we feel and act is real, exists; as soon as we reflect on our feeling or action, it is already a bit of the dead, unchangeable past. We cannot keep our own being more than a moment.

But if our temporal experience is thus in its essence beset with imperfection, we could only attribute it to God, if He is to that extent imperfect, and if He is imperfect at all, He no longer is what we mean by "God." Christian theologians seem therefore to have been fully justified in saying that if there is a Being than whom none greater can be conceived, His life cannot be a temporal sequence like man's. But it may be questioned whether they were wise in going beyond this negative statement, in trying to give, under Neo-Platonic influence, a statement which sounded positive about that in God's life to which our temporal experience is analogous. To call it eternity says nothing, eternity is a mere *x* denoting something of which all we know is that it cannot be Time like the Time we experience. Still less is it helpful to describe it by such a phrase as a *Nunc Stans*; for the only meaning we can connect with "now" is the meaning it gets from our experience of the present in contrast with past and future, and to be stationary means nothing except to persist without change throughout a period of time.

It seems to me utterly idle for us to speculate in this way at all on what God's life is for Him; but that also makes it idle to deny that there is anything analogous to successiveness in God's apprehension of the universe. I referred in my last lecture to the suggestion of Royce and Sorley that God apprehended the time-series as a succession, but a succession grasped in a single act of cognition, like man's apprehension of the "specious present." I indicated that the theory did not seem to me easy to accept. Yet it may come nearer the truth than the idea of a *Nunc Stans* in which there is no temporal after and before. It is better to confess that we do not know and cannot know.

With regard to the picture of the cosmic consummation of the time-process or the picture of what awaits the individual after death, it would be absurd to take literally the imagery given us in the traditional Christian eschatology. But to substitute the mythology of Plotinus, in regard to the Higher World and to *Aion*, for the Christian mythology in regard to the end of the world and the coming of the Son of Man, is, I think, a doubtful advantage. The Christian traditional eschatology may be truer than the mythology of Plotinus in the value it gives to the time-process and to the consummation of the Purpose of God in Time.

Any Theism which recognizes God as the Creator must at least say that, if Time is an essential characteristic of the universe we know, God must will that there should be such a thing as Time, even should it be only a form of the experience of His finite creatures. And if we can speak of God as being interested in the volitions of human beings —or, as it might be put, as caring at all for righteousness (and it may be remembered that not only has this been basic with Hebrew religion, but that Plato in his latest work, denounces with unwonted passion the idea that the Divine is not interested in human volitions)—Time must for God Himself at any rate have the value of making the volitions in which He is interested possible.

Even Dr. Inge recognizes the value of Time, in so far as it is the necessary condition of soul-making by moral volitions: the idea apparently which he cannot away with is that the time-process as a whole carries out a Divine Purpose, and that there is therefore some future consummation (as the Christian Church has always believed) to which we have to look forward for the satisfying realization of values. He allows us to believe in a multiplicity of separate Divine purposes carried out in different parts of the time-process, but we must not say that there is one

Divine Purpose subserved by the whole.[1] The antithesis seems to me quite false. One single inclusive Divine Purpose or plan is not in the least incompatible with any number of subordinate purposes embraced within the whole. If you suppose that the time-process is ever going to come to an end and be succeeded by a timeless state of things, and if it is by the will of God that there has been a time-process at all, its final consummation must obviously show the meaning of the whole complete: the 'Purpose' in the process would then correspond with the ordinary type of purpose expressed in action which has a definite end and is fulfilled when that end is reached. But even if you suppose that the time-process will never have an end, it is still not impossible to regard it as realizing a Purpose: the ancient philosophers distinguished activities which aimed at some result beyond themselves and activities whose purpose was in themselves. Dancing is given as the stock example of the latter kind of activity. The purpose, the production of a particular kind of beauty, is being realized all the time the activity goes on. It would be possible to conceive an endless time-process as similarly realizing a Divine Purpose, the production of some particular kind of value, as it goes on for ever. There are some purposive processes which combine both characteristics: they are achieved only in the final result, but the value of the result depends on its having been achieved in that way, so that in a sense the purpose is being *progressively* realized all through the process. The attainment of moral virtue or of spiritual perfection is a process of the latter kind. It would not be the same thing if the moral virtue or the spiritual perfection were suddenly conferred and not won by a series of free volitions.

Since the time-process goes on throughout a universe

[1] *God and the Astronomers,* p. 12.

of which our planet is, spatially, only an infinitesimal part, it would seem an unlikely supposition that the series of events on this planet is the whole of God's purpose. Supposing there are other rational or sentient beings anywhere else in space—a view to which Dr. Inge inclines, though apparently on no ground except that the hypothesis satisfies a certain aesthetic exigence, offended by the huge disproportion between material extent and value if you suppose conscious life confined to this planet[1]— supposing, however, there are rational beings elsewhere, it would no doubt be difficult to see how God's dealings with them and His dealings with us could form parts of one world-plan. Yet our not being able to see how this might be is a poor argument. The supposition that God's dealings with the universe consist in a number of different purposes, disjointed and uncoordinated, is a far greater offence to the aesthetic ideal of order and harmony in the human spirit than the disproportion of material extent and value, if life is confined to this planet. And if the work of God in creation reveals His being at all, it must reveal, one would think, unity as well as richness in variety.

Dr. Inge, in his first chapter, examines various modern philosophies which identify God Himself with a Power or Tendency working through the time-process, and regard the process as bringing God Himself progressively into being as it realizes a richer life of the universe. Since I have just ventured to question some things said by Dr. Inge, I should like to say with the greater emphasis that his exposure of the utter unsatisfactoriness of such philosophies in his first chapter seems to me admirable

[1] "From the astronomical point of view we are only creatures of a day; and even if the other globes in our system are permanently unfit to be the abode of life, it is wildly improbable that among thousands of millions of stars there is only one planet capable of being the abode of 'living souls.' . . . There is, I think, something derogatory to the Deity in supposing that He made this vast universe for so paltry an end as the production of ourselves and our friends" (*God and the Astronomers*, p. 249).

and conclusive. I do not know that Dr. Inge proves that such a Power or Tendency, or whatever it should be called, as these philosophies suppose, is not there in the time-process, but he does show—unanswerably, I should say —that, if it is there, Christians, Jews or other Theists could never regard it as identical with what they mean by God.

There is an ambiguity to be guarded against when we speak of a future consummation. One may mean a consummation which is itself within the time-process, the final phase of the time-process with a definite temporal duration, such as the Messianic age on earth is conceived to be in some Christian and Jewish eschatological schemes. Of course, even if such a hope is warranted, it cannot be regarded as satisfying the exigence of the spirit: that exigence can never be satisfied by any earthly Paradise. One may, on the other hand, mean a consummation in a state of being wholly different from our present existence under the laws of material space, and that different being may be conceived as altogether timeless, or as having unending temporal duration, or as having something analogous to time which we cannot now imagine. Supposing it is timeless it would nevertheless be in temporal relation to the world-process in which we now live: it would have no successiveness in itself, no before and after in itself, yet it would stand in the relation of *after* to the present world process: the world process would get its meaning by leading up to it. If any human spirit enters into this eternal timeless state, it would be *after* his temporal experience. One would think of his temporal experience as like a river flowing between banks into an unbounded, unmoving ocean. It would be nonsense to say his perfected state in eternity was just as much *before* his earthly experience as *after* it, that, if it is reached through the process of soul-making in this earthly vale, the individual's existence in the eternal state after his

116

earthly experience was no different from his existence *before* he had his earthly experience. But if you can speak of his eternal existence as *after* his temporal existence, and cannot speak of it as *before* his temporal existence, then his eternal existence, even if itself timeless, is in a temporal relation to his experience in Time.

If one asks why Dr. Inge and other philosophers who have taken a similar view of Time, such as the late Professor Bosanquet, so hate the idea of a consummation, for the individual or the world, which is future, either in the sense of being the last stretch of Time or of being beyond the latter end of Time, it is perhaps because they refuse to think that a man cannot here and now enter upon complete possession of everything he can ever reasonably desire to have or to be. A value—let us say beauty, for example—is something timeless, therefore all a man has to do is to immerse himself in the contemplation of something beautiful, and that enjoyment is such that it is unreasonable for him to want anything more in the time to come, or beyond it. Even if he has entered, I suppose, into the eternal world of beauty for ten minutes only of his earthly time he ought to be satisfied: because the world he apprehended is eternal, he has thus already appropriated what exceeds all measure and he should crave for no more. Dr. Inge quotes with approval Bosanquet's dictum that "to throw our ideals into the future is the death of all sane idealism."[1] I confess that if

---

[1] The dictum of Bosanquet which Dr. Inge likes is profoundly anti-Christian. It is perfectly true, of course, that a right relation to God in this world implies, according to the Christian view, the present possession of a great deal of ultimate good (the believer, St. John says, already has eternal life); but the Christian view also insists that all present realization of good is imperfect, and that for the complete realization the Christian must look to *the future*. "Beloved, *now* are we the sons of God, and it doth *not yet* appear what we shall be." It is the combination of the "*now*" and the "*not yet*" which characterizes the Christian *Weltanschauung*. Dr. Inge would be quite right in condemning a view which eliminated the "*now*" and made the realization of ideals merely future; but it is no less a mistake to eliminate the "*not yet*."

117

I try to represent to myself what this means in actual practice, I can make no sense of it. There seems a strange confusion between the eternity of values—values are, of course, timeless—and the eternity of our apprehension of values. Granted that there is all round us, close to us, this eternal world of values, what makes us look forward to a future is that apprehension of these values under earthly conditions cannot be anything but broken and transient and partial. It reminds one of the Turk's answer, when his boat was caught in a squall at sea and his companion sought to cheer him by enunciating that God was great: "Yes, I know that Allah is great, but what troubles me is that this boat is so very small." It is no good going on telling us that the world of values is great and eternal, when we are so small and so subject to time.

If ever the exigences of any human spirit are to be satisfied, it cannot be in life under earthly conditions. If God does mean them to find fruition at all, it would obviously be absurd to say that they have already been satisfied at some past time: it would be equally absurd to say that they are being satisfied at the present moment; we know too well they are not: their satisfaction then can only be, if at all, in the future. Bosanquet, indeed, seems to represent the brief and scrappy apprehension of eternal value which is all any of us can have in this life, not as all we might wish for, but as all we shall ever get, and he seems to make wisdom consist in resignation, the acceptance of such a destiny because it is the law of the world. Such a view has no doubt an undertone of pessimism, though Bosanquet apparently thought we ought to be quite cheerful about our limitations, because, if we could have no more than this, the Absolute had everything, and that ought to make us happy. If Professor Bosanquet denied that the individual had ground for expecting any existence after death, this was logical, in so far as he maintained that a man ought to be satisfied with such apprehension of the eternal as he can have under the conditions of this life. Dr. Inge, while apparently quoting this doctrine with approval, shrinks from going all the way with Professor Bosanquet, and still clings to belief in the existence of individual spirits in a beatified state, only we must not, he tells us, say that this state is somewhere, because there is no region of space where it could be, and we must not say that it is in the future, because it is an enjoyment of values which are timeless. I confess that in thus trying to combine belief in an existence beyond death for human spirits made perfect, while forbidding us to look forward to the future for the realization of values, he seems to me to entangle himself in hopeless contradictions. Perhaps he would say that it is impossible to speak about what lies outside time and space except in language whose figures are borrowed from time and space, and that verbal contradictions are therefore inevitable. But if this line of defence were taken, one would be bound to make equal allowance for the mode in which the Christian eschatological hope is expressed: it would be hardly legitimate, after having poured scorn on a particular view because it seems to you confused and contradictory, and then, having put in the place of it something still more confused and contradictory, to turn round and say: "Ah, but you know it is impossible to speak of these things without contradictions."

Of course, even if it is true that in the life of God there is nothing like Time, it does not follow that any finite spirit ever attains a condition which is timeless. It may be so, but I do not think we have any right to affirm it. And if it is true that beatified human spirits attain a timeless condition, it does not follow that they do so immediately after death. For all we know, human spirits may go through experiences in Time for ages before they reach the timeless state, if they ever do. Dr. Inge's argument, that there is no region in the space we know in which they could be, can hardly be taken seriously.

In our earthly experience the passage of Time is so strongly marked with loss that we can with difficulty imagine Time without that characteristic. We lose the past continually because the vivid apprehension of the present moment instantly grows blurred and our memories fade. What small fragments we remember now of all we have seen and felt and thought and done during the past years of our life! But if there were a form of existence in which every present was full of unmixed joy and the contents of that present were possessed eternally in a memory which let nothing go, and if the only change experienced were one of ever-increasing apprehension and richness of life, I do not see that any *Nunc Stans* could be superior to such duration. Such a life might combine the highest activity with the most complete rest. And there is, I think, one great difficulty in thinking of the life of beatified spirits as timeless. Beatitude must consist in an apprehension of God. But if God is infinite, no apprehension of Him by a finite spirit can be more than partial. If, therefore, you suppose that at any stage in the life of a spirit it reaches timelessness, that is, that any further change becomes impossible for it, you have to suppose that it can never, never, apprehend more of God than it does at the moment when its present apprehension is fixed in an eternal Now. It is not to be thought that after a given number of million years any of us will have found out all there is in God, that we shall then have got to the end of Him, and have nothing further to explore. This is a difficulty: I do not wish to deny that it may be God's purpose for finite spirits that for each a measure of apprehension is finally assigned beyond which it can never go, but I would suggest as a more acceptable view that *finiteness* and *time* go together, and that since no spirit other than God, however immense its expansion may be, can ever cease to be finite, no spirit other than God can ever cease to live, after some mode or other, in time, with always greater possibilities of attainment beyond all that it has attained hitherto.

With regard to God Himself, I have expressed my full agreement that the application to Him of temporal duration, as it is experienced by man, is only a symbol or analogy for a life incomprehensible to us. I pointed out in my last lecture that a universe in which there was no change at all would be one in which there could hardly be, in any sense, Time, and therefore not duration; but that if there were change in the mind of some one person observing an otherwise changeless universe, that changelessness would be apprehended by the observer as duration. Somewhat after such an analogy, it may be that the inconceivable life of God, though not duration to God Himself, can be apprehended by any finite mind cnly as duration, the changeless contemplated from the standpoint of someone who is changing.

I should agree also that in some way it is possible for men, even in their earthly life, to apprehend partially, for moments, a mode of existence, unaffected by the succession of temporal events and strivings in which the spirit, as time is experienced on earth, is distracted and wearied. A sense of this may, I think, be discerned behind the imagery of an old and familiar document, the first chapter of the book of Genesis, in which an ancient Hebrew writer makes the pageant of the six days of creation pass before us, followed by the Creator's Sabbath rest on the seventh day. There is nothing in the actual history of the earth to correspond with such a day. Yet, for some reason, to the visionary or poet or priestly philosopher it seemed appropriate to imagine, at the end of the six days, a period of empty time in which God is there, but the activity of creation has ceased. It is not, I think, extravagant to see the same truth about God which we ordinarily express by the spatial metaphor of transcendence expressed here by a symbol taken from Time. Transcendence presents the symbol of an empty space in which God is alone *above* the space filled by the created universe: the symbol in Genesis i. presents the idea of an empty period of time in which God is alone *after* the activity of Creation. The image of transcendence and the Sabbath rest are equally symbols which it would be absurd to take literally in regard to God. There is no such empty space and no such empty time, but each symbol expresses imaginatively something that in human language we can only express by metaphors—that the being of God extends infinitely beyond the world, that God is much more than the world. The moving time-process in which the Divine activity is seen in the production of continual change does not show all that God is. There is a sphere in which God rests, into which the unrest of the earthly time-process does not enter. It is not necessary to suppose that the old priest-poet who wrote the first chapter of Genesis had a clear philosophic conception, that he thought like a modern European and deliberately clothed these conceptions in an imagery which he knew to be symbolic only. He may have had quite a *naïve* conception of God literally resting on the Sabbath day. We do not know. But we have here again a case, I believe, in which we may see a man at a more primitive stage of thought led by a feeling of appropriateness in the association of ideas, which he could not, perhaps, himself justify or explain, but simply felt. The image of God which showed His being to extend into a quiet beyond the activity of creation seemed to him somehow more worthy of God than an image which showed God as only active in the world process. Looking back from a stage of human thought further on, we may hold that such a feeling in the old writer was a veridical intuition, whether we regard it as due to some action of a personal Reality itself upon his mind, as, in that sense, revelation, or not.

If this is a true account of the idea underlying the symbol of God's Sabbath rest, the association with it of the Sabbath, as an institution for man, has particular point. There is an appearance of absurdity in a commandment which says that men must rest from their works every seventh day on the ground that God rested from His on a particular Sabbath day long ago. But if the image of God's rest after the activity of creation was a dim apprehension of God's transcendence, and if the belief is true, that men can come into contact with God Himself by a movement in which they escape from the multiplicity and changefulness of the world to the unchangeable One, then we may see the old Israelites led by a true feeling of appropriateness, not only when they conceived the empty space of time in which God rests after creation, but when they required something corresponding to be reproduced in the life of man. Man, too, is a being who extends potentially beyond the world he handles and sees. It is right that a great part of his time should be taken up with activities in dealing with that world. "Six days shalt thou labour and do all that thou hast to do." In that world, too, he meets God at every turn, for God is the ground of the world and is active in all its movement. But the nature of man is such that he cannot be satisfied with meeting God only in the things of the world: if he practises the right way of withdrawal, he can meet God in the sphere of God's Sabbath rest too. The religious life, Baron von Hügel used to insist, involves tension and difficulty because it means continual alternative movement from the Many to the One, and back again from the One to the

Many. The particular form in which the requirement of movement from the Many to the One was couched in the old Jewish Sabbath Law may have been of temporary usefulness, but the underlying principle of the explanation given, the principle that the potential being of man extends beyond the world, and that man must therefore seek to meet God in God's own quiet beyond the world— that seems something fundamental to any spiritual Theism.

LIGHT

A SYMBOL which has been used in the religions of the world, perhaps as widely as that of height, is that of light. It is curious that light should be at the present moment one of the mysteries for Science, with characteristics hitherto supposed irreconcilable. It has certainly been one of the things in the physical environment of man which, from the earliest times we know of, has peculiarly impressed him and been most closely associated with his thoughts of the Divine.

Some years ago (in 1915) a monograph was published by a Swedish scholar, Gillis Wetter, with the title of *Phōs*. It is an inquiry suggested by the observation how frequently the idea of light is brought in throughout the literature of what is described as "Hellenistic Piety"— that is to say—the Hermetic literature, the magical papyri, semi-Christian Gnosticism and Manichaeism.

Wetter admits that the use of light as a religious symbol is found in earlier Greek literature, before the Hellenistic age, but he insists that it is found in the Hellenistic literature, just indicated, with very much greater frequency. That no doubt is true. The reason may be partly that this literature largely proceeds upon the idea of an occult knowledge—a knowledge at any rate not possessed by the ordinary man—which is communicated to the adept, and which enables him to attain salvation—deliverance from death, deliverance from the tyranny of the stars, deliverance from the bodily passions which hold the soul down in the lower world. Between the boon given by knowledge, which enables a man to know what the laws of the universe are and by what course of conduct he can secure his good in view of them, and the boon given by light, which enables a man to see his physical environment and to guide his steps rightly, the analogy is so obvious and close, that to describe the knowledge imparted to the adept as "light," to call his attainment of it "enlightenment," is not something which calls for any elaborate explanation. In Christianity, too, the view of the universe imparted to the *catechumen* was contrasted as *knowledge* with the *ignorance* of the pagan world which led men to mistake stocks and stones or the heavenly bodies or devils for gods, so that it is perfectly natural that in Christian language too the metaphor of light should frequently occur and that initiation into the Christian Church by baptism should come to be spoken of as *phōtismos* (enlightenment).

In the earlier days of Greek culture, the days of *naïf* polytheism, reflected in the greatest works of Greek literature, the idea of *knowledge* was not so prominent in religion. Men needed indeed in many conjunctures of life to know what the will of the gods was, so that they might order their steps aright, and men sought such knowledge by resorting to omens or oracles or soothsayers, but it was not commonly thought that there was a special knowledge of the universe possessed by a particular group or community of persons, in contrast with which the ideas of the ordinary man were as darkness to light. The ideas attached to the great gods of the state religions were taken as being the real truth about the world and they were known to everybody.

That, probably, is, generally speaking, true. But, of course, from the sixth century B.C. there were also the Orphic sects or individuals who claimed to possess an occult knowledge, and at an even earlier date a particular experience, the sight at any rate of certain sacred objects not known to the ordinary man, was obtained in the Eleusinian mysteries, whereby a happy future was secured after death; but neither Orphism nor mystery-cults seem to have occupied much place in the thoughts of the ordinary Greek citizen in the great days of Greece. It seems possible that, if we had more of the Orphic literature, we should find the symbol of light for special knowledge brought in more or less as it is brought in in the later Hellenistic literature. The great literature we possess, historical, dramatic, philosophic, political, of the fifth and fourth centuries was largely produced by people who show relatively little interest in Orphism or mysteries, whereas it was just people who *were* mainly interested in occult knowledge who produced the kind of Hellenistic literature with which Wetter deals. And it is noticeable that Plato occasionally uses the light simile. In the Seventh Epistle he describes the beginning of knowledge in the soul as like a light lit by a sudden jet of flame (341 d). In the famous parable of the cave, the world of reality is the world of light outside the cave, by which those who first come to it are dazzled (518 a).

We should, however, not get a true idea of the part played by the light symbol in religion if we thought of it simply as a symbol for salutary knowledge. We have, I think, to recognize that light is welcomed by men for different reasons, which need not go together.

Men fear darkness not only because they cannot see their way in it, but because it may conceal beings of malignant will, human or spiritual enemies. It is a vague fear of something hostile that may be there which makes darkness a terror to children: if I may speak of my own childish terrors, I certainly saw in the dark, with a vividness which in later life belonged only to actual dreams, monsters like the giants depicted in the coloured illustrations of the nursery *Pilgrim's Progress*. Unquestionably the fear of spirits goes largely with primitive man's fear of the dark. "The Australians peopled the darkness with a variety of horrible beings ready to pounce upon men."[1] But the concealed enemy need not be a spirit; it may be a human enemy. And sometimes concealment is just what a man desires for himself. It may be he who is lying in wait for the enemy ignorant of his presence. Or he may desire concealment simply because he is doing something of which his community disapproves, of which he is ashamed. Light, in this way, comes to be associated with actions which men do not mind being seen, with honesty, with goodness. This is markedly so in certain passages of the New Testament. "Men loved darkness rather than light, because their deeds were evil. For everyone that doeth evil hateth the light, neither cometh to the light, lest his deeds should be reproved. But he that doeth truth cometh to the light, that his deeds may be made manifest, that they are wrought in God."[2] A similar idea seems to lie behind some of St. Paul's phrases: "Ye are all children of light and day"—"have no fellowship with the works of darkness," and so on.

Quite early darkness must have become associated in men's minds with evil—whether the malignant will of some being directed against me, or evil deeds which I myself may wish to do undiscovered. And when once the association of light with goodness and darkness with evil had become established, it was carried out in ideas of the fate awaiting men after death. Good souls enter a world

---

[1] MacCulloch, in Hastings, *Encyclopedia of Religion and Ethics*, "Light and Darkness," p. 50, col. 2.   [2] John iii. 19–21.

of light and wicked souls a world of darkness. In some primitive forms of belief, it is true, no distinction is made between the destiny of the good and the destiny of the wicked after death. In the Old Testament itself one shadowy world, thought of from its connexion with the grave as underground, is conceived to await all souls alike. It is a pious man who, desirous that his life may be prolonged, addresses to God the appeal: "Shall thy wonders be known in the dark? And thy righteousness in the land where all things are forgotten?"[1] Similarly, in the Homeric poems, there seems no distinction between the lot after death of good and bad—unless we take account of the punishments inflicted upon certain great sinners in *Odyssey* xi, which is believed to be a later addition. But the idea which connects the good souls after death with the upper light world and the wicked souls with the lower darkness, is apparently found among some very primitive people where the influence of higher religions is unlikely. "In Nanumea" (Polynesia) "the wicked go to a place of mud and darkness."[2] In the earliest form we have of Indian religion, the Rigveda, it is only certain privileged persons, of higher worth than the ordinary man, whose souls go to the sky, where the gods live, "a heaven where there is light everlasting." "We hear of a deep abyss made for those who are false, like women unfaithful to their husbands; a hymn against demons consigns to an abode under the three earths the one who plots against the singer, and there are references to the wicked being consigned either to a pit, or to the lowest darkness." [3]

In all great religions of antiquity the chief gods are characterized by their connexion with light. In Egypt

---

[1] Psalm lxxxviii. 10.
[2] MacCulloch, *Encyclopedia of Religion and Ethics*, p. 50.
[3] A. Berriedale Keith in *Encyclopedia of Religion and Ethics*, xi. p. 843.

this led to the chief god being identified with the sun—
the Ra or Re of Heliopolis combined at Thebes with the
local god *Amen*. If Osiris, the special god of the dead, was
originally a god of the dark lower world, the belief came
to prevail that he rose again into the light-world and
carried the pious dead with him in his boat. "Light plays
the principal part, although the obstacle of darkness has
to be surmounted before the goal of light can be reached.
One of the charms in the Book of the Dead is for making
the transformation into the god that giveth light for
darkness."[1] In Egypt, again, "the demons of darkness
were an awful power of evil."[2]

When the sense of the numinous in primitive Aryan
religion, Rudolf Otto says, took the form of a visionary
hallucination, it was regularly the vision of something
shining, burning, just as in the Old Testament the
presence of the Divine is revealed to Moses by the
appearance of a burning bush. Both the very early general
terms for numinous forms, *vasu* and *deva*, connote in
their root meaning, brilliance, radiancy.[3] The numinous
is essentially the luminous.

It is Zoroastrianism which most signally among
religions gives prominence to the idea of light as representing the Divine in contrast to darkness representing
the Evil Power, which sets the light creation of Ahuramazda against the dark creation of Angramainyus. In the
oldest bit of Zoroastrian literature which has come down
to us, the Gathas, believed by most modern scholars to
go back to the Founder Zarathushtra himself, it must be
admitted that the light-symbol can hardly be said to
appear. In one passage of the Gathas, indeed, Ahuramazda
is represented as the Creator of *both* light and darkness.
"Tell me truly, Ahura," the prophet asks, "what artist

[1] W. Cruickshank in *Encyclopedia of Religion and Ethics*, viii. p. 66.
[2] Ibid., p. 64.   [3] *Gottheit und Gottheiten der Arier*, p. 31.

130

made light and darkness? What artist made sleeping and
waking? Who made morning, noon and night, that call
the understanding man to his duty?"[1] The question
implies, of course, that the prophet attributes the creation
of all these things to God. A parallel is pointed out in a
Hebrew prophet who represents Jehovah as saying: "I
form the light and create darkness; I make peace and
create evil. I am Jehovah that doeth all these things."[2]
That passage in Isaiah is the very one brought forward
by the Jewish Rabbi Perles in his polemic against
Bousset's book, *Die Religion des Judentums im hellenis-
tischen Zeitalter*, to prove how wrong it was of Bousset to
exalt Zoroastrianism, with its dualistic division between
the light-creation of Ahuramazda and the dark-creation
of Angramainyus, to a level with Judaism.[3] He reproaches
Bousset with not having referred to the passage in Isaiah.
He was himself evidently unaware how close a parallel
to Isaiah xlv. 7 was to be found in the Gathas.

Yet it may be that the parallel is really not quite as
close in sense as the closeness of the language makes it
appear. For in the Gatha passage darkness does not seem
to be used with any metaphorical suggestion; the contrast
spoken of is simply that of night and day in the literal
sense. It is combined with the phrases, "sleeping and
waking," "morning, noon and night," and the meaning
would thus be only that the order of the world, with its
alternation of day and night, is ordained by God. On the
other hand in the Isaiah passage, "I form light and create
darkness" is followed immediately by the more explicit
statement, "I make peace and create *evil*." Perhaps no
Zoroastrian would have said that.

If we leave out of count this passage in the Gathas, as

---

[1] Yasna, 44. 5 (Moulton's translation).   [2] Isaiah xlv. 7.
[3] F. Perles, *Boussets Religion des Judentums im neutestamentlichen Zeitalter
kritisch untersucht* (Berlin, 1903), p. 31.

not connecting any religious symbolism with the mention of light, we cannot say that any other passage in the Gathas shows that the symbol of light was specially connected in the prophet's mind with God. One passage[1] speaks incidentally of the "felicity that is with the heavenly lights." Another represents Ahuramazda's creative thought in the beginning: "Let the blessed realms be filled with lights."[2] The future hell in which the wicked will suffer is described as a state of darkness.[3] That, I think, is all; and considering the length of the Gathas, 45 pages in Moulton's *Early Zoroastrianism*, and the prominence of the light-symbol in Zoroastrianism later, it is certainly remarkable that it should be thus absent in the early document.

It must, however, have become a characteristic element in Zoroastrianism before the Sassanian reformation, since Plutarch found in his sources that Ahuramazda was "born of the purest light" and Angramainyus from the darkness.[4] A similar statement was picked up by Porphyry. "The body of Ahuramazda," according to this, "resembled light, and his soul resembled truth."[5] It would be a waste of time to attempt here to collect passages from the later parts of the Avesta and from Zoroastrian literature in which light or radiance is connected with good and darkness with evil.

If we find the light-symbol play a greater part in the religious and theosophical literature of the Graeco-Roman world at the beginning of the Christian era, in the Hermetic literature, in magical papyri, and in Gnosticism, this may no doubt have been to some extent due to the influence of Zoroastrianism. In Manichaeism, a religion itself partially Persian in origin, the identification of the good with light is fundamental. In the New Testament

---

[1] Yasna, 30. 1. [2] Ibid., 31. 7. [3] Ibid., 31. 20.
[4] *De Iside et Osiridi*, 47. [5] *Vit. Pyth.*, § 41.

too, light is prominent as a religious symbol. Wetter, whose monograph *Phōs* has been already referred to, seems to suppose that the symbol in early Christian literature can be explained as derived from the "Hellenistic piety" of the environment. It seems oddly not to occur to him that in this case something might be derived from the Old Testament as well. Indeed, the Old Testament as a whole comes hardly at all into Wetter's purview. That is rather characteristic of the *religions-geschichtliche* school of which Reitzenstein was the chief exponent, whose disciple Wetter seems to be.

While we are speaking of light as a symbol in religion, we must look at a use of the symbol in later forms of Greek philosophy and in Christianity, due to properties of light different from those so far considered. One of these is the characteristic of light, or of the luminous body, to reveal itself at the same time that it reveals other things. This characteristic furnished Chrysippus, the second Founder of Stoicism, with an analogy for the sense-impression (φαντασία in the Stoic terminology) which reveals both itself and the object from which it comes.[1] But when once this characteristic of light had been dwelt upon, it might suggest to others an analogy of something on a higher plane. For Philo it is God whom the symbol of light in this respect may be used to typify.

"How," he asks, "the approach to God has been effected it is worth seeing by means of an image. Do we need any means to behold this material sun beside the sun itself? Do we behold the stars by any light beside that of the stars themselves? Speaking generally, do we not perceive light by light? Just in the same way God, being His own illumination is be held by means of Himself

---

[1] ὥσπερ οὖν τὸ φῶς ἑαυτό τε δείκνυσι καὶ πάντα τὰ ἐν αὐτῷ, οὕτω καὶ ἡ φαντασία (Sextus Empiricus, vii. 162; Arnim, *Stoicorum Vet. Fragm.*, II. frag. 63, p. 24).

alone. Nothing else co-operates, or can co-operate, towards
the pure apprehension of His Being. The guessers indeed
are concerned to behold the One without beginning, the
Creator of the universe, from the things which have been
made. That is as if one sought to grasp the nature of the
number one from the number two. It is in the reverse way
that one ought to proceed—start from the number one
to the consideration of the number two. Those who follow
Truth are those who get their impression of God by God's
own virtue, who behold light by light."[1] Moses in another
place is represented as saying to God: "As light is not
made known by something else, but is its own evidence,
so none can reveal Thee save Thou thyself alone."[2]

The other property of light which has made it serve for
a symbol is the way in which a luminous body apparently
sends forth, without any force coming into play or any
loss being suffered, emanations of its substance, which,
to whatever distance they may reach, remain always one
with the luminous body, derivative from it not by a
momentary event accomplished and done, but by a mode
of derivation continuous and always the same. The religious application of this property of light would naturally
not be suggested till the idea had come up of derivative
Divine beings emanating from God or begotten by God,
or proceeding from God, who had an existence of their
own and yet remained one with God. Such an idea of
Beings in one way identical with God and in another way
distinct from God might obviously seem to involve a
contradiction, and when men cast about for some figure
which might make the apparent contradiction intelligible,
the analogy of a luminous body and the ray proceeding
from it almost immediately presented itself.

The first ancient writer in whom we find definitely the

[1] *De Praem.*, 45, 46 (Cohn and Wendland, Vol. V. p. 346).
[2] *De Monarch.*, 42 (Cohn and Wendland, Vol. V. p. 11).

idea of the Logos, a derivative Divine Being proceeding from God, is Philo of Alexandria. It used to be said that Philo had borrowed this idea from the Greek philosophical schools. Since there was no doubt a good deal taught in Greek philosophical schools in the last century b.c. of which all record has perished—it must be remembered that the works of every Greek philosopher between Aristotle and Philo himself have perished except for a few fragments—it would be rash to deny that Philo may have found a doctrine like his Logos doctrine somewhere current among the Greeks of Alexandria. On the other hand, the assertion that Philo derived the doctrine from Greek philosophy rests upon no actual bit of previous Greek philosophy that we know. There is nothing like it in Plato or Aristotle. The Stoics, although they used the term *logos* for the scheme of the universe, in no existing fragment use it for a Divine Being in any way distinct from God. The Stoics did indeed believe that all minds in the universe were derived from the One Divine Mind and remained portions of the Divine Mind because, conceiving Mind like a material substance, a fiery gas, they held that it was the same substance in God and in the individual man. This is perhaps the nearest thing to an emanation in Greek philosophy before Philo. The symbol of the ray of light may have been used for it in the Stoic books. It is noticeable that in one place,[1] where Philo expresses a view of the human mind like that of the Stoic, he says that man, in respect of his mind, is akin to the Divine Logos, being a fragment (ἀπόσπασμα) or a light-ray (if that is what is meant by ἀπαύγασμα) of the Blessed Nature. The word ἀπόσπασμα, we know to have been used by the Stoics in this connexion,[2] so that it may well be that Philo had

[1] *De Opif.*, § 146 (Cohn and Wendland, Vol. I. p. 51).
[2] σὺ δὲ προηγούμενον εἶ. σὺ ἀπόσπασμα εἶ τοῦ θεοῦ (Epictetus, ii. 8. 11) αἱ ψυχαὶ μὲν οὕτως εἰσὶν ἐνδεδεμέναι καὶ συναφεῖς τῷ θεῷ ἅτε αὐτοῦ μόρια οὖσαι καὶ ἀποσπάσματα (Idem, i. 14. 6).

found the word ἀπαύγασμα, which brought in the symbol of light, used as well in some Stoic book.

Since the word ἀπαύγασμα is used in the Book of Wisdom for the personified Wisdom (ἀπαύγασμα γάρ ἐστιν φῶτος ἀϊδίου, vii. 26), "which is the ἀπαύγασμα of the eternal light," and is used again in the Epistle to the Hebrews for the relation of the Son to the Father, the Son being the ἀπαύγασμα of the Father's glory, its meaning is of some importance in this connexion. If it means a ray of light or a volume of radiancy emitted direct from a luminous body, we should have in the verse of Wisdom just quoted the earliest appearance in extant literature of the idea which describes by the figure of luminous body and emitted ray the relation between the primal God and a Divine Being conceived of as in some sense distinct from Him and at the same time one with Him. But it is not certain that ἀπαύγασμα does mean a ray of light directly proceeding from a luminous body. The ἀπ- in the word may signify the indirectness of the light, that it comes by reflection from some other body, just as ἀπήχημα means an echo. In one passage of Philo[1] this is apparently what it must mean: the world is called an ἀπαύγασμα of the holy things, and this is explained as equivalent to saying that it is an imitation, μίμημα, of the archetype. When you look at the visible world you do not see the real νοητὸς κόσμος: you see only a reflection of it. And in the passage quoted from Wisdom, as well as in the passage in Hebrews, the word may possibly have this meaning: Wisdom is a reflection of the eternal Light: the Son is a reflection of the Father's glory. It is true that reflected light comes from the luminous body in the first instance; but if you emphasize its being a reflection, you emphasize its difference from the original emitting body: it is the figure of the direct ray which illustrates the unbroken one-

[1] *De Plant*, § 50 (Cohn and Wendland, Vol. II. p. 143).

ness of the being emitted with the being who emits and which was used for the purpose certainly later on both by the Neo-Platonists to explain the relation of the Νοῦς to the primal One, and by the Christians to explain the relation of the Son to the Father.

Does Philo use the figure to explain the relation of his Logos to God? It is stated in many modern books that he does, but I have been unable to find any passage of Philo which supports the statement. The figure of light is very common in Philo for the knowledge of divine things. Such knowledge comes, of course, from God, who is the fountain of the purest radiancy.[1] Or the light-symbol may be used for God's own knowledge of the world. His rays penetrate into every part of it.[2] In visible things God is symbolized by the sun.[3] None of these ideas, however, dwell on the solidarity of the emitted ray with the luminous body in order to illustrate the relation of God with His semi-personified Logos. In two passages the Logos himself is called light. In one the first-created light spoken of in Genesis is said to be an "image of the Logos."[4] In the other we read "God is light, and not only light but the archetype of every other light, or rather something higher than an archetype, something which is to be explained as an example, λόγον ἔχον παραδείγματος. The παράδειγμα indeed is his immensely rich Logos, light, of whom it is written, 'God said: Let there be light,' but God Himself is not like anything which has had a beginning."[5] This rather confused passage in which the text may be corrupt (for, as it stands, it speaks first of God Himself as having the character of a παράδειγμα and in the next sentence of

---

[1] πηγὴ τῆς καθαρωτάτης αὐγῆς. De Mut. Nom., § 6 (Cohn and Wendland, Vol. III. p. 157).

[2] De Cherub., § 97 (Cohn and Wendland, Vol. I. p. 193).

[3] De Somn., i. § 73.

[4] De Opif., § 31 (Cohn and Wendland, Vol. I. p. 9).

[5] De Somn., i. § 75 (Cohn and Wendland, Vol. III. p. 221).

the Logos as the παράδειγμα) is the passage which comes nearest to making the Logos a secondary light emitted from the primary. But it is doubtful whether the point of the passage is the relation between the Logos and God. When it calls the Logos light, it may mean only that knowledge is bestowed upon man through the Logos.

In Plotinus, at any rate, the figure of the luminous body and the emitted ray is one commonly used to explain the emanation of Νοῦς, Ψυχή and the world from the ineffable One. "A parable of the One," he says, "may be found in the sun, which is a centre to the light proceeding from him and is connected with him: everywhere the light abides with him and is not cut off from him: nay, if thou wilt seek to cut it off in one direction, there in the direction of the sun the light is still" (I. vii. 1). "The Soul can never cease to abide in the Νοῦς, being attached to νοῦς by a connexion far firmer than that by which the light surrounding the sun is attached to the sun" (III. v. 2). "Just as, so long as the sun exists, the light cannot fail to stream from him, similarly, so long as Νοῦς and Ψυχή exist, the seminal formulas cannot fail to stream into this Soul of the lower world" (II. iii. 18). "If there is any second term after the One, it must come into existence without any movement on the part of the One, without any inclination of the One towards it, any act of will. How then can it come into existence? How are we to think of it abiding round the One? It is like the light of the sun, the brilliant light which runs all about him, ever begotten by him, while he remains still" (V. i. 6).

The idea is a regular constituent of the Neo-Platonic theosophy prevalent in the Graeco-Roman world in the last centuries of paganism. In the Hermetic literature, for instance, we find: "What is the incorporeal? It is Νοῦς entire and wholly self-encompassing . . . standing firm-fixed in itself . . . whose rays are the Good, the Truth, the archetypal Light."[1] "*Noῦs* is not severed from the substantiality of God, but is, so to speak, spread abroad from that source, as the light of the sun is spread abroad."[2] Or in the *De Mysteriis*, which is probably by Iamblichus, the Supreme God is described as "the Wellspring of the Universe, the Base of the first things apprehended by *Noῦs*, which are Ideas." "And from Him, the One, the [second] self-sufficing God radiated himself forth."[3] Amongst the Christians the figure had come into use to explain the relation of God the Son to God the Father before the end of the second century.

If we now turn to the Old Testament, we find that the symbol of light there could not certainly, if the different contexts are examined, be regarded as standing simply for useful or salutary knowledge. There are indeed some passages in which such an interpretation of the symbol might be adequate. "The entrance of thy words giveth light."[4] "Thy judgments are as the light that goeth forth."[5] "Send out thy light and thy truth."[6] Though even in these it may be questioned whether other associations, besides that of knowledge, do not enter into the symbol. Although "light" and "truth" are coupled in the last quotation, the "truth" of God to an Old Testament poet had a different connotation from that which *aletheia* had to a Greek philosopher: it meant something else than the intellectual apprehension of reality. In a number of other cases the idea of light as meaning knowledge does not seem to come in at all. It is here quite a different characteristic of light which underlies the symbol, the immediate effects of light upon the emotions. Two distinct effects come into consideration. One is the exhilaration produced by light. "Truly," says the

---

[1] *Corp. Hermeticum*, ii. 12.   [2] *Corp. Hermeticum*, xii. 1.
[3] ἐξέλαμψε ἑαυτόν. Iamblichus, *De Mysteriis* (G. Parthey, 1857), viii. 2.
[4] Psalm cxix. 130.   [5] Hosea vi. 5.   [6] Psalm xliii. 4.

Preacher, "the light is sweet, and a pleasant thing it is for the eyes to behold the sun."[1] And since what survives of the person after death is thought of as going out of the region of light into a place of darkness, light may come to stand for the relatively cheerful world of the living: the "light of the living" is a stock Hebrew phrase. "Lighten mine eyes," says a Psalmist, "lest I sleep the sleep of death."[2] The idea is so natural to man that we find close parallels in other literatures: in Greek poetry, of course, βλέπειν φῶς, "to behold light," is a regular synonym for the verb "to live." But it is not only in connexion with the contrast of life and death, that light sometimes seems to mean, not knowledge, but joy. "Unto the upright there ariseth light in the darkness"[3] cannot mean "Unto the upright there comes a sudden accession of knowledge," but "there comes the relief of deliverance and joy in exchange for sorrow and trouble." Darkness indeed is used analogously, not only for ignorance or intellectual bewilderment, but for emotional distress, as when Amos says (v. 18): "Wherefore would ye have the day of the Lord? It is darkness and not light . . . even very dark and no brightness in it." Here again, the Greek parallels are close.

When once the symbol of light or glory had come into general use as a way of indicating the character of the Divine, you may have phraseology in which the different ideas connected with literal material light are fused in such a way as to make it impossible to say which idea predominates. Take, for instance, the familiar language in a book of the New Testament. "God is light, and in him is no darkness at all. If we say that we have fellowship with him and walk in darkness, we lie and do not the truth. But if we walk in the light as he is in the light, we have fellowship one with another."[4] Is it the chief idea

[1] Ecclesiastes xi. 7.   [2] Psalm xiii. 3.   [3] Psalm cxii. 4.   [4] 1 John i. 5–7.

140

that apprehension of God means true knowledge of the universe, so that the man who has it can order his conduct aright? Or that in God supreme goodness is found with no admixture of evil? Or that a peculiar kind of wonder, exhilaration and fear is created by the disclosure of God? Probably all these ideas run together. One could not translate the phrase "God is light" into a statement of any one of these ideas singly without robbing it of its power, because it involves all those ideas together and yet presents the imagination with something which has apparent unity and simplicity. We feel that we know best what is meant by the declaration that "God is light" when no attempt is made to explain it. We have come almost to lose the sense that light is only a symbol; we almost feel it to be a literal statement of recognized truth.

But light may produce another emotional effect beside joy, a peculiar kind of admiration. It is the diffused light, the light of day, which produces joy: it is concentrated light, looked at directly in a blaze or in a shining surface, which produces admiration. In some Old Testament passages it is this effect of light to which the symbol points. "Arise, shine, for thy light is come," says the prophet to Israel.[1] Here plainly what is spoken of is not something received by Israel, whether knowledge or joy, but something given forth by Israel: it is the admiration to be created in others by the spectacle of the Israel of the future that the prophet is thinking of. It is especially in regard to manifestations of the Divine that this application of the light symbol comes in. The Lord "covereth himself with light as with a garment."[2] Light in an extreme degree, splendour, is the normal characteristic of Divine manifestations, and the Hebrew word *kābhōdh*, originally meaning "weight" and then coming to mean the impressiveness of very bright light, is the word for this effulgence

---

[1] Isaiah lx. 1.   [2] Psalm civ. 2.

141

which the Hebrews brought into use. The idea has passed through the Greek δόξα and the Latin *gloria* into the language of all Christian peoples, though neither δόξα nor *gloria* had the meaning in question till they were used to translate the Hebrew *kābhōdh*.

In English we indicate the particular kind of admiration evoked by a concentration of bright light when we apply to such a phenomenon the terms "glory" or "splendour." The languages of mankind bear witness to the fact that this sort of feeling connected with bright light is universally human. It would probably be possible to find in all of them words which mean literally "shining," "radiant," used metaphorically to express an admiration for persons or actions which is felt to be analogous somehow in the moral sphere to the admiration evoked by bright light in the material sphere—ἀγλαός, φαεινός, φαίδιμος, in Greek, *clarus*, *splendidus* in Latin, and so on. It may be repeated, as a capital point, that such an admiration caused by concentrated light is wholly distinct from the joy in diffused light or the sense of the usefulness of light in showing up the environment. The concentrated light, the glory or splendour, may sometimes, so far from showing up the environment, have the opposite effect of dazzling. The admiration is not due to any usefulness in the bright light, but is an immediate emotional reaction to it. I think it is, further, true that the particular kind of admiration evoked is a feeling *sui generis*, and cannot be analysed into a combination of other more primary feelings; any attempt to define it would inevitably bring in the notion to be defined by the use of some such word as "splendid" or "glorious." We all know what the emotion is and can indicate it to each other for that reason, but we could not explain it to anyone who had never experienced it. The admiration, or the quality in the object which evokes the admiration, is

142

thus closely analogous to the sense of the beautiful, or beauty; the sense of the unclean, or dirt; the sense of the sublime, or grandeur. And there is one thing which ought to be noticed giving a special character to the impression made by a high degree of concentrated light, by a dazzling blaze, as against the impression made by mild, diffused light: the glory may have in it a quality of terror. The Divine, the Holy, as Rudolf Otto has made us realize, has in it an awfulness akin to terror. When therefore the symbol of glory is applied to God, its appropriateness may be due not only to the admiration aroused by concentrated light, but to the fear. "God," says a passage of the New Testament, "dwelleth in light which cannot be approached."[1]

Most people, I suppose, would now recognize that the beautiful was something ultimate which could not be resolved into anything else. An attempt was made by Grant Allen, forty years ago, to find the origin of beauty in sexual attraction. Certain colours and shapes had come to have a particular kind of appeal because they once served in animal evolution to attract the female to the male, or *vice versa*. A little thought shows that such a theory is a ridiculous putting of the cart before the horse. The tail of the peacock could not impress the peahen unless the peahen had already found such colours impressive independently. It is only with creatures who have already a sense of the beauty of bright colours that bright colours could be used as a means of sexual attraction. No doubt, different species of creatures, even different individual men, may differ very much in what they think beautiful: the huge red beak of the toucan looks to us grotesque, perhaps even repulsive; but the toucan of the opposite sex evidently admires it. This variation of judgment, however, in regard to the question:

[1] 1 Timothy vi. 16.

143

What particular things are beautiful? does not show that beauty does not mean something definite which is fundamentally the same for all. A good deal of confusion of thought might have been avoided in this connexion if people had attended to the distinction made in text-books of Formal Logic between that which a term "connotes" and that which it "denotes." The fact that there is wild difference of view regarding the things which such terms as beautiful, just, honourable, denote, does not prove that the connotation of the words "beautiful," "just," "honourable," varies. It is impossible, of course, to say how far the emotion aroused in the breast of the female toucan by the sight of the red beak of the male is the same as the admiration of the beautiful in men, since the psychology of toucans must always be largely inaccessible to us; but in regard to differences between men respecting the beautiful or the just, we may believe that we all mean the same thing when we say that something is beautiful, even when we disagree what things are beautiful. In fact there could be no conflict in regard to the denotation except in so far as there is agreement as to the connotation. If one man says that the Albert Memorial is beautiful and another man says that it is not, there is no conflict unless they mean the same thing by "beautiful."

It would, I think, be generally conceded to-day that in all men a particular kind of feeling is aroused by the sight of certain objects or the hearing of certain sounds, which they express by saying that what they see or hear is beautiful, and that this kind of feeling belongs to human nature everywhere. It apparently is connected with a feeling which is wider than human, is broadly animal, as the tail of the peacock and the song of the nightingale show, but in the human mind, the attraction to beautiful colours and shapes and sounds must obviously have a quality which it cannot have in minds infra-human.

The feeling may have a physical element common to men and toucans, but in the human mind it sets in activity distinctively human apprehensions, has an intellectual or spiritual resonance which it cannot have in the lower animals. But all men, we must believe, have a sense of what is called "beautiful" in English, καλός in Greek, "*pulcher*" in Latin, and some equivalent word in each human language, though they may apply the term differently.

What, of course, is controversial, is not the distinctive character and universal distribution of this feeling, but the question whether it is the sense of anything real apart from the human, and animal, mind. All theories of the universe which deny the existence of any mind beyond those of men and animals must necessarily say that the feeling which we call a sense of the beautiful is not truly a sense at all, since a sense implies the apprehension of something that is really there. This feeling, like all the other feelings connected with values, must simply be modes of emotional reaction to the environment which happen to have been developed in the human species by the chances of whatever physical process it was which brought man into being. Certainly when we, any of us, say that a thing is good or is beautiful we do not feel our statement to be merely a statement about our own psychology, or even human psychology generally; our statement expresses a conviction—it may be a momentary conviction, while we utter it—that the thing of which we speak *is* good or *is* beautiful. If we hold a certain scientific theory, we may, when we examine afterwards the feeling behind our statement, pronounce that it was an illusion. Such ideas as goodness, beauty, and so on, we may then say have no real validity: they are merely expressions of the way the human mind happens to react to the matter of the universe: if the chances of the evolutionary process had been different, quite a different set of feelings might have been developed in the being which would have been where man is now. These perhaps would have had just as much validity as our supposed sense of goodness and beauty have—that is, in any proper sense of the term "validity," none at all.

Any theory of the universe which confines mind and spirit to species of creatures on this planet—or to creatures on any number of planets—seems logically shut up to such a conclusion. It is only a view of the universe which extends spirit to the whole of it, which makes the Reality behind phenomena spiritual, so that the spirit in man is a special representation of something which is, in its full being, the Whole enclosing man—it is only such a view which can claim real validity for human judgments of value—and such a view must be in some sense theist— even if it puts a pan- or a poly-, and not a mono-, before theist. An atheistic view of the universe can exalt human ideas of goodness and beauty to the rank of really valid ideas, of ideas which have a right to command or claim men's acknowledgment, only by a logical confusion.

All Theists would, I take it, hold that the sense of beauty in man is the sense of something that is really there apart from man, that the beautiful is a revelation of the being of God. This may be taken for granted amongst Theists to-day. What I want rather to urge here is that what is admitted to apply to the sense of beauty, applies equally to the sense of various other values, where such a sense is found to be broadly human. In an article published some years ago I ventured to argue that the sense of clean and unclean was *sui generis* and unanalysable and was of importance in connexion with judgments of moral value, and I have had the satisfaction of knowing that Professor A. E. Taylor agreed with this view. That would be another case in which a Theist would, I think, logically hold that

146

a human idea widely prevalent had a validity beyond the human mind, that for God too there was such a thing as uncleanness, just as there is such a thing as beauty. But in the present lecture what we are specially concerned with is the admiration produced in men, all over the world, by bright concentrated light, the sense of glory. No doubt it might be argued that the glorious was only one variety of the beautiful. But, if so, I think you want two different terms for the two different applications in which we should now use the one term, "beautiful." The sense of beauty in its more specific acceptation, the quality we recognize in a beautiful face or a beautiful flower, seems to me something really different both from the sublime and from the glorious. That they are akin, I admit. Of the beauty of some flowers it has been said that "Solomon in all his *glory* was not arrayed like one of these." Similarly, Plotinus, where he is speaking of the admiration evoked by concentrated light, describes it as a perception of the beautiful. "Fire is beautiful in a pre-eminent degree beyond all other bodies" (I. vi. 3). In the tract entitled Περὶ τοῦ νοητοῦ κάλλους (v. 8), the description of the supreme beauty whose home is in the world above sense, it is sometimes definitely called "light" φῶς. "All things there are translucent and there is nothing dark or resisting; everyone is manifest to everyone in his inner being, through and through: it is light apprehending light" (§ 4). "Everything there shines" (§ 10). We must remember that Greek had no commonly used term for "glory," till that meaning was put into δόξα by Jews and Christians. There is, indeed, the word αἴγλη which Plotinus twice uses in the tract referred to and which seems to mean very much what we mean by glory, but it never became a word regularly used in connexion with the Divine, as "glory" is in Christian parlance. Yet I think it is true that both the glorious and the sublime are different from what we ordinarily mean by the term "beautiful." Of the sublime I have spoken in a previous lecture, which dealt with the symbol of height. It is with the glorious that we are at present concerned.

We have seen that everywhere among men the idea of glory is one of those connected with the divine: gods are imagined as beings who shine or are clad in shining garments: the Jehovah of the Old Testament is surrounded by His glory, sometimes called fire. And if we believe that men's idea of the beautiful is an apprehension of something which is really in God, it is reasonable to believe that man's idea of the glorious is likewise an apprehension of something really in God. What that something is it may be impossible for us to say. On the one hand since light is a phenomenon of the material world, we could only attribute light in a literal sense to God, if we supposed God to have a material body—which some Christians, like Tertullian, *have* supposed, but which the recognized theology of all Christian Churches now repudiates. On the other hand, if the peculiar feeling evoked by bright concentrated light, the sense of glory, is, as I have argued, unanalysable, it must be impossible to explain what we mean when we ascribe glory to God otherwise than by bringing in the symbol itself, and so offering a definition in a circle.

But that the figure of glory may be used where literal light is not intended we see by the ordinary language which applies the metaphor to manifestations of intellectual or moral greatness—a brilliant piece of writing, a glorious deed. If we were called on to explain what we mean in such a connexion by "brilliant" or "glorious," we could only say that the things in question excite in us a feeling which we recognize to be in a certain way analogous to the admiration evoked by bright concentrated light. We could no more explain to anyone who had never had the feeling in regard to literal light what we mean when we use such terms as "brilliant" or "glorious" metaphorically than we could explain to a person born blind what we mean by "scarlet." If we said, for instance as we might in speaking to a man born blind, that what we mean is that the deed excites in us a high degree of admiration, that would not be the whole truth. When we use such words as "glorious" or "splendid" we do not only express admiration, but we indicate a particular quality or note in the admiration. And we can indicate that in no other way than by saying it resembles the feeling aroused by bright light, and anyone who has had the feeling in regard to light understands.

We can apply the metaphor to that which God reveals of Himself within the range of our earthly experiences. There are moments, which come no doubt to poets and mystics oftener than to us ordinary men, when the natural world round us is seen clothed in a glory, analogous, in the feeling it arouses, to bright concentrated light. Still more, as the highest expressions of the spirit of man, may the great utterances and heroic deeds be regarded as manifestations of the glory of God. All these things are within the range of our experience, and we know what the reality is which we describe as glorious. But when we speak of the glory of God, as the mode in which Christians believe that He manifests Himself to beings on a higher plane than ours, to those human spirits who attain, beyond their earthly experience, to the Beatific Vision, we use the symbol to indicate something which in our present plane of being we cannot even imagine. If our idea of God, as a whole, is an act of faith, our attribution of glory to God will necessarily be part of such an act, not a matter of demonstration. What we mean is that we believe that, if we could have a more perfect apprehension of God's being than we can have under earthly conditions, that apprehension would involve something analogous to the feeling now aroused in us by bright concentrated light, something which cannot possibly be described in human language, except by our pointing to that feeling. Thus the light metaphor would not here be the use of a figure for mere poetical or imaginative embellishment, in order to say something which we could say more precisely in other terms: it would be the most precise way in which the Reality can be expressed in human language. And yet, while we use it, we have to recognize that it is only a figure, not a literal description.

SPIRIT

A SYMBOL which, in the Christian religion at any rate, has had a use even more constant than the light-symbol which we considered in our last lecture is that of *spirit*. "The spirit," in a phrase of the poet's, "does but mean the breath"; and that, of course, is true of its original meaning. It would be idle here to try to do over again what has been done abundantly in books dealing with the ideas of primitive men, show by examples how the soul was identified with the breath. It was a perfectly natural operation of reason at the outset, in view of the fact that, in each case of death, the cessation of breath exactly coincided in time with the apparent cessation of conscious life, to infer that the breath and the conscious life were the same thing. But one may notice that the words chosen on this theory to denote the soul did not in the Semitic languages and in Latin mean "soul" only, but generally "air in motion": they meant "wind" as well as breath or "soul." This, of course, is the case with the Hebrew *ruakh*; and the Latin words for soul, "*animus*" and "*anima*," are analogous formations to Greek *anemos*, which means "wind." Paul Volz in his book *Der Geist Gottes im Alten Testament*, declares that the original meaning of *ruakh* must have been "wind," and that the word will then later have been applied to the breath as well. His apparent ground for this assertion is that the wind is a more noticeable phenomenon than the breath, and therefore more likely to have been named first by primitive man. This argument seems to me very shaky. I do not think it possible, when primitive man is found using the same word for "wind" and for "breath," to say that one meaning is prior to the other, any more than to say in regard to our use of the verb "to blow" whether it primarily denotes the action of the wind and is then metaphorically used of the action of a man who forcibly ejects his breath, or the other way round. But even if the words for soul originally meant breath, in Greek and Latin, when they became literary languages, different words had come to be used for breath, spirit, and for wind: *psyche* in Greek, as we have it, means "soul," and not "wind"; and so does "*anima*" in Latin, although *anima* could still be used for the wind in poetry —"*impellunt animae lintea Thraciae.*"[1] It is an oddity in the history of words that the Greek *anemos* means "wind" and never "soul" while the Latin corresponding words mean "soul" and no longer (except in such poetical phrases) "wind." In Hebrew the word *ruakh* continued to be used equally for "wind" and for "spirit."

We must take into consideration that of all material substances known to ancient man, air may be regarded as the least material. Ἐγγύς ἐστιν ὁ ἀὴρ τοῦ ἀσωμάτου ("Air is near to the bodiless") is a phrase preserved from the old Greek philosopher Anaximenes. It has not either the visibility or the tangibility which seem the most essential characteristics of matter. And the wind has one notable positive characteristic in common with spirit: just as man from the beginning found out that feelings and volitions, things belonging to the spirit, caused the material masses constituting his limbs to move, so the

[1] Horace, *Odes,* iv. 12, 2.

152

wind, being invisible, could move material masses in the world round about him, sometimes in a terrific way. The wind also had a voice whose cadences seemed to express sorrow or grievance or rage just as a human voice did.

Further, air was often associated with the other substance which early attracted the attention of men as something peculiar and akin to the mind, fire, the source of light, fire which was a thing apparently self-moving like something alive. It cannot be accidental that throughout the thought of men in the field of religion fire and air are found associated. Wind and fire were, of course, actually associated by nature in the thunder-storm; and they therefore both entered into the idea which the ancient Hebrews had of a theophany, a manifestation of God. Ezekiel's description of his vision begins by saying, "I looked, and behold a stormy wind came out of the north, a great cloud with a fire infolding itself, and a splendour round about it" (i. 4). For the Greek thinkers of the sixth and the early fifth century B.C., air and fire seemed the two rival candidates for recognition as the primal substance. If Anaximenes chose air, Heraclitus chose fire. Later on, when the Stoics constructed a theory of the world on the basis of the old Ionian cosmogonies, air and fire were combined in a single substance, conceived as the Divine power and wisdom ordering and interpreting the world: it is sometimes called air, *pneuma*, and sometimes fire, the πῦρ τεχνικόν, and sometimes both together, a fiery *pneuma*. You find the two again closely combined in a stratum of Jewish religion in Palestine at the beginning of the Christian era which seems little touched by the ideas current in the Hellenistic environment, in the preaching of John the Baptist. The Coming One will baptize with the Spirit and with fire. And in the account of the coming of the Spirit which the author of Acts must have derived from some Palestinian

153

source the coming is manifested to the senses by the sound of a rushing mighty wind and by tongues of fire.

It was indeed not only a *naïve* idea of primitive man which identified the soul with the breath, or with air in motion. When philosophical speculation had got with the Greeks in the sixth and fifth centuries B.C. far beyond the primitive level, air still seemed a factor in the phenomenal world of peculiar significance. We all know that Anaximenes in the sixth century regarded air as the world substance in its form of greatest rarity, every solid thing being simply the same substance condensed. But it is noteworthy in our present study that Anaximenes is specially said to have insisted upon the identity of the air in the universe with the air which was the life of an individual. "Just as our soul, being air, holds us together, so do breath and air encompass the whole world."[1] This suggests that Anaximenes thought of the air in the universe not as simply a material substance, that he attributed to it some of the quality which air had as human soul. We have the word of Cicero, for whatever it is worth in this connexion, that Anaximenes regarded air as a god.[2]

There can be little doubt that we should go wrong if we supposed that when Anaximenes said that all solid and liquid things were air more or less condensed, such a statement meant for him only what it would mean for us who think clearly of air as an inanimate substance which Science can analyse into its material constituents. Unquestionably for an old Greek philosopher in the sixth century such a phrase as "the world is air" had a fringe of suggestion which made the meaning much nearer than we might suppose to that of the man who

---

[1] Οἶον ἡ ψυχὴ ἡ ἡμετέρα ἀὴρ οὖσα συγκρατεῖ ἡμᾶς, καὶ ὅλον τὸν κόσμον πνεῦμα καὶ ἀὴρ περιέχει. Diels-Kranz, *Die Fragmente der Vorsokratiker*, I. p. 95. [2] *De Natura Deorum*, i. 10, § 26.

would say in later phraseology that the whole world was brought into being by Spirit, was encompassed and interpenetrated by Spirit. Even when people still identified the Spirit quite frankly with material air, as Anaximenes did, the material air, as he thought of it, was more like what we mean by Spirit.

This comes out more plainly in the theories of Diogenes of Apollonia, the fifth-century philosopher, which were confessedly a development of those of Anaximenes. It is ideas resembling those of Diogenes which Aristophanes attributes in the *Clouds* to Socrates. One interest in the theory of the world put forward by Diogenes is that you have in it already what was to be, a century and a half later, the Stoic theory almost complete. The universe, Diogenes said, had come into being by the condensation of one substance, which, although material, had the characteristics of mind, was conscious and omniscient. This universal substance, wherein there was much activity of thought, νόησις πολλή, might be called Zeus or God. The mind in us was a part of it, "a little piece of God" (μικρὸν μόριον τοῦ θεοῦ). This comes close to the Stoic phrase which describes the human soul as an ἀπόσπασμα of God or Zeus, a little bit broken off. Following Anaximenes, Diogenes called this substance *air*, whereas the Stoics, following Heraclitus, generally described it as fire. But the Stoics, as we saw just now, sometimes also described it as *pneuma* or as fiery *pneuma*; and similarly, Diogenes, in one of his books, seems to have described the substance as something between fire and air (μεταξὺ πυρὸς καὶ ἀέρος,)[1], so that the difference here too between him and the Stoics is small. The universal substance, Diogenes said, by its supreme wisdom ordered all the processes of the universe in the way which realized the maximum of good and beauty (ὡς ἀννστὸν κάλλιστα);

[1] Diels-Kranz, *Die Frag. d. Vorsokratiker*, II. p. 52.

it is in fact the order of the world which proves that it is governed by a supreme Mind. And Diogenes probably applied this teaching of the Divine all-encompassing, all-wise Air for ethical control, just as Epictetus does the Stoic view of God. "Thou, God, seest me" is a consideration enforced apparently on the lines drawn by Diogenes of Apollonia in a fragment of the fourth-century comedian Philemon: "He from whom no action that is being done by any being can be hidden, nor any action that will be done in the future or has been done in the past long ago, whether by a god or by a man, I am He, Air, who may also be called Zeus. I, for such is the manner of God's working, am everywhere—here in Athens, in Patrae, in Sicily, in all cities of men, in all houses, in each one of you. There is no place in which Air is not. And to Him who is everywhere present everything of necessity is known."

Is there any special significance to be found in the fact that the Stoics said πνεῦμα where Diogenes of Apollonia said ἀήρ? *Pneuma*, Plato says in the *Cratylus* and the Stoics said in one of their definitions of *pneuma*, is simply air in motion, ἀὴρ κινούμενος or ἀέρος ῥύσις. When used in connexion with the wind it meant something which blew and moved things; when used in connexion with the breath, it meant something which a man might direct by blowing; there was in the word the idea of an activity which produced a definite result. When the medical writers used *pneuma* or *pneumata* to explain phenomena in the human body, it conveyed the notion, not only of enclosed air but of air which worked in a certain way. Thus the Stoics may naturally have felt it a better word than *aër* for the divine substance which worked actively in all the processes of the cosmos.

Pneuma, as used by the Greeks, apart from Jews and Christians, meant something material, not something

156

spiritual in our sense—properly, the breath, but then also, in poetry, the wind, and in the language of early physicists and physicians, a kind of invisible substance or gas which could account for various affections in organic bodies. It is curious that it was never used in classical Greek for the soul or the higher part of the soul, as "spirit" is used in modern languages shaped by Biblical usage. Nor is it used for disembodied persons, whether the spirits of dead men or gods or daemons. It was no doubt a commonplace of Greek poetry that at death the man's body went to earth and his *pneuma* into the air; but *pneuma* means there simply his life-breath: the moving air inside his body, in virtue of which his body was alive, has now left his body and mingled with the great volume of air outside. If you wanted to speak of the departed spirit in our sense, the spirit which might be conceived as still conscious somewhere, or possibly appearing in the form of a ghost, you called it not the man's *pneuma* but his soul, $\psi v \chi \acute{\eta}$.[1] This is the usage we find in Greek classical literature from Homer onwards. There is, it is true, one fragment of Epicharmus in which a disembodied spirit seems to be called a *pneuma*. "If thou hast been pious in mind, thou wilt suffer no ill after death: the *pneuma* will still exist up there in heaven."[2] But this may be simply a modification of the commonplace just spoken of, which Epicharmus himself formulates in the ordinary way in another fragment (fr. 9). Epicharmus may have believed that the *pneuma* still had individual consciousness after death; but the phrase hardly implies that a disembodied spirit could in general

---

[1] This contrasts curiously, as we shall see, with the Semitic usage. If the Hebrew word corresponding to $\psi v \chi \acute{\eta}$ is *nephesh* and the Hebrew word corresponding to $\pi v \epsilon \tilde{v} \mu a$ is *ruakh*, it is noteworthy that a bodiless spirit is called a *ruakh*, never a *nephesh*.

[2]   Εὐσεβὴς νόῳ πεφυκὼς οὐ πάθοις κ' οὐδὲν κακὸν
    κατθανών· ἄνω τὸ πνεῦμα διαμένει κατ' οὐρανόν.
                                        (Frag. 22, Diels-Kranz, I. p. 202.)

speech be called a *pneuma*: the fragment would rather mean, "When you die, the non-corporeal element in your present constitution will continue in the upper world," leaving it undetermined whether that non-corporeal element would be an individual spirit in our sense or not.

It appears to have been the Stoics who made *pneuma* a current term for the conscious Divine Being diffused through all things, for what Diogenes of Apollonia had called *air*. They arrived at the use of the term by starting from the meaning of *pneuma* as a gas or effluvium proceeding from things, or as man's bodily breath: because such a gas or effluvium was naturally diffused through surrounding space, the term seemed to express the universal diffusion of the Divine activity. We seem to have come here very near to the Jewish and Christian conception of the Divine omnipresence. Both Stoics and Greek-speaking Christians describe the God everywhere present in the universe as a *pneuma* and as a being who has the characteristics of mind in a supreme degree. What made the great difference was that *pneuma* in the mouth of a Christian had, embodied in it, the ideas which had attached to a term outside the Greek sphere, to the Hebrew *ruakh*. For a Hebrew, *ruakh* had denoted the mind of man in its higher activities; for a Greek, as we have seen, *pneuma* denoted a material substance, and it was only because the peculiar metaphysic of the Stoics identified mind with a material substance that the Divine Being diffused through the universe could be regarded as having the characteristics of mind as well as of material gas. He had those characteristics not because of His being *pneuma* (as a Christian might have said), but in spite of His being *pneuma*. So far as the Stoics wanted to designate those characteristics of the omnipresent Being to which the mind of man was analogous they used other words than *pneuma*, such a word as *nous*. Already in the fifth century, before the birth of the founder of Stoicism, some Greek thinkers had come to believe that God was most appropriately described by applying to Him terms used to describe the inner life of man. Plato, expressly in his latest work, the *Laws*, speaks of God as a *psyche*, a Supreme Soul. In a celebrated passage of Euripides Hecuba cries to the Supreme Being as One who is hard to know by guessing "whether Thou art the fixed Law of Nature or the Mind of man" (εἴτ' ἀνάγκη φύσεως εἴτε νοῦς βροτῶν).[1] It is interesting to set this against a fragment of Menander which speaks of the Power governing the universe—εἴτ' ἐστι τοῦτο πνεῦμα θεῖον εἴτε νοῦς—"whether this is a divine *pneuma* or a Mind." The idea of *pneuma*, observe, is not identical with that of *mind*, but is an alternative to that of mind: *pneuma* implies a material substance, and mind does not.

But, although *pneuma* was never used in classical Greek for what we mean by spirit, for the inner non-material life of man or the non-material Divine personality, there are phrases in which *pneuma* was used, even in classical Greek, for certain manifestations of the inner life and for certain abnormal psychic phenomena. In these phrases its usage seems to overlap with that of the Hebrew *ruakh*, and they therefore require examination, if we are going properly to discern the Christian use of the word *pneuma*, where it differs from the classical use. For such an examination one must acknowledge indebtedness to a book which some of you may know, Hans Leisegang's *Der Heilige Geist*, published in 1919. No scholar should speak of this book without gratitude because it is the most systematic inquiry into the ideas connected with the word *pneuma* as used by Greeks, Jews and Christians, and puts together a great amount of useful material.

[1] *Troiades*, 886.

Nevertheless, it seems to me a book whose theories should be carefully checked by the student's ascertaining what the documents on which Leisegang builds really say: in some cases footnotes seem to me to give no support to Leisegang's constructions in the text. With regard first to the phrases in which the name *pneuma* or the verb *pnein* are used for manifestations of the life of the soul, these are practically confined to poetry, in which they serve as metaphors.

Probably from the fact that the manner of breathing is very much affected by emotions, it was possible in Greek to describe a man's temper by saying that he breathed in a certain way—μένεα πνείοντες, "breathing valour" in Homer, phrases like κότον πνέων, "breathing wrath" in the Tragedians. And from this use you could go on to speak, in poetry, of a mood or temper as a *pneuma*. "Receive this suppliant band," a Chorus says in Aeschylus, "to the land of Argos, αἰδοίῳ πνεύματι χώρας, "with a gracious breathing of the country,"[1] that is, in a kindly spirit.[2]

We ought to note the other usage in classical Greek of words derived from *pnein* "to breathe or blow" which seems to overlap with the Hebrew use of *ruakh*, that in reference to mantic inspiration. When men went into abnormal states in which they uttered things believed to be messages from the unseen world of daemons and gods, that was described in Greek by saying that some god had breathed upon them (*epipnein*); inspiration was *epipnoia*;[3]

[1] *Supplices*, 28.
[2] At this point, Greek usage coincides closely with Hebrew: *ruakh* in the Old Testament is sometimes used for mood or temper: "A garment of praise for the *spirit* of heaviness" (Isaiah lxi. 3).
[3] One of Leisegang's principal theories is that *pneuma* was a word used by the common people in classical times for mantic inspiration, but that it was regarded as a vulgar word and was avoided in this sense by the writers who composed the classical literature which has come down to us. The evidence which he brings forward for this theory seems to me quite insubstantial and

160

just as the Hebrews described people in such a condition as possessed by a *ruakh* or the *ruakh* of Jehovah. In a well-known passage of Aeschylus the *epipnoia* of Zeus is said to have produced, not only a mood, but actually the physical process of parturition in Io: her son Epaphus is born miraculously, without a human father, by Zeus breathing upon Io and laying his hand upon her (ἐξ ἐπιπνοίας Ζηνός · ἔφαψιν ἐπωνυμίᾳ δ' ἐπεκραίνετο μόρσιμος αἰών).[1]

Pneuma was, it is true, often brought in to explain mantic inspiration in later Greek times, as it is by Plutarch in his dialogues about the Delphic oracle. But it is brought in, notice, as a would-be scientific explanation of the Pythia's trance condition. It is supposed that a peculiar material exhalation from the ground, a *pneuma* in this sense, produced the Pythia's trance, and a speaker in one of the dialogues suggests that the reason why the Pythia had ceased to deliver oracles in verse was that the *pneuma* in question had become exhausted by the same sort of process as brings about other changes in the material world. What we have here is not the application of a primitive belief that a medicine-man was literally filled with some spirit's breath, but the application of a tentative rationalist science to account for an apparently supernatural phenomenon.

What remains of our time in this lecture will be devoted to considering the uses of *ruakh* in the Old Testament. The important difference between *ruakh* and

one passage of Pollux, of which he makes a great deal, he has, I think, mis-understood. Although *epipnoia* is no doubt a good classical word for mantic inspiration, I do not think that there is any reason to suppose that *pneuma* by itself was commonly used for this among any stratum of the people in classical times. Possibly one might have said that a person in mantic frenzy was full of the *pneuma* of such and such a god : you certainly could not call the thing possessing him a *pneuma* in the sense of a quasi-personal being, as we to-day might say that someone was possessed by a spirit.

[1] *Supplices*, 45, 46.

pneuma in classical Greek, as was indicated, is that *pneuma* meant something material, whereas *ruakh*, although that too had originally meant something material, a *wind*, and although this material sense of *ruakh* continued in Hebrew to the end (*ruakh* remained the ordinary word for "wind"), had also come to be regularly applied to the inner non-material life of man, to mean what we still call the *spirit* of man. It was one of three words mainly used to describe the inner life of man, volitional, intellectual and emotional. The other two words were *lebh*, heart, and *nephesh*, commonly translated "soul." It is probably a mistake to try to get any clearly-marked psychological theory out of the language of the Old Testament. All the three terms were used in a vague popular way, perfectly adequate to convey the poetical, dramatic or religious sense required, but not to furnish precise terms for scientific psychology. It is often pointed out that the spheres covered by the use of the three words overlap.

But while in many contexts you could say *ruakh* or *nephesh* indifferently, there were contexts in which you could say *ruakh*, but not *nephesh*, and others in which you could say *nephesh*, but not *ruakh*. When these divergent uses of *ruakh* and *nephesh* are examined, it becomes plain that *ruakh* is a term of higher dignity. It is used for the stronger and higher activities of man's inner life, for which *nephesh* would not be appropriate; *nephesh* on the other hand is used for bodily appetites, for the merely animal life, to which it would be derogatory to apply the term *ruakh*. When Greek-speaking Jews came to use *pneuma* as the translation of *ruakh*, and *psyche* as the translation of *nephesh*, this same difference of dignity distinguished the two Greek words in the speech of Jews. *Pneuma* shed that material connotation which it had always had in classical Greek and now denoted not only a constituent of the immaterial inner life of man, but the highest constituent, something superior to mere *psyche*.

But *ruakh* was used in Hebrew not only for the spirit in a living man but for a daemonic being without a human body, just as to-day we can speak of a "spirit." In 1 Kings xxii. when Jehovah propounds to the host of heaven the problem how Ahab is to be induced to go up to Ramoth-Gilead and fall, the being who comes forward and undertakes to act as a lying spirit in the mouth of the king's prophets is called a *ruakh*.

A somewhat staggering theory about the *ruakh* in this passage is maintained in a book to which I owe large acknowledgment—*Der Geist Gottes im Neuen Testament*, by Friedrich Büchsel, published in 1926—a fine book, it seems to me, probably the fullest and most discerning treatment in recent times of the problem of the "Spirit" in the Old and New Testaments. In regard to this passage, however, I cannot say that Büchsel's view seems to me probable. As we read the story in our English Bibles, Jehovah, sitting on His throne in heaven, with all the host of heaven standing by Him, asks who will go and entice Ahab. One member of the heavenly host says on this manner and another on that manner. Then, we read, there came forth a spirit and stood before Jehovah and offered to be a lying spirit in the mouth of the king's prophets. But in Hebrew the word *ruakh* has the definite article attached to it, "the *ruakh*," not "a *ruakh*," and the term *ruakh* is not applied in the passage to the other members of the heavenly host. Büchsel therefore maintains that the *ruakh* here spoken of is actually the *ruakh* of Jehovah Himself, the Spirit of the Lord. He thinks that the *ruakh* of Jehovah can by a poetical fiction be represented as another person who carries on a dialogue with Jehovah, just as in other passages the "arm" of the Lord is poetically personified as a being who can be called upon to awake and who is said to help the Lord, or rule for Him. Büchsel admits that it is to us a strange conception that the Spirit of God should act as a lying spirit, but he thinks that this belongs to an early and crude stage of Israelite religion, when the character of Jehovah was conceived rather as power and sovereignty than as moral according to human standards. But I do not think that there is any need for us to strain our own conceptions of the God of the Old Testament to the point of seeing in the spirit who here acts as a lying spirit the Lord's own Spirit. My brother, Professor Ashley Bevan, whom I have consulted as an authority on Hebrew, tells me[1] that the definite article here makes no real difficulty if the being mentioned is understood in the ordinary way as one of a multitude of spirits forming the host of heaven. It is, he says, according to Hebrew usage in narrative for an individual introduced for the first time to be spoken of with the definite article, for instance, "the maidservant" in Samuel xvii. 17, where we should say "a maidservant." And the parallel which Büchsel adduces of passages in which the arm of Jehovah is poetically personified is not really a parallel to a dialogue between Jehovah and His Spirit.

This, however, brings us to the question of the *ruakh* of Jehovah in the Old Testament, and it is this application of *ruakh* which we have specially to consider in view of the idea of the Spirit in the Christian Church and in the languages of modern Europe.

P. Volz, the author of a monograph on the subject already mentioned (*Der Geist Gottes*) has put forward the theory that originally, in the stage of *naïf* polytheism, Hebrews had spoken of *ha-ruakh*, the Spirit, to denote a daemonic being distinct from Jehovah, and that later on, in the Old Testament as we have it, the *ruakh* has

---

[1] When this was written, my brother was still living.

been fitted into a monotheistic scheme by attaching it to Jehovah as a manifestation or activity of Jehovah Himself. That is speculation about a prehistoric state of things of which we cannot have any direct knowledge. All we know is that among the Hebrews whose ideas are preserved in the Old Testament certain manifestations in men of what was apparently a power not their own—the sort of heroic frenzy which came at particular moments upon national champions and impelled them to astonishing exploits, but chiefly the impulse which drove the prophet to a special kind of utterance—were attributed to the *ruakh*, Spirit, of Jehovah. The *ruakh* was in so far different from the men who acted or spoke, as it was felt by themselves, and seemed to others, to be a power not themselves; yet it was not exactly Jehovah's personal presence, since Jehovah Himself was in heaven. It was something proceeding from Jehovah and operating in men, something like a wind from a world men could not see. And if *ruakh* was a term applied to the more explosive exhibitions of this superhuman power in hero and prophet before it was applied to the quieter manifestations, it certainly came to be used of these quieter manifestations also. There might be something uncanny about the skill of a craftsman, something more than human; that was the *ruakh* of Jehovah;[1] so, too, the sagacity of a king or judge;[2] how could anyone be so wise, if it were not for a power in him, not himself?

Of course, one has to distinguish different conceptions attached to the *ruakh* of Jehovah in the Old Testament according to the dates of the different documents. The association of the *ruakh* with feats of physical or warlike prowess belongs to the earliest period; we find it in the legendary stories of the Judges and Saul. In regard to the utterances and abnormal behaviour of prophets under

[1] Exodus xxi. 3, 31. [2] Isaiah vii. 11; xxviii. 6.

control by the *ruakh* there are, as Professor F. C. Burkitt pointed out in his contribution to the S.P.C.K. Commentary, two distinct ideas of the prophet according as his state is one of frenzy, in which his normal consciousness is blotted out or superseded, the state of a howling dervish, or as his normal consciousness and judgment of moral and religious values remains, unimpaired, though certain overmastering convictions or impulses to action emerge in him, which seem to him the pressure of a power not himself. An example of the first kind of prophets are those whom Saul meets on the road and from whom he catches the frenzy by a kind of infection —"Is Saul also among the prophets?": as an example of the other kind of prophet, Professor Burkitt points to Samuel in the same story.

It is possible, of course, that the dervish type of *nabhi*, prophet, had been the earlier type, and the type of the prophet without ecstasy appeared as the religious life of Israel matured. The author of the document embodied in I Samuel states that the type of prophet exemplified by Samuel had in Samuel's own day been distinguished by a different name, *"rō'ē,"* "seer," from the dervish type, to which the name *"nabhi"* was applied.[1] The "Seer," he says, was the kind of man to whom people resorted in practical difficulties for counsel drawn from Jehovah—a man in whom was a kind of *clairvoyance* or second sight. Such a man, as we know from examples to-day, need not enter into any ecstasy. On the other hand, there is no indication that people resorted to the dervish type of *nabhi* with questions: they would have regarded the abnormal utterances of *nabhi* frenzy with awe as manifestations of a non-human power, possibly as omens given by Jehovah, but they could hardly have communicated with such a *nabhi* as they could with a

---

[1] I Samuel ix. 9.

clairvoyant. If this is a true construction of the evidence, the type of *nabhi* seen in the great prophets of the Old Testament is an amalgamation of something which had belonged in old days to the *nabhi* with something which had belonged to the *rō'ē*, seer. Prophets like Isaiah and Jeremiah had in common with the dervish *nabhi* that they were moved to utterance, not in answer to people consulting them, but by an overmastering impulse, by a spontaneous action upon them of Jehovah: they had in common with the old *rō'ē* that they delivered their messages in their sober senses, without going into an ecstasy, and were sometimes consulted by people who desired guidance from Jehovah about some concrete problem of the day.

In whatever way, however, men seemed to themselves and to others to be moved by a power not themselves, that power was described as *ruakh*, and in certain cases as the *ruakh* of Jehovah. It is important to notice that this idea of the operation of *ruakh* was not confined to the abnormal actions and utterances of heroes and prophets but that a certain mode of its activity was seen in the ordinary life of men and animals. Life remains to-day, in spite of all our science, in its essence a mystery. All life, in old Hebrew thought, was due to the *ruakh* of Jehovah. In the document which forms chapter two of Genesis the beginning of life in the progenitor of the human race is said to be brought about by Jehovah's breathing into his face: true, the actual word *ruakh* is not there used for Jehovah's breath, but the same idea seems to be expressed as is elsewhere expressed by *ruakh*. It is possible that this idea is also contained in Genesis vi. 2, if the words attributed to Jehovah are rightly understood to mean "My *ruakh* shall not abide in man for ever; yet his days shall be a hundred and twenty years," my *ruakh* being here the conscious life which

167

men possess in virtue of God's breathing upon the first man. But both text and meaning of the Hebrew in this passage are uncertain. In any case the phrase frequently applied to God in the Priestly Code, "the God of the spirits of all flesh," indicates a belief in the divine origin of all conscious life as such.

May we say that an operation of God's *ruakh* was conceived in the Priestly Code to be not only the origin of conscious life, but the origin of all the orderly process of the universe? In the second verse of Genesis we are told that the *ruakh* of God moved, or brooded, over the primal waters before God made an orderly world out of chaos. Our Bibles translate, probably rightly, "the Spirit of God," but the old Rabbis seem generally to have understood it of literal wind. "Nowhere," Strack and Billerbeck tell us, "do we come across an attempt in Rabbinic literature to see in this Divine *ruakh* the creative life-power of God; the term is held to mean either the wind blowing across the expanse of primal waters, or the spirit of Adam, which is sometimes taken to stand allegorically for the spirit of the Messiah."[1] In the Phoenician cosmogony given by Philo of Byblus, which has points of resemblance to the cosmogony in Genesis i., we are told that the first men were procreated by the wind Kolpias and a woman called Baaut.[2] Robertson Smith, I believe, conjectured that the wind Kolpias is the *ruakh kol-peah*, "the wind of every quarter," and Baaut is supposed to be the Hebrew *Bohu*, the term used together with *Tohu*, to denote the primal chaos. Thus it seems likely that the writer of Genesis i. was spiritualizing a bit of traditional folk-lore which in its imagination of the primal chaos had added to the horror of vast waters and darkness the blowing of a great wind. For the writer

[1] *Kommentar zum Neuen Testament aus Talmud und Midrasch*, I. p. 48.
[2] Eusebius, *Praeparatio Evangelica*, I. 10, § 34.

of Genesis i. it seems probable that this primitive idea had given place to the idea of spiritual energy proceeding from God, still denoted by the old word.

If originally for the Hebrews the idea connected with *ruakh* was simply uncanny power or vitality, something breaking into the course of things from the unseen divine or daemonic world above or behind, how did ideas of goodness, righteousness, holiness come to be connected with it? Büchsel answers this question, surely rightly, by saying that from the close connexion of Jehovah's *ruakh* with Himself, the conception of the *ruakh* became ethical and spiritual, just in proportion as the idea of Jehovah Himself became ethical and spiritual. In Isaiah xxviii. 6, while the prowess of the Israelite warrior who in the better time coming will repel the alien foe will be the strength of Jehovah in him, the word *ruakh* is specially connected with the judge who will be guided by a power not himself in giving judgment. "Jehovah will be for a spirit of judgment to him that sitteth in judgment and for strength to them that turn back the battle at the gate." The idea connected with *ruakh* in Isaiah xxx. 1 seems to be simply the old one of prophetic inspiration. The people are rebuked because they take counsel but not of Jehovah, and cover themselves with a covering but not of His spirit. This would mean that they formed designs in public policy without safeguarding themselves by ascertaining first the will of Jehovah through the inspired directions given by the prophet. The parallel phrase in the next verse is: "They have not asked at my mouth." The plainest assertion in Hebrew thought at this time of the *ruakh* of Jehovah as a power making for *goodness* is in Isaiah's description of the future ideal king. "The spirit of Jehovah shall rest upon him, the spirit of wisdom and understanding, the spirit of counsel and might, the spirit of knowledge and of the fear of Jehovah"

F*   169

(xi. 2). P. Volz, in a book already referred to, because, on his theory, it was not till later that the *ruakh* of Jehovah became essentially a spirit of moral goodness, would make this passage a later insertion; a similar view was taken by Buchanan Gray: but there seems no ground for this supposition except a preconceived theory.

In one important passage of Isaiah *ruakh* is spoken of as if it were the substance of Jehovah's being. "The Egyptians are men and not God; and their horses flesh, and not spirit" (xxi. 3). Does this mean that Isaiah thought of God as having a body of air, a body like the invisible but powerful wind? Isaiah's metaphysical conceptions may quite well have been marked by primitive *naïveté*; yet when we consider that *ruakh* meant not only wind, but the mind of man in its higher activities, we may be justified in holding this utterance to come near to what we mean when we say that God is immaterial and spiritual. What we mean is that the spirit of man must furnish us with the analogy after which we conceive the being of God, and that is pretty much what Isaiah probably meant. But in this context Isaiah is not interested in the metaphysical difference between material and immaterial. The characteristics of flesh he is thinking about are its weakness and perishability: God is conscious life unrestricted by the infirmities of a mortal body.

"Isaiah," says Büchsel, "grasps with clear consciousness that the knowledge of God and the fear of God are essential characteristics and operations of the Spirit. So far as we can tell, Isaiah was the first to do this. Thus Isaiah is of decisive importance in the history of the idea of the Spirit, so far as that is known to us. I should not like to express Isaiah's importance by the formula, 'Isaiah moralized the conception of spirit,' because this would imply that before Isaiah the Spirit had had no moral quality at all. That would not be true. But it would be true to say that Isaiah deepened the conception of spirit, and that the depth he gave it was distinctively moral depth."[1]

It is a very odd thing that in Jeremiah there is no allusion at all to the Spirit of Jehovah. Volz supposes that Jeremiah avoided the term because for him it was associated with the dervish ecstasy; he wanted to keep his presentation of Jehovah's action clear of all such lower accompaniments. That is a mere guess without much ground. The absence of the term *ruakh* of Jehovah in Jeremiah may be accidental: Jeremiah has clear descriptions of the thing, the consciousness of being laid hold of and impelled by a power not himself. Only he does not call it *ruakh*. Ezekiel, on the other hand, is always bringing in *ruakh*. In our English Bibles, he seems often to speak of the Spirit of God as simply "the Spirit"— "the Spirit lifted me up" comes several times. This seems to contradict something stated by Dalman—that when in the New Testament you find the Spirit of God spoken of as "the Spirit," that is a usage which would have been unintelligible to the Jews who wrote the Old Testament. In the Old Testament, Dalman says, the Spirit of God is always denoted by some qualifying word attached to *ruakh*, the "Spirit of Jehovah," the "Spirit of holiness," "my Spirit," "thy spirit"—never "the Spirit" alone.[2] When the phrase in St. Mark, "Jesus saw the Spirit descending as a dove upon him" is translated literally into Hebrew, as it needs must be in present-day translations of the New Testament issued by the Bible Society, an ancient Hebrew would have understood by that, he says, nothing except that Jesus saw the wind descending, or saw some daemonic being. Yet here, in Ezekiel, you

[1] *Der Geist Gottes im Neuen Testament*, p. 19.
[2] G. Dalman, *Die Worte Jesu* (2nd ed., 1930), p. 166.

171

read continually "the Spirit" in our English Bibles. As a matter of fact, our English Bibles here mis-translate. There is no definite article in the Hebrew. What Ezekiel says is simply that "spirit lifted me up." There is no indication of a personal being distinguishable from Jehovah, but only of a supernatural force, something like a wind. "I was lifted up by invisible agency."

When Ezekiel describes the power which comes upon him and impels him to utterance as the *spirit* of Jehovah, he is not going beyond the old usage in regard to prophetic inspiration. Where there seems something new in Ezekiel's conception of the Divine *ruakh* is in his anticipation of its effecting a spiritual conversion in the nation at large. "I will give them one heart," he represents Jehovah as saying. "I will put a new *spirit* within you: I will take the stony heart out of their flesh and will give them an heart of flesh, that they may walk in my statutes and keep mine ordinances and do them" (xi. 19, 20). The *ruakh* will be seen, not in abnormal states of prophetic possession, but in a right direction of will towards God. It is possible that the idea has been already hinted at by Isaiah, in a passage (xxxiii. 15) which describes the future time of blessing "when spirit will be poured upon us from on high." But it is questionable both whether that verse is not a later insertion in the book of Isaiah and also questionable what it means. Duhm thinks that the pouring of the *ruakh* from on high does not mean any moral renovation but a transformation of the natural world in the coming age. Certainly in Chapter xi., Isaiah had spoken, as we have seen, of the *ruakh* of Jehovah producing great spiritual qualities in the ideal future king, and, in so far, the ideal state will be due to the operation of the divine spirit. But it is only in the head of the nation that the spirit works, so far as the conception there goes. In Ezekiel a right heart is produced in the nation at large. "Israel," in Büchsel's phrase, "becomes a people whose members individually are men of the spirit." The idea does not seem to have established itself after Ezekiel as an element in the Jews' imagination of the coming Kingdom of God. In the second Isaiah indeed, half a century later, it is there: "I will pour my spirit upon thy seed and my blessing upon thine offspring" (xliv. 3). But it is doubtful whether it can be traced in the later Old Testament documents. The passage in the work of a late prophet attached to the book of Zachariah which speaks of a spirit of tenderness and supplication being poured out by Jehovah upon the nation which has been guilty of some murder[1] (the historical incident referred to is not known) may only mean that Jehovah causes a mood of compunction in reference to this particular murder, not indicate a hope like Ezekiel's, the hope of a general moral and spiritual renewal. Again, the well-known passage in Joel which speaks of an outpouring of Jehovah's spirit upon all flesh in the latter days seems to have in view not so much a spiritual change of heart as prophetic inspiration. It will be a feature of the latter days that prophetic inspiration, dreams and visions, are common, and granted even to slaves.

If we turn to the expressions of Jewish piety in the centuries between the return from exile and the establishment of the Hasmonean dynasty, we find a conception connecting the *ruakh* with the life of the God-fearing individual in everyday conduct, quite apart from exceptional prophetic gifts. "Teach me to do Thy will," a Psalmist prays, "for thou art my God: let thy good *ruakh* lead me in the land of uprightness" (cxliii. 10). "Whither can I go from thy *ruakh*? Or whither can I flee from thy presence?" another Psalm (cxxxix. 7) exclaims.

[1] Zechariah xii. 10.

The *ruakh* [Büchsel comments] is the presence of God. . . . Yet one cannot exactly say, I think, that we have there the possession of the Spirit by the individual godly man. Certainly the godly man is regarded as led by the Spirit, but the relation of the individual and the Spirit does not seem to me close enough to warrant our speaking of the individual as filled with the Spirit, as a vehicle of the Spirit. The Spirit leads, but it does not "rest upon" the man. The two things are not the same.

The working of the Spirit [he says] now extends over a wider field, but at the same time, it has become vaguer, less obvious to the eye. . . . For the broadly human, for what makes direct and strong appeal, you may look in vain in post-exilic Judaism. Gone are the great heroic figures, gone the rich poetic vision, the things in which the primitive force of religion breaks forth. As a compensation, this religion has ethical depth and purity. Man is small in Judaism, but God is great (p. 33).

It is, of course, important to grasp that in all these Hebrew conceptions of the action of the Divine *ruakh* upon man, whether in the days of the great prophets or in post-exilic Judaism, the distinction, one might say the distance, between God and man is maintained far more firmly than in surrounding paganism. There is never any suggestion of the Divine Being Himself entering into the human individual as there is in Greek ideas of mantic possession. The Greeks spoke of a man so possessed as ἔνθεος, "with the god inside him," or perhaps rather "steeped in the god." Such a phrase would have been abhorrent to the Hebrews. The *ruakh* of God is not Jehovah Himself, it is the power of Jehovah working at a distance, a breath or wind, as it were, coming from Jehovah: Jehovah abides in His holy heaven. The figure of a wind which travels over vast spaces served admirably to convey the idea of something coming from God which moved and controlled men— coming from God as a wind comes from somewhere far away and breaks the trees here close to me. It is noteworthy too that, even in regard to the *ruakh*, it is not commonly spoken of as entering into the prophet, but as coming *upon* him. We are told indeed that the crafts-

174

men who made the tabernacle were filled with the Spirit of God;[1] but elsewhere the Spirit "comes upon," or "rests upon" the man. It remains a power working from outside, felt by the man as essentially not himself. It is sometimes described as a hand laid upon the man which he cannot resist. This forms a signal contrast to all Greek and Indian ideas, according to which a man looking into the centre of his own being can discover his fundamental identity with God.

There is one problematic document which has to be considered in this connexion, the Fifty-first Psalm, in which a man prays: "Take not thy Holy Spirit from me." It is now apparently believed by most Old Testament scholars that this poem is not an expression of merely general piety or that the person who is heard speaking represents the God-fearing community as a whole: it is believed to be the cry of some particular man in regard to some particular event, an intense page torn from some personal history long ago, which must remain for ever dark to us. We shall never know what the action was which has fastened upon the speaker that horror of blood-guiltiness. It is a question what he understood by God's *ruakh* of holiness, of which he so dreaded to be deprived. "The strength to live a good life," some commentators have explained. "The Divine Being bestowed upon the pious," Volz says, "the bond of fellowship which unites the man essentially with the Deity." Such a conception, Büchsel insists, would be quite incompatible with the Hebrew sense of the difference between the human and the Divine. But neither does the explanation "strength to live a good life" seem satisfactory. The *ruakh* never became a force which was a constituent of a man's own life, it remained always the action of God upon a man from outside. And the speaker, Büchsel believes, cannot

[1] Exodus xxxi. 3.

175

have been an ordinary member of the community; it is indicated that he was someone whose office was to teach sinners the way, and who for such an office had been endowed, as a prophet, with the *ruakh*. In spite of that, he had fallen into his great sin; and now he was afraid that God would no more act upon him as of old. So long as he had not offended the *ruakh*, he had experienced a happy sureness and promptness of will. He had felt himself in the presence of God. Could he ever get all that back again? "Renew a steadfast spirit within me: cast me not away from thy presence: uphold me with thy willing spirit." If we knew something of the personal history behind this document, we could understand better how the lost good so bitterly desired was conceived. But we can understand enough to see, as Büchsel says, that "this whole personal conception of what possessing the Spirit means shows the prophetic idea of spirit raised to peculiar purity and strength."

We have not yet considered one aspect of the *ruakh* of God in the Old Testament which is important in view of later Christian beliefs—the apparent attribution to the *ruakh* in certain passages of a personality distinct from that of Jehovah Himself. With that we shall begin our next lecture.

SPIRIT

(continued)

OUR last lecture left us in sight of a problem in regard to Old Testament conceptions of the *ruakh*, Spirit, of God—the apparent attribution to the *ruakh* in certain passages of a personality distinct from that of God Himself. The most signal passages are in Isaiah lxiii., a document belonging, of course, to the period of Persian rule. The children of Israel are there said to have had the *ruakh* of Jehovah for their leader in the wilderness— "as the cattle that go down into the valley, the Spirit of Jehovah caused them to rest" (v. 14).[1] And this *ruakh*, the Holy Spirit in verse 10, they are said to have grieved by their rebelliousness.

This kind of personification or quasi-personification of the *ruakh* of Jehovah is plainly analogous to the usage according to which the action of Jehovah, in leading

[1] Similarly, Nehemiah ix. 20, speaking, in a prayer to God, about Israel's passage through the wilderness says: "Thou gavest also thy good *ruakh* to instruct them"—though that passage may mean only that prophetic inspiration was bestowed upon the leaders of the people in those days. In Haggai ii. 4, 5, according to what is probably the true text, omitting a clause which appears in our Bibles, the presence of the *ruakh* is asserted in the prophet's own day: "Be strong, all ye people of the land and work, for I am with you, and my Spirit abideth among you." A like conception may perhaps be seen in the utterance of Haggai's contemporary, Zechariah: "Not by might, nor by power, but by my Spirit," saith Jehovah of hosts (iv. 10).

Israel, is attributed to the angel of Jehovah. It is a commonplace of Old Testament scholarship that the angel of Jehovah seems sometimes to be a way of speaking of Jehovah's own action in the world of men. The story which describes how the angel of Jehovah appeared to Gideon goes on to speak as if the angel were Jehovah Himself. And, in regard to the leading of the children of Israel through the wilderness, this is attributed to the angel in Exodus xxiii. "Behold I send an angel before thee" (v. 20). "Mine angel shall go before thee" (v. 23). The same chapter of Isaiah which, as we saw, spoke of the children of Israel as having been led by the Spirit of Jehovah, had said two verses before "The angel of his presence saved them"—as if the angel and the Spirit were identical.

We have already in such passages the example of a mode of expression in Jewish religion which gives rise to a problem still unsettled—the mode of expression which seems to make of God's activity in the world, or God's appearance to men, a personal being distinguishable from God Himself, the Wisdom of Proverbs and the Apocrypha, the Logos and the other Powers in Philo, the Memrā of the Targum, the Shekinah and Metatron in other Rabbinical books. How far was this separate personification of the Divine activity or the Divine self-manifestation taken as purely poetical metaphor, how far was there belief in any real angelic subordinate to God as a distinguishable person, or in any distinction of persons within the Divine? It is probable that no ancient Hebrew felt the need of a clear metaphysical definition when he used this kind of language and that any attempt on our part to say precisely what was meant thus leads inevitably to misrepresentation: the images floating before the mind had vague edges and we should do the old Hebrew wrong if we tried to pin him down to any

178

clearly articulated conception. Even in the case of Philo, who had gone through the schools of Greek philosophy, no one has been able to define precisely how far he thought of his Logos as a separate personal being and how far as a figure of speech. Perhaps Philo himself did not know.

In the case of Philo, it is commonly explained that he introduced his Logos in order to avoid bringing God Himself into contact with matter. The ancient Hebrews had had no such sense of the essential unworthiness of matter as Philo learnt from Greek Platonists, but they had had no doubt a sense that the holiness of God meant His abode in some region higher than the world of men and His invisibility to eyes to flesh, so that to attribute His activity in the world and His visible manifestations to something that was Himself and yet not quite Himself met an instinctive exigence of Hebrew religion. The conception of the *ruakh*, the wind-like power proceeding from God, was a way of combining the idea of God's distance from the world with the idea of His operation within the world. To think of the *ruakh* as something personal in itself was easier, we may believe, because *ruakh* meant not only wind, but the higher activities of mind and will in man. It is a problem for any view of the universe which holds strongly to the idea of God as transcendent, in what sense the power working in the physical world and upon or within the mind of man is to be regarded as Divine. Where the minds of men have not yet emancipated themselves from spatial conceptions in regard to the spiritual, where God, that is to say, is conceived as an individual Person literally distant in a region above the earth, it may be almost a necessity of thought to postulate a *ruakh*, or something analogous, as the extension of God's activity away from Himself.

That this is so may be shown by the fact that in the

other religion which offers so many points of resemblance to the religion of Israel, in Zoroastrianism, the Supreme God has attached to him a number of divine beings, regarding whom the very same question arises as arises regarding the *ruakh* of the Old Testament and the Logos of Philo: How far were these beings, the seven Amesha Spentas, Holy Spirit, Good Thought, Right, Desirable Dominion, Piety, Welfare, Immortality, believed to be real persons distinguishable from God? How far were they understood to be merely imaginative personifications of constituents making up spiritual good? Except the name of the first, Spento Mainyus, ordinarily translated "Holy Spirit," the names sound curiously abstract, unlike personal names. Modern Jewish scholars who have concerned themselves with Zoroastrianism, anxious perhaps to secure the prerogative of Israel's religion, seem disposed to insist that the phraseology of Zoroastrianism must be construed in the most realistically literal way. Thus Scheftelowitz contends that the Supreme God was believed to be literally and physically the father of Armaiti, Piety, that Vohumanah, Good Thought, was believed to be literally a being in human form, nine times taller than Zarathustra, and clad in a robe of silken material, and so on.[1] It seems to me quite arbitrary to take this view at any rate in regard to the primitive Zoroastrianism of the Gathas (there were no doubt all kinds of popular and priestly coarsening of the Zoroastrian religion from the time of the Achaemenian kings onwards)—just as arbitrary as it would be to force a literal meaning upon the language used in Proverbs about the Wisdom whom God brought into being at the beginning of His ways.

The fact that the chief of these quasi-personal divine

[1] J. Scheftelowitz, *Die altpersische Religion und das Judentum* (1920), pp. 8–11.

beings attached in Zoroastrianism to God bears a name, Spento Mainyus, which is commonly translated "Holy Spirit," seems to make the parallel to the Old Testament remarkably close. But it is not quite so close as it seems. The adjective *spento* does not, Avestan scholars tell us, really mean what the Hebrew word translated "holy" means: Lommel thinks that in German it should be translated *"klug,"* that is, "sagacious," rather than *"heilig"*;[1] and the noun *mainyus,* translated Spirit, has nothing to do with the idea of breath or wind. Its root is that of words for mind or thought, like the Latin *mens,* and it would thus correspond with the Hebrew *ruakh* only in the derivative meaning which *ruakh* has as denoting the spirit of man, not in its root-meaning. How far the Zoroastrian conceptions had influence upon Hebrew conceptions in the days of Persian, Greek and Roman rule is, of course, a much debated question. It is possible that the seven archangels who appear in the Jewish tradition from the book of Zechariah onwards, and who are perhaps meant by the seven spirits before the throne of God in the book of Revelation, were suggested by the Zoroastrian Amesha Spentas, though it is equally possible that the number seven, both in the case of the Persians and in the case of Jews, was derived from a common source, the seven planetary gods of Babylonia. It does not seem likely that conceptions of the Holy Spirit in Judaism and Christianity owed anything to Spento Mainyus.

When the terms of Jewish religion had to be translated into another language, into Greek, for the Greek-speaking Jews who spread through the countries of Hellenistic culture after Alexander, the Greek *pneuma* was taken as the regular word to represent the Hebrew *ruakh*. *Pneuma* had already a history in the Greek poetical and philo-

[1] H. Lommel, *Die Religion Zarathrustras* (1930), pp. 18, 19.

sophical vocabulary, which we surveyed in our last lecture. But it would be a mistake to suppose that in the mouths and in the writings of Jews, and later on, of Christians, *pneuma* had the same connotation it had for pagan Greeks. By being used to translate *ruakh* it acquired for Jews and Christians a new connotation, that of *ruakh*, which in some of its meanings indeed overlapped with the connotation of *pneuma*, but in others was used in a way which would, I think, have been hardly intelligible to a Greek of the time of Plato. (To glance on for a moment at the language of the New Testament, it is doubtful whether a pagan Greek who heard for the first time the phrase which we translate "Blessed are the poor in spirit" would have been able to attach any meaning to it. "Blessed are the grovellingly poor by their breathing" or "by gaseous substance.")[1]

I believe that the view stated in books of the last generation, by Siebeck for instance and Cremer in his Lexicon of Biblical Greek, that the word *pneuma* did not get a connotation which was spiritual in our sense till it was adopted by the Jews to translate *ruakh* and passed on from the Synagogue to the Christian Church, is substantially true. Or perhaps we should enlarge this statement to allow for the possibility of *pneuma* having also been adopted by Greek-speaking Semites other than Jews in Hellenistic times to translate the word which in their languages corresponded with the Hebrew *ruakh*. If other Semitic peoples beside the Jews did this, then, when we find the word used in popular Hellenistic literature, such as magical papyri, in a sense closer to the Biblical sense than the one it had in classical Greek, we could not say definitely that its use was due to Jewish

[1] The more honourable word for "poor" in Greek, $\pi \acute{\epsilon} \nu \eta \varsigma$, had been to some extent superseded in the language of Greek-speaking Jews by the word $\pi \tau \omega \chi \acute{o} \varsigma$, which in classical Greek had had a suggestion of contempt; it was connected with the verb $\pi \tau \acute{\omega} \sigma \sigma \epsilon \iota \nu$, "to cringe," "to cower."

or Christian influence, though it would still be true that its use was due to the influence of Hellenized Semites.

Personal beings without bodies, whether non-human beings, angels and devils, or discarnate human spirits, could now be spoken of as *pneumata*. But the more proper Greek usage continued amongst Hellenistic Jews side by side with the new Hebraizing usage. "The souls (ψυχαί) of the righteous are in the hand of God," says a well-known verse of Wisdom. There seems no certain use of the term *pneuma* for a discarnate human spirit in the Apocrypha, but in Enoch xxii., the discarnate spirits are called indiscriminately ψυχαί, and πνεύματα and the two terms are even curiously run together in a single phrase ("These hollow places wherein the spirits of the souls of the dead are assembled," xxii. 3). If the verse in the Song of the Three Children, "Ye spirits and souls of the righteous," means discarnate spirits, as Church tradition and Walter Bauer's *Wörterbuch zum Neuen Testament* hold against Fritzsche's old commentary and the late Dr. Bennet in Charles's *Apocrypha*, who thought that it meant the spirits and souls of righteous men still in the flesh, then you have there too a coupling of the two terms, apparently simply for fullness of sound, without any difference of meaning between the two being implied. In the New Testament there are undoubted instances of discarnate human spirits being called *pneumata* (the "spirits of just men made perfect" in Hebrews xii.: the "*pneumata* in prison" in 1 Peter iii.).

In the voluminous works of Philo we have our greatest monument of Hellenistic Judaism outside the Septuagint. But from Philo's usage we can draw conclusions only with great caution and discrimination regarding the way Greek-speaking Jews ordinarily expressed themselves in the matter of religion. Philo's ambition was to write beautiful literary Greek, and he avoided ways of speaking which had not a sanction in the Greek literary tradition. Thus he evidently used the word *pneuma*, so far as he could, with its proper Greek connotation, not with the connotation of *ruakh*. He could not help bringing it in sometimes just because it was there in the Septuagint text which he made the basis of his discourse. But he confines himself, so far as he can, to senses which had classical precedent, either that of a material air or gas or that of prophetic afflatus which might be justified by the classical *epipnoia*. He never talks of *pneuma*, to mean the higher principle in the universe, opposed to matter, or the higher principle in man contrasted with the animal soul, what we mean by "spirit." That he avoided other uses of *pneuma* because they were old but vulgar Greek, as Leisegang supposes, seems to me, as I said in my last lecture, a conjecture without basis. It was a sufficient reason for his avoiding them that they were new Jewish Greek. For the higher principle in the universe or in man he uses the proper Greek term, *nous*. Unlike Philo, the writers of the New Testament were, for the most part, little concerned to write literary Greek; they used the phrases which were the ordinary ones used by Greek-speaking Jews in daily life: we cannot therefore get much light on the meaning of New Testament terms from the language of Philo.

The other work of Hellenistic Judaism which stands near to Philo, the Book of Wisdom, is written in a style which follows much more closely that of Old Testament poetry. The author accordingly did not feel the same shyness of the word *pneuma* in the Old Testament sense which Philo felt. There is indeed no trace in the Book of Wisdom of *pneuma* being used for the higher part of man's soul as distinguished from the lower part. If the author uses any term to denote this it is the same term

184

as Philo uses, *nous*. At least, in one phrase, human souls seem to be distinguished from merely animal souls by their being called πνεύματα νοερά, that is *pneumata* possessed of *nous* (vii. 23). But in this very phrase the use of *pneumata* to mean individual conscious beings is, as we have seen, Hebrew, not Greek, and various other uses of *pneuma* analogous to that of *ruakh* are found in this book. The most interesting thing, however, in the book, is the application of the term *pneuma* to the Divine Wisdom pervading the universe. For what you see here happening is something which it was antecedently probable would happen. It was not likely that if a term with a rich connotation attached to it in Greek was used to cover the connotation of a Hebrew word its new sphere of meaning would remain altogether uncontaminated with the meanings which belonged to the term in pagan Greek; it was likely that the two connotations would sometimes become fused; the word would look back to two different lines of tradition which met and mingled at this point. When the author of Wisdom writes: "For Wisdom is more mobile than any motion; yea, she pervadeth and penetrateth all things by reason of her pureness. For she is an exhalation (ἀτμίς) of the power of God, and a clear effluence of the glory of the Almighty. . . . From generation to generation passing into holy souls she maketh men friends of God and prophets. . . . She reacheth from one end of the world to the other with full strength and ordereth all things graciously" (vii. 22–vii. 1), and when the author expressly describes this world-pervading Wisdom as a *pneuma*, it is quite impossible that he was not consciously reproducing current Stoic language about the *pneuma* which was also a peculiarly pure and subtle fire, identical with God, which penetrated all the kosmos and ordered everything with perfect wisdom, which, lastly, constituted the reason in man and made those obedient to it sages and friends of God.[1]

To deny the pagan Greek antecedents of the language in these passages of the Book of Wisdom would be absurd. Yet it would be no less a mistake to suppose that the writer uses this language in the purely Greek sense. The word *pneuma* for a Jew could not but have the spiritual sense which belonged to *ruakh* as standing for something in the sphere of consciousness, mind and will. The Stoic *pneuma* never ceased to be a material gas, even if it had characteristics of spirit at the same time. Again, in representing this *pneuma* as sent forth from a personal God, the book of Wisdom is definitely not Stoic. The Stoic *pneuma* pervading the world was not something sent forth from God: it was God.

We come now to some of the problems connected with the use of *pneuma* in the Christian Church which took over the language of Greek-speaking Jews, but put into it some new meanings. It is, of course, mainly from the language of the primitive Christian Church that the English word "spirit" and analogous words in other European languages have come to have the range of meaning which they have to-day.

That the Christian use of the term *pneuma* had to some extent antecedents in the Old Testament no one, of course, could deny. In some cases it was used by Greek Christians precisely as *ruakh* was used in Hebrew, to describe the non-corporeal part of man. When the Gospel narrative says "Jesus knew in his spirit"[2] or "Jesus groaned in his spirit"[3] that reproduces a Hebrew phrase, with the meaning that Jesus perceived something by direct intuition without the perception being mediated by a bodily process, or that Jesus felt stress internally

---

[1] ἐλεύθερος γάρ εἰμι καὶ φίλος τοῦ θεοῦ, ἵν' ἑκὼν πείθωμαι αὐτῷ (Epict., iv. 3. 9).   [2] Mark ii. 8.   [3] John xi. 33.

apart from the vocal groan. St. Paul sometimes uses it in this way. When he says that the "spirit" of Titus was refreshed by the reception he met with at Corinth,[1] he means simply that Titus had a refreshing experience in his inner conscious life. Even in application to God, when Jesus in the Fourth Gospel says: "God is *pneuma*"[2] —a phrase which a Stoic might have used, though with another meaning, as an exact expression of his own doctrine—we need not interpret it by the pagan parallel. For there is after all the well-known passage in Isaiah (xxxi. 3) which equates God and *ruakh*. "The Egyptians are men and not God; and their horses flesh, and not spirit."

In two respects the Christian use of *pneuma* offers a problem. One is the conception of the Holy Spirit as a personal Being distinguishable from God the Father. This was not altogether new. We have seen in the Old Testament a kind of separate personification of the *ruakh* of God, in Proverbs the personification of the Wisdom of God, and in Philo that of the Logos. But in all those cases the personification does not get decidedly beyond the character of a figure of speech, a poetical metaphor. It is an image which the mind entertains for a moment as a pictorial symbol: there is no assertion in sober prose that a personal Being exists distinguishable from God, who has the functions of the Spirit of God or of Wisdom or of the Logos. The new thing in the Christian Church was that the distinct existence of a personal Holy Spirit was taken seriously as a truth about the Divine Being.

The emergence of this belief was, of course, a new fact of importance, of which various explanations can be given. It may be explained by a Christian theologian as a new apprehension of Reality in consequence of a new illumination vouchsafed to human minds by God, and the theologian may endeavour, by applying metaphysical

[1] 2 Corinthians vii. 13.   [2] John iv. 24.

187

notions prevalent in his own time or thought out by himself, to make the belief intelligible. Or it may be explained by an anthropologist as a new illusion, and the anthropologist may endeavour to show psychologically how it came to be formed in the minds of men in the first century. Since the Christian doctrine of the Holy Spirit is one which could not be demonstrated as true by rational metaphysics, and requires the belief in some kind of revelation, it lies outside the province of a Gifford Lecturer either to defend or to impugn the claim of the doctrine to give truth about the universe. Only certain observations about it may be advanced, which do not pretend to do more than take note of probable matters of fact.

One thing of which we may be certain is that, whatever the ideas attached to the term "Holy Spirit" in the first days of Christianity were, they have been shaped not only by the traditional Old Testament associations of the term "Holy Spirit" but by new actual experiences with the primitive community—that apparent control by a Power not themselves, sometimes coming upon believers abruptly at particular moments and impelling them to abnormal utterance, sometimes simply quickening their thoughts and supplying words in controversy or exhortation or prayer. Whether in these unusual experiences there was a real inrush from the world above man or whether they could be wholly explained by human psychology, it cannot be questioned that they formed a determining element in the life of the first Christian generations, and that whenever the term "Spirit" or "Holy Spirit" was used, what was essentially meant was the Power conceived to be operative in these actual experiences. The Power entering into men seemed essentially to be Divine, to be God Himself; on the other hand, the activities to which the Spirit impelled seemed to be largely directed towards God as Someone different from the directing Power. The prayer uttered by someone in the assembly, when possessed by the Spirit, was an utterance addressed to God, the Spirit interceding with groanings which could not find expression in any normal human language. And apart from these more abnormal manifestations of the Spirit's working, the new love towards God, which might be a permanent part of the Christian's inner life, was regarded as shed abroad in men's hearts by the Holy Spirit dwelling in them, so that here too the Spirit was felt as something both coming *from* God and directed *to* God.

It must be recognized that in Rabbinical literature passages may be found which speak of the Holy Spirit as interceding for Israel with God, as crying to God and weeping. But with the Jews such language remained merely figurative: it never implied any belief in a real personal Power beside or within the Godhead. The occasional personification of the Holy Spirit in Rabbinical utterances simply carried on the poetical personification of the Spirit in the Old Testament. But if the same modes of expression stood, in the case of the Christians, for a belief which issued in the explicit recognition of the Holy Spirit as a distinct "Person" within the Godhead, and in the case of the Jews remained a mere figure of speech, why should there have been this difference? It can hardly, I think, be questioned that the difference was due to the young community having begun its life in the world with a peculiarly vivid feeling that a Spiritual Power was at work within it, and within its individual members, the thrilling sense of actuality coming from real experiences and real events, regarded as manifestations of this Power, to which there was no parallel in the Jewish community at that time. This view may be denied on the basis of a few Rabbinic passages which speak of the Holy Spirit as resting upon, or working in, some eminent pious Jews of later times. That such passages, however, do not imply anything which amounts to the assurance of the early Church is proved, I think, by other Rabbinic passages which indicate the general feeling of the time that the operation of the Holy Spirit, connected almost exclusively with the gift of prophecy or second sight, not with the piety of the ordinary man, belonged to the great days of the past, not to the commonplace present. "When the last prophets, Haggai, Zachariah and Malachi died," says a Rabbinic book,[1] "the Holy Spirit ceased out of Israel." The Jewish writer Dr. J. Abelson indeed maintains that experience of the Holy Spirit was frequent in Rabbinic times.[2] But passages such as that which asserts that Hillel (early first century) and Samuel the Small (early part of second century A.D.) were worthy to have had the Holy Spirit, that is, the gift of prophecy, bestowed upon them, if the wickedness of their times had not prevented, seem to prove the contrary. It would no doubt be excessive to say that there was no consciousness at all in Judaism of the piety, even of the ordinary man, being due to the operation of the Holy Spirit. An isolated utterance is adduced which says: "All that the righteous do they do in the Holy Spirit."[3] The contrast between the early Christian Church and the contemporary Synagogue, in regard to their feeling of being moved by a supernatural Power, was, we may believe, one of degree. The ecstatic outbreaks of what was believed to be the Holy Spirit in the Church, shown us in the New Testament, the sense of being led by the Spirit in the actions of every day—one might have looked long in contemporary Judaism for anything quite like that.

---

[1] *Tosefta Soṭah*, xiii. § 2 (before A.D. 500).
[2] *The Immanence of God in Rabbinical Literature*, pp. 37, 208, 260, 271 ff., 279.   [3] *Tanḥuma*, ed. Buber, *Vayeḥi*, § 13, f. 110a.

When Christians had to think out, and express in definite terms, what they were to conceive the relation between this Power, so vividly experienced, and God to be, its double character, Divine itself and directed towards God, no doubt made a difficulty. The solution of the difficulty was ultimately found in a distinction of Persons within the Godhead, the Spirit was truly God, and yet the Spirit proceeded from the Father and turned back in prayer towards the Father. Thus the personification of the Spirit in the Christian community cannot be explained merely by the influence of earlier forms of religion which personified or semi-personified divine Beings intermediate between God and Man—Philo's Logos or the Zoroastrian Spento Mainyus. It was an attempt to explain an actual experience.

It may be objected that the more signal experiences belonged to the first Christian generations and it was not till long after that the dogma was ecclesiastically formulated. True, but the formulation was confessedly an attempt to reconcile the various texts in the New Testament, and the New Testament enshrined the experiences of the first two generations, and the convictions which, for these generations, had arisen out of the experiences. It seems unlikely indeed that the first generation of Christians, even St. Peter or St. Paul, had as sharply-defined an intellectual idea of the distinct personality of the Holy Spirit as the theologians had who drew up the formula of the Council of Constantinople in A.D. 381. We should probably think of the state of mind of the first Christian generations in regard to the Holy Spirit as something between that of the Old Testament writers who spoke of the Divine *ruakh* as a Being distinguishable in imagination from God, though not distinguishable in fact, and that of later theologians who defined the Christian belief in Greek metaphysical terms.

Even if the first Christians would not have been prepared to state in these precise terms what they believed about the Holy Spirit, they certainly felt the Holy Spirit as a distinct Person much more than the Old Testament writers had done, and that feeling was so far effective belief as their volitions and actions were determined by it. It is especially difficult to say what ideas were attached to the words "Holy Spirit" in the earliest circle of disciples, which constituted the Aramaic-speaking community of Nazoraeans in Judaea, because we have no document emanating from that primitive community which has not passed through a Greek-speaking Christian medium. It is very unlikely that the Nazoraeans at any rate can have been influenced by any associations attached to the Greek word *pneuma*: for them the Holy Spirit was still *ruakh qodshā*.

Here then a term which at the beginning of its history meant simply breath or air in motion has come, at the end of a long process, to stand in the minds of men for a Person within the One Godhead. That is an event in history of which anyone can take cognizance, whether they think the belief of the Christian Church a revelation or a delusion. The word "spirit," which inevitably still suggests to the imagination characteristics associated with its original meaning—the wind that bloweth where it listeth—or even a fluid substance which can be poured out upon a multitude of individual men—is at best a symbol thrown out in human language at the Supreme Reality. One arrives here at a threshold beyond which we may not now attempt to penetrate.

The other application of the term *pneuma* in the New Testament which constitutes a problem is its use to denote an element in man—the problem of the apparent trichotomy in St. Paul's phrase "your spirit and soul and body" (1 Thessalonians v. 23)—which also appears in the distinction between the spiritual man (*pneumatikes anthropos*) and the natural man (*psychikos anthropos*).[1]

There has been a good deal of controversy round the question whether for St. Paul *pneuma* was a constituent of human nature, as such, present, together with the *psyche* in all men from their birth, or whether it was something possessed only by the regenerate, the new element which corresponded with the new divine life, in those who were members of the Body of Christ. In the judgment of many scholars to-day, the second is the true view. The *pneuma* in Christians, they think, as understood by St. Paul, was simply the portion which each individual had of the one Divine Spirit, practically identical with the "new man." And this *pneuma* was what survived bodily death and remained alone, apart from the *psyche* and the body in the interval between death and the Resurrection. There is, it is pointed out, one passage in which St. Paul speaks of the *pneuma* of a man being saved in the life to come, but no passage in which he speaks of a soul (*psyche*) being saved.

The difference of opinion on this subject goes back to early Christian times. In a Latin tract published by Batiffol in 1900, for which the superscription in the manuscript claims that it is the translation of a work of Origen's—a work otherwise unknown, though Batiffol believed that the claim was true—"*Tractatus de libris sanctarum scripturarum*"—we are told, "The spirit is not born with a man, but is bestowed on him subsequently by God, through merit, through the grace of faith" (I. p. 4).[2] Similarly, a fragment of an unknown commentator quoted in Cramer's *Catenae* says: "The apostle never speaks of the three elements, spirit, soul and body,

---

[1] 1 Corinthians ii. 14; cf. xv. 46.

[2] *Verum animalis homo, qui necdum Spiritum Dei acceperit, duabus rebus, ut dixi, constat, id est corpore et anima* (Origen, *Tract.*, p. 4).

in connexion with unbelievers, but only with believers. These possess soul and body by nature, but spirit only as a Divine boon—spirit being in fact the *charisma* bestowed upon those who believe."[1] With this the Gnostic view corresponded in so far as the Gnostics distinguished a particular class of men who possessed the divine element, *pneuma*, in addition to their human *psyche*, from the rest of men who possessed either only the lower human principle described as "flesh (*sarx*)," or, at any rate only the higher human principle as well, the "soul (*psyche*)." But the Gnostics seem commonly to have believed that a man was born into one or other of the three classes and remained in it: in that respect their view would have differed from St. Paul's. And in another way the Gnostic doctrine must have differed essentially from that of St. Paul. The Gnostic trichotomy was, like that of Plato, a division into three *of the inner life* of man, whereas St. Paul's was only a dichotomy, so far as the inner life of man went, the third element in St. Paul's case being the material body, something outside the inner life. For St. Paul indeed, as for the Gnostic, the "flesh," *sarx*, extended as a lower element into the inner life, thus differing from the external *sōma*, but for the Gnostic *sarx* was an element differing from the *psyche*. A *sarkikos anthrōpos*, a "fleshy man," was a different kind of man from a *psychikos anthrōpos*, a "soul man." For St. Paul to be a *psychikos anthrōpos* was apparently the same as to be a "man in the flesh." Where the *psyche* is opposed to the *pneuma*, the *psyche* is practically identical with the *sarx*. Thus for St. Paul, the inner life is divided into two only, *pneuma* and *psyche*, with the body as the third constituent of man outside: for the Gnostics, the inner life was divided into three, so that if you are going

[1] J. A. Cramer, *Catenae in S. Pauli Epistolas ad Galatis*, etc., Oxford, 1842, p. 374.

to reckon the body as well, the Gnostic theory would give us not a trichotomy, but a tetrachotomy.

The view which has come to prevail in the Church rejects the idea that the mental constitution of a believer differs from that of an unbeliever by the addition of a new element; it holds that *pneuma* is an essential part of human nature as such, present in unbelievers as well as in believers. Only in believers, it is held, the human *pneuma* is brought into a new kind of activity by the action upon it or within it of the Divine Spirit. So far then, as the existence of body, soul and spirit can be called a trichotomy, the trichotomy extends to mankind as a whole; only the theologians of the Roman Church apparently object to the term trichotomy being used to express this view, because they attach to the term trichotomy an idea such as the Gnostic one, which makes a sharp distinction between *psyche* and *pneuma* as two distinct elements, whereas in the Catholic view there is never more than one soul, and the distinction between *psyche* and *pneuma* indicates only a diversity in that one soul's operations.

The difficulty raised by the old commentator, that St. Paul never speaks of the *pneuma* in connexion with unbelievers, might be met by the consideration that St. Paul, as a matter of fact, says practically nothing about the psychology of unbelievers. And if he once speaks of a man's *pneuma* being saved, but never of his *psyche* being saved, it has to be considered that St. Paul apparently did not like the word *psyche* in any reference to the inner life of men. It is curious how seldom the word occurs in his writing; and then it is only in a few current phrases. So far as his language was determined by the Jewish tradition he used *pneuma* where one speaking in Hebrew might have used *ruakh*, of the inner life which belonged to anyone as a human being. Certainly he regarded the *pneuma* as being active in a new way in the believer, and in some passages it is impossible to say whether by *pneuma* he means the human *pneuma* of the believer now filled by the Divine *pneuma* or the Divine *pneuma* itself. Roman theologians, shy as they are of anything like Gnostic trichotomy, would admit that there is this new state of things in the believer; only they would insist that it is not the accession of a wholly new element.

It is noteworthy that Friedrich Büchsel, in that book of his to which I referred more than once in my last lecture, *Der Geist Gottes im Neuen Testament*, speaks of the passage in 1 Thessalonians in which the three, body, soul and spirit, are spoken of together, as containing a problem hitherto unsolved. Büchsel's own suggestion is that the threefold formula is used merely for rhetorical emphasis, to enforce the apostle's prayer that the Thessalonian believers may be preserved "whole and complete (ὁλοτελεῖς)" to the Parusia. The coupling of soul and spirit would then express simply an emotional urgency in the apostle's mind, not a clear psychological distinction. It would no doubt be a mistake to try to get out of St. Paul's language anything like a scientific psychology in our sense. Yet it seems impossible to take Büchsel's view, that in the coupling of the two words "soul and spirit" there is merely rhetorical emphasis, in view of the fact that elsewhere St. Paul makes such an emphatic distinction between the *pneumatikos anthrōpos* and the *psychikos anthrōpos*. That surely implies that there was a very strongly felt difference between *pneuma* and *psyche* in St. Paul's mind.

Our examination of the distinction between *ruakh* and *nephesh* in the Old Testament shows that St. Paul might well have derived from that an association of *psyche* with the lower activities and operations in mental life, and of

196

pneuma with the higher. So far as he did that, we have obviously an analogy in the Christian conception to the distinction made in Greek philosophy between the rational and the irrational part of the soul.

The tripartite division of the soul in Plato, as Professor A. E. Taylor has argued, may not improbably go back to the Pythagoreans. But it has just been seen that what you want, in order to have a parallel to what is called St. Paul's trichotomy, is a dichotomy, so far as the inner life goes. And this *is* provided by Greek philosophy. The Platonic trichotomy of the soul easily appears as a dichotomy if you reckon together τὸ θυμοειδές and τὸ ἐπιθυμητικόν as the irrational part of the soul in contrast to the νοῦς or reason. In Plato himself you find in some passages the division of the soul into two, the rational and the irrational part, and this division became a commonplace of later Greek philosophy. In Aristotle the dichotomy is marked: the νοῦς has a different origin and a different destiny from all the rest of the soul. When the Neo-Platonists made the *Nous* and the *Psyche* the two elements in the inner life of man, they were not going beyond what was implicit in Plato and Aristotle. The analogy between this Neo-Platonic dichotomy and St. Paul's distinction of *pneuma* and *psyche* is all the more striking that in both cases the lower element is described by the same term, *psyche*.

What we have to note here is that in the Christian phraseology the higher element is described by the word which meant originally breath or air in motion. Dr. Inge in his deservedly admired Gifford Lectures on Plotinus translated the Neo-Platonic *Nous* by the Christian term *Spirit*. This no doubt truly marked the analogous place held by *Pneuma* or Spirit in the Christian scheme. In other ways the translation seems to me unfortunate, since the term Spirit inevitably brings with it a host of associations, got from its use in the Christian Church, which did not attach to the *Nous* of Plotinus. St. Paul and Plotinus alike made a distinction between something called *psyche* and the higher part of the Soul. But they drew the line in quite a different place; St. Paul would certainly not have denied to the natural man, the *psychikos anthrōpos* who was governed only his *psyche*, the perception of mathematical truth, while for Plotinus as certainly the perception of mathematical truth belonged to the *Nous*. The scale of relative dignity which Plotinus draws between the constituents of man's inner life is strongly marked by Greek intellectualism; true knowledge of existing reality is the highest thing, the right direction of will is subordinate to that, is only *kathartic* virtue, and the element of emotion, if it can be called emotion, in the supreme elevation to the One, is just the radiance of knowledge perfected. St. Paul goes upon the scale of values which had come down from Israel, will and emotion having a higher place because it is not so much a question of the contemplation of existing reality as the creation of new reality. Will and Emotion enter far more powerfully into *Pneuma*, Spirit, than they do into *Nous*. There remains in the word Spirit always something of the idea of a great wind.

This contrast between the two attempts to mark off a higher and a lower in the life of Soul shows where the real problem is, to determine how we are going to place the values which we find or recognize in a scale of relative worth. Professor Sorley showed in his Gifford Lectures that to determine such a hierarchy of values was an essential part of the problem of conduct. In some way or other we, each of us, have to do it, by the very fact that we decide to act in a particular way. The question whether there is any absolute scale, or whether one man's way of arranging the scale is as good as another's, need not be raised here. Even if it is only a scale for his own acts of will that a man is going to put before himself, he has to make up his mind what he considers a greater and what a lesser good. We all of us to-day connect with the term Spirit certain kinds of inner activity, good in themselves or apprehensive of a good beyond themselves, and we contrast this order of good from other goods, from the pleasant bodily sensations, for instance, which are the good of the animal, and the good of man so far as he is animal. It is perhaps impossible to say precisely what is included under *our* use of the term Spirit because the word has now gathered to itself a mass of associations from the life of the Christian society through the centuries. But for each of us the word calls up a whole range of things we know; it would include the joy in beauty and the scientific interest in truth as well as what was specifically religious by conscious direct reference to God.

The German *religionsgeschichtliche* school believes that the true meaning of phrases used by St. Paul in regard to *pneuma* can be understood only when there is seen behind them a conception widely current in the pagan Hellenistic religion of the time. The *pneuma* was thought of, we are told, quite realistically, as a material substance, a kind of fluid which belonged to the being of gods and daemons, and could enter into men—could be induced by certain rites or practices to enter into men; and when it did so, it superseded the ordinary consciousness of the man so possessed, his human *psyche*, and made him to all intents and purposes a divine being with supernatural perception of the divine world and supernatural knowledge. The contrast of *pneumatikos* and *psychikos* was not, it is held, something new in Christianity, but was taken by St. Paul from the Hellenistic environment.

With regard to this theory, it must be admitted at

199

once, it must be admitted by everyone, that there is an analogy between Christian ideas of men being directed by the Spirit of God and ideas of spirit-possession outside Christianity. It is a fact which no one has ever questioned that the shamans and medicine-men of primitive people profess—and in many cases no doubt really believe themselves—to be possessed and directed by a spirit not themselves which enables them to communicate things inaccessible to ordinary human consciousness. The belief in an unseen world of spirits, gods and daemons which can occupy and control living men in this way went on through all the ancient civilizations. No doubt Christians differed immensely from pagans in the character they attributed to the unseen Power which acted upon the mind of men and in the way they thought men could come into communion with the Power, but that an unseen Power of some kind existed outside man and that man could bring himself by some kind of actions to be controlled by that Power, this fundamental belief Christians and Pagans had in common. So far as the documents brought forward by Reitzenstein and others prove this, they prove the obvious. But there seems no ground for saying that the contrast between a person acting under divine or daemonic control and a person ruled only by his human soul was commonly expressed, before Christianity adopted them, by the terms *pneumatikos* and *psychikos*. The main ground on which they have been attributed to the Hellenistic world outside Christianity is that they were used by Gnostics in the second century and the Gnostics carried on a certain number of ideas current in the non-Christian Hellenistic world. But the argument breaks down in view of the fact that the Gnostics also claimed to be Christian and mixed with the elements of pagan origin in their theories large bits of Christianity. So far as I know, there is no real reason

200

to doubt that the Gnostics derived their use of *pneumatikos* and *psychikos* from St. Paul. It is true that in a writer on alchemy, Zosimus, a passage has been found in which the phrase *pneumatikos anthrōpos* is used in a way analogous to the Christian and that Zosimus was a pagan,[1] but Zosimus belongs probably to the fourth century A.D., when the term in this sense, through Christians and Gnostics, had no doubt become familiar generally. Otherwise, Reitzenstein quite ingenuously admitted that he had found one instance only of the term *pneumatikos* in the sense required: a magical papyrus speaks of the god Eros as "Lord of all spiritual perception of all secret things," πάσης πνευματικῆς αἰσθήσεως κρυφίων πάντων.[2] The magical papyri exhibit, as we know, a wild mixture of pagan, Jewish and Christian elements. With regard to the other adjective, *psychikos*, Reitzenstein admitted that of this too he had found only a single instance, in the papyrus published by Dieterich with the title *Mithras-liturgie*.[3] The votary prays that he may be enabled to behold the god Aion in virtue of immortal *pneuma* "while for a little my human psychic power abides sanctified beneath me" (whatever that means), ἁγίας ὑπεστώσης μου πρὸς ὀλίγον τῆς ἀνθρωπίνης μου ψυχικῆς δυνάμεως. Out of all that remains of occult Hellenistic literature there is that one instance picked from the gibberish of a magical papyrus, which dates from the beginning of the fourth century A.D. (!) though the writer may, of course, have been copying an earlier document or embodying bits of earlier documents. In any case the phrase in the papyrus is very poor proof of a general depreciatory use of *psychikos* in contrast with *pneumatikos* in the Hellenistic world apart from Christian suggestion. In the Christian

[1] Berthelot, *Collection des anciens Alchemistes grecs* (1887), II. 230.
[2] Wessely, *Denkschr.*, 1888, p. 89, line 1778; R. Reitzenstein, *Die hellenist. Mysterienreligionen*, 3rd ed., 1927, p. 311.
[3] 3rd ed. by Weinreich, Teubner, 1923.

community such a use of *psychikos* may no doubt have early become common, since it is found, not only in the Pauline epistles, but in James and Jude.

What makes the conclusions of the *religionsgeschlichtliche* school seem startling and new is the suggestion implied that the Christian belief is not only analogous, in the way just spoken of, to pagan belief, but that you only understand what the Christians meant by their language when you discern behind it a number of ideas which went with similar language in the pagan world. If, for instance, you find that mantic possession in the pagan world was thought of as a *pneuma* in the sense of a material fluid penetrating into a man, you get wonderful new light on St. Paul's language, it is thought, the moment you see that St. Paul too, when he speaks of the spirit, is thinking of a material divine fluid. But the supposition that, when a certain set of ideas adhere together in a certain *milieu*, therefore, when you find one of the ideas in quite a different *milieu*, all the other ideas go with it—are to be conceived there in the background although they are not indicated—this supposition is precisely what needs to be proved. Even if a particular word or phrase is borrowed by one *milieu* from another one, it is quite unsafe to assume that all the ideas attached to it in the original *milieu* go with it in the new one.

We may take, as an illustration of the fallacious mode of argument to which the *religionsgeschichtliche* school is liable, the case of Aion. Reitzenstein and others have believed that they have made out the widely-spread conception in the Hellenistic world of a god Aion, with whom the idea of unending time was specially connected. Some of the phrases used in connexion with Aion resemble phrases used in the book of Revelation about Jesus. "I am Alpha and Omega, the beginning and the end."

Reitzenstein accordingly pronounced that Jesus was Aion.[1] The fallacy lies in the ambiguous assertion of identity. If "Christ announces himself as Aion" means that an idea of eternal time attached by a pagan to the god Aion is attached by the Christian writer to Jesus, that Jesus has so far an analogous place in Christian thought to that held by Aion in some pagan thought, the statement may well be true. But if "Christ is Aion" means that you can only properly understand what the Christian writer meant if you suppose behind his language the whole mass of ideas attached by a pagan to the god Aion, then the statement seems to me to have no basis at all. And yet it is just because the statement suggests this that it seems significant and interesting. Now what we have seen in the case of Aion applies equally to the Christian language about the Spirit. It is, I think, quite gratuitous to infer that because *pneuma* meant a material fluid for pagan Greeks it meant a material fluid for St. Paul—for St. Paul, who drew largely on the Jewish tradition, in which *pneuma* had acquired the connotation of the Hebrew *ruakh*.

It has to be remembered that the language of the New Testament has been in continuous use to express Christian thought from the time of St. Paul to our own. Now when any writer's language both has a tradition in the past behind it and itself becomes part of a continuous tradition afterwards, we can get to its meaning in two ways: we may argue forward from the meaning which such forms of expression had in the tradition behind the writer, or we may argue back from the meaning which they have in the later tradition. Neither procedure is absolutely sure: the writer may use the terms in question with a

---

[1] "Dann aber scheint mir . . . sicher, dass die Selbstankündigung Christi in der Offenbarung Johannis . . . ihn als den Aion bezeichnen soll" (*Das iranische Erlösungsmysterium*, p. 244).

more or less different connotation from that which they had had in the earlier tradition, and equally the later tradition may modify the connotation which they had for the writer. While, however, neither argument is sure, each has to be taken into account, for whatever it is worth. Now we note that in interpreting the language of St. Paul the *religionsgeschichtliche* school proceeds entirely upon the argument from meanings found attached to terms in the tradition of the non-Christian Hellenistic world from which St. Paul may be supposed to have drawn, and takes little or no account of the meaning attached to the terms in the Christian tradition which derives from St. Paul.

We certainly to-day do not understand a material fluid when we speak of "Spirit"; we can say of Christians for many centuries back, that they have not understood a material fluid; if St. Paul did, then plainly the connotation of the term must have changed at some moment between St. Paul's day and our own. It is admitted that with primitive man such words as *pneuma*, *spiritus*, meant literally material breath or air in motion: we use them to-day to denote something non-material: therefore that the change in meaning did occur at some time or other is certain. But why should we suppose that it occurred after St. Paul, and not before? Why should not St. Paul have found *pneuma* already understood by Greek-speaking Jews in what we call a spiritual sense? Why should phrases which spoke of the Spirit being poured out have been understood by the first generation of Christians otherwise than as figures of speech, otherwise than we understand such phrases to-day? If you want to put the moment when the meaning changed after St. Paul, between St. Paul and ourselves, you will, I think, find considerable difficulty in making out a likely date for it.

204

"Breath," Wind—there are common phrases in which these things stand for types of what is transient and elusive and insubstantial—"nothing but a breath" we say, and the Preacher, when he declares that all human activity is vanity of vanities, uses, as an equivalent, the phrase "a hunting after wind." It is an odd accident that Europeans have come at the same time to denote that which seems to them to have the highest value of anything in the constitution of man, of anything in the universe, by a word which means literally breath or wind.

THE WRATH OF GOD

WHILE it is generally recognized to-day that all modes of speaking about God which represent Him as having a material form or a local habitation—all those familiar phrases about the hand of God or the eyes of God or the throne of God—are symbolical, are merely poetical metaphors, it is felt that the modes of speech which attribute to God characteristics of the human mind and spirit are, if not literally true, at any rate much nearer the reality. Yet among those too there are grades of resemblance to the reality, it is held: not all of them are as true as, for instance, the language which speaks of God as wise or just or loving; and amongst those which, though free from material suggestion, are nevertheless set down as symbols a good long way from the reality is the attribution to God of anger. Only very old-fashioned people, only very crude Fundamentalists, it is largely thought, can regard such a phrase as the "wrath of God" as meaning that God can be thought of as really angry in any sense of the word. The phrase is a symbol very far away from the reality. But, if the reality it symbolizes can be more truly described in other terms, what, we have to ask ourselves, is the reality? When people repudiate the attribution of anger to God, their doing so implies a belief that they do have a conception of the reality which enables them to describe it in truer terms.

All primitive polytheism attributes anger to its gods. They are conceived like men who react in their volitions and emotions to the conduct of their worshippers as human kings react to the conduct of their subjects. One need not amplify this assertion with examples. They are too familiarly known. If you take Greek polytheism alone, you can find all the terms describing anger, ὀργή, μῆνις, κότος, and so on, or the verbs connected with them, attributed quite commonly to deities. There are two things especially which make deities angry. One is some omission in the modes of worship and tendance which they require: Artemis sends the boar to ravage Calydon because the king had failed to offer her the proper sacrifices. The other thing is the utterance of proud words which brave the gods, like those of Capaneus in the *Seven against Thebes*, or boast that in some particular respect a human being is superior to this or that deity—those of Niobe vaunting against Leto—or declare that the man uttering them can do without the deity's help—those of Ajax to Athena in the play of Sophocles. When Rudyard Kipling in a well-known poem described men's boasting of their independence of divine help in reliance upon their weapons as "heathen"—"such boastings as the heathen use"—he was singularly far from anthropological fact. If there is one thing strongly marked in pagan religion it is the extreme danger of such boasting, because it makes the deity angry. It is true, of course, that this is also found in the old religion of Israel, but it is not something which distinguishes Biblical religion from pagan religion: it is something which Biblical religion has in common with pagan religion.

In its idea of the Deity as capable of anger the Old Testament seems altogether on the same level as Greek paganism. A large number of characteristics which belonged to the heathen deities are eliminated from the Old Testament conception of Jehovah—He has no physical body, is without beginning, has no other being akin to Him, but in respect to His capacity for anger Jehovah seems to go even beyond the gods of Greece. "Now will I shortly pour out my fury upon thee, and accomplish mine anger against thee, and will judge thee according to thy ways . . . mine eye shall not spare, neither will I have pity."[1] "God," says a Psalm (vii. 8), "is angry with the wicked every day." And the same two things which especially provoke the gods of Greece, a fault in the offering of sacrifice and proud words, are also spoken of in the Old Testament as provoking Jehovah. Nadab and Abihu, the sons of Aaron, are consumed by fire from Jehovah because they put the wrong sort of fire into their censers (Leviticus x. 1, 2). Jehovah, a Psalm again says, "will cut off the tongue that speaketh great things" (xii. 3). "There shall be a day of Jehovah of hosts upon all that is proud and haughty, and upon all that is lifted up; and it shall be brought low."[2]

It is true that in one respect Hebrew religion, in the form given it by the great prophets of the eighth and seventh centuries, differed markedly from the primitive Greek paganism at which we have just glanced. It repudiated the idea that the Deity cared much about ritual practices. "I will not reprove thee for thy sacrifices," a Psalmist represents God saying: "I will take no bullock out of thy house, nor he-goats out of thy folds. . . . Will I eat the flesh of bulls or drink the blood of goats? Offer unto God the sacrifice of thanksgiving."[3] The story about Nadab and Abihu being consumed by fire, although found in a book whose compo-

[1] Ezekiel vii. 8.   [2] Isaiah ii. 12.   [3] Psalm l. 9–14.

208

sition is generally believed by scholars to-day to be much later than Amos and Isaiah, shows merely, it would be held, a primitive element subsisting still in later legalistic Judaism, side by side with the ideas of the great prophets of the time before the Exile. But while the prophetic religion repudiated the idea that Jehovah could be provoked to anger by a ritual omission or mistake, it by no means repudiated the idea that Jehovah could be angry. It asserted the wrath of God as strongly as ever primitive religion had asserted it. The things conceived to make God angry were now moral wrong-doing, injustice between man and man, oppression of the weak, but the anger was depicted as vividly as ever. In the very same great chapter in which Isaiah denounces the idea that Jehovah cared for ritual worship apart from moral goodness, he describes the Divine anger as impatient to vent itself upon the wrongdoers. "Ah, I will ease me of mine adversaries, and avenge me of mine enemies."[1]

"Yes, yes," many say, "that is the old Testament Jehovah; but it is not the God of Christians. We are to-day in a position to see on what a low level Old Testament religion stood; we no longer stand in awe, as our Puritan and Evangelican ancestors did, of an angry despot in heaven. There is indeed to-day a movement which aims at doing in another way very much what Marcion wanted to do in the second century, cut Christianity quite loose from Old Testament religion. Marcion and many people to-day agree in saying that the God of the Jews was a definitely inferior being and that Jesus brought in something wholly new which repudiated the Old Testament God: only whereas Marcion believed that the Old Testament God was a really existing being inferior to the high far-off God of pure loving-kindness and grace, people to-day would say that the Old

<hr/>

[1] Isaiah i. 24.

Testament Jehovah was simply a figment of primitive imagination."

The trouble is that when we look at the facts in connexion with the coming of Christianity into the world this modern view seems strangely at variance with them. The Christian Church rejected Marcion's suggestion with the utmost vigour and held resolutely to its connexion with Old Testament religion. It was in those days a commonplace of the pagan philosophical schools that the Deity could not be thought of as capable of anger. Greek philosophy had long ago repudiated emphatically the conception common to primitive and popular Greek religion and to the Old Testament. Anger was a weak and discreditable emotion, it taught, in men, and to attribute such an emotion to a divine being was absurd and blasphemous. Deity, every novice in Greek philosophy knew as an axiom, must be *apathēs*, without disturbing emotions of any kind. The idea of the Divine anger was not something which penetrated into Christianity from its pagan environment: it was something which the Church maintained in the face of adverse pagan criticism. An early Christian writing, the Apocalypse, accumulates words to describe it—"the cup of the wine of the fierceness of the wrath of God,"[1] and the Christians of the first generations pictured Jesus returning from the sky in flaming fire, rendering vengeance on them that know not God.[2]

One must recognize, of course, that you find a view similar to the Greek philosophic view—the view that God cannot be angry—asserted both in the writings of the pious Jew, Philo of Alexandria, and in the writings of some Christian fathers. But that is because Philo and those Christian fathers were strongly influenced by the tradition of the Greek philosophic schools. In view of

[1] Revelation xvi. 19.   [2] 2 Thessalonians i. 8.

the Old Testament accepted by Jews and Christians as inspired, in the view of the sayings attributed to Jesus, and of the writings other than Gospels belonging to the first two or three generations of Christians, it would be obviously a mistake to take these utterances of Philo and later Christian writers as giving the genuine Jewish and Christian view.

Some people [Philo says] who hear the threatenings in the Old Testament suppose that the Supreme Reality (τὸ ὄν) feels wrath and anger. But that Reality can be touched by no passion of any kind: mental disturbance is a mark of human infirmity; to God irrational passions of the soul can no more be attributed than bodily parts and limbs. Nevertheless, utterances of this kind are used by the Law-giver (Moses) during a certain introductory phase of teaching, in order to admonish those who could not be brought to exercise restraint in any other way. . . . It is said of God "As a man chasteneth his son, so the Lord thy God will chasten thee."[1] Note, these utterances are for the sake of chastening and admonishment, not because God is really like that.[2]

"It is enough," Philo says in another place, "if men can be made to exercise restraint by the fear which these descriptions induce."[3] The attribution of anger to God is a pure fiction (προσαναπλάττομεν);[4] but it is a useful fiction, in so far as sinners can be frightened by it.

This way of explaining God's "wrath" passed from Philo to his Christian successors in Alexandria two centuries later. It is reproduced precisely by Clement of Alexandria. It is just as much a figure of speech, Clement repeats, as to speak of His hand or His eyes.[5] If God inspired the Old Testament writers to declare His anger, that was God's benevolent artifice (τέχνη) in order to prevent us sinning by fear: it is against our own interests that we should leave the way of righteousness, and so all the threatenings have a benevolent intention.[6] We

[1] Deuteronomy viii. 5.
[2] *Quod Deus sit immut.*, §§ 52–54.
[3] *De Somn.*, i. § 237.
[4] *De Sacr. Ab. et Caini*, § 96.
[5] *Strom.*, v. 68.
[6] *Paed.*, i, 8. p. 130.

find this theory continued in Clement's disciple, Origen, who intimates expressly that he is following an earlier writer, no doubt Philo. When God threatens, Origen says, it is as when we pretend to a child that we are angry in order to make it take its medicine, when we say that we shall run a knife into it, if it does not. (Children, I suppose, really were threatened in that way in antiquity.)[1] If Scripture sometimes seems to make the revelation of God's wrath more prominent than the revelation of His love, that, Origen says, is adapted to human psychology: God knows that fear is a powerful motive in keeping men from sin, whereas they are liable to be demoralized, if things are made pleasant for them and they can count on God's good nature. Origen laid hold of the phrase in St. Paul that the sinner "treasures up wrath for himself in the day of wrath," to show that it did not fit a conception which made God's anger a strong emotion like anger in men, but indicated that what was meant by "wrath" was simply the inevitable painful consequences which sin in the end by its own nature must have for the sinner.[2] But such a theory as that of Philo and the Alexandrine Fathers, does not show the mind of the first generations of Christians, if one may go by the New Testament.

"Ah yes," it may be said, "but the early Christians departed very quickly from the religion of their Founder. If we want to know what conception of God is essential to Christianity, we must go to Jesus himself. Jesus had no hesitation in correcting the utterances of the old Law: 'It was said to them of old time. . . . But I say unto you.' Jesus taught men to think of God as the loving Father in heaven." Yet people who talk like this usually get their notion of what Jesus taught and of what Judaism taught from modern popular authors and journalists who

---

[1] *Comm. on Jeremiah*, p. 157, K1.　　　　[2] *Comm. on Romans*, i. 18.

212

go on repeating the same kind of statements, taking them over one from another, rather than from any serious study of the documents. It is true that in our first Gospel Jesus claims authority to amend the old Jewish Law, but He never, be it observed, amends it by way of relaxation, never by saying that God required less than the Old Law said, but by tightening it up, declaring that God required much more. Not only the act of adultery, but even the eye, if allowed to go on ministering to adulterous desire, would bring a man to hell, where the worm died not, and the fire was not quenched. There is never a word in any saying attributed to Jesus in any of our four Gospels to suggest that he repudiated as too severe the Old Testament conception of God. "Fear him," He is reported to have said, "who after he hath killed hath power to cast into hell; yea, I say unto you, Fear him" (Luke xii. 5), and the attempt of some modern interpreters[1] to escape from the implications of such a saying by supposing that Jesus was referring to Satan, not to God, is a vain expedient which has against it the general consensus of scholars, whether of the conservative or of the extreme radical wing.

It is true, indeed, that Jesus spoke of God as the loving Father, always ready to welcome home the sinner who turned to Him; but this was nothing alien to the Old Testament conception of Jehovah. Jehovah's anger in the Old Testament falls only upon the impenitent: it belongs equally to the Old Testament idea of God that He forgives freely and welcomes home the penitent. When Jesus spoke of God as "your Father in heaven" he was probably using a phrase current already in the Judaism of those days, as it certainly was in Judaism a century or two later. Mr. Claude Montefiore has made the interesting observation that it seems to have been

---

[1] C. W. Emmet, *The Lord of Thought* (1922), p. 244.

something new in Jesus that he went after sinners and associated with them, in order to bring them to repentance: if so, while the parable of the Prodigal Son would not go much beyond accepted Jewish belief, the parable of the Shepherd who goes to seek the lost sheep on the mountains would strike a new note. But there is nothing incompatible between the belief that God is always ready to receive the sinner who repents, and even goes after him into the wilderness to draw him home, and the belief that the anger of God comes ultimately upon the sinner who does not repent. And if Jesus asserted the former belief strongly, he seems to have asserted the latter belief no less.

Now if we accept the idea of the ancient Greek philosophers and the idea of very many people to-day, that to think of God as in any sense angry is wrong, the facts just noted are very awkward for those who profess Christianity. If no more is true than that the Christian conception of God is, on the whole, the best conception, one would expect to find in the stream of tradition which produced it a marked superiority from the beginning in its conception of God, as compared with that produced by other traditions in the religious history of mankind. But here we should have to register a marked inferiority to the conception of pagan philosophers, both in the Old Testament conception from which the Christian was derived, and in the conception of the Founder of Christianity. If, on the other hand, you go so far as to think the Christian view of God on the whole superior, you can hardly help asking whether perhaps the idea of God's anger does not stand for something in the Supreme Reality which in truth belongs to it, something which was asserted by means of anthropomorphic imagery in Old Testameut religion and in the religion of Jesus and which was wrongly left out in the Greek philosophic view of God.

Of course, everyone who believes in God at all would admit at once that anger in men has characteristics which it would be absurd to connect with the Divine Being. So far as to be governed by an emotion is a weakness which is not in accordance with reason, so far as an emotion is a disturbance—and that is what is meant by *pathos, passion*—we should all say that if there is any Being corresponding to the term *God*, He must be *apathēs*, without passion, as the old Greek philosophers asserted, and as is repeated in the first of the Thirty-Nine Articles of the Church of England. Anger in men is in the vast majority of cases an unworthy and irrational emotion. It includes the desire that the person against whom it is directed should suffer pain, and in a large number of cases the thought of the person suffering pain gives pleasure because it salves an individual grievance; the feeling is selfishly vindictive. There are, however, kinds of anger which we do not think it unbecoming a good man to feel, indeed it might seem to us a defect if a man did not, in certain circumstances, feel anger. In the presence of such things as cruelty to the helpless, to a child or an animal, or acts of disgusting meanness, we should not like a man who felt no stirring of anger. To that kind of anger we commonly apply the special term *indignation*, and perhaps we may get light by considering what is the root meaning of that word.

If *dignus*, worthy, implies merit, that the person so described deserves to have some kind of good, honour or love, or whatever it may be, the term *indignus* implies demerit, that the person deserves to go without some kind of good or perhaps to have its opposite, shame instead of honour, pain instead of pleasure. Indignation is thus strictly a strong feeling of demerit in the person against whom it is directed. It is an emotion in so far as it implies a desire, not at present gratified, that the appropriateness which we feel to join together particular kinds of conduct and painful experience, should be realized in actual fact, that the man who has been cruel to a child should actually himself suffer. The desire to bring together in act two things already associated by the kind of appropriateness which is connoted by the idea of justice or merit may be a desire of vehement urgency. There might perhaps be a clear perception of unworth which was not accompanied by any emotion; we should in that case simply see that suffering was appropriate to the cruel man, but be without desire that he should actually suffer. We could hardly call the mere perception, apart from the desire, indignation or anger. It is, however, very hard to conceive anyone having a perception of the appropriateness without some desire that the connexion should be established in fact.

We can now see the kinship between righteous indignation and the anger which is personally vindictive. They both imply a desire that someone should suffer or should go without some kind of good; they may both imply the will actually to inflict the suffering, as when a strong man seeing a child ill-treated might strike the ill-treater; only in one case the desire is based on the perception of appropriateness in justice, and in the other case, it is a desire for personal revenge. Yet it is to be noticed that the selfishly vindictive anger almost always borrows something from the feeling of righteous indignation. Men like to represent to themselves that the suffering they desire to see experienced is appropriate in justice and not merely a return for annoyance inflicted upon themselves. When anger vents itself in terms of abuse, "You beast," and so on, the angry man declares, not that the other person has done something which is annoying or painful to him personally, but that his character generally is of a kind which makes suffering appropriate in justice. He instinctively makes his vindictive anger take on the appearance of righteous indignation. This may often in particular cases make it doubtful whether what an angry man believes to be righteous indignation is not really personally vindictive anger in disguise; for we did not have to wait for present-day Psycho-analysis in order to know that people very commonly represent their motives to themselves as different from what someone who could detect the psychological genesis of these motives would see them to be.

In spite of this running together of the two kinds of anger, it remains true that the appropriateness of suffering to ill-doing, which is connoted by the words "demerit," "deserve," is something which seems to be immediately obvious to the human spirit all the world over. The question is raised to-day whether this feeling of the appropriateness of suffering to ill-doing is not really an illusion, inherited from primitive man but dissipated in the light of modern knowledge. Is there really such a thing as *desert*? You can no doubt make a plausible show of tracing the idea to the need of the primitive tribe to secure its survival by inflicting death or suffering upon its enemies, the desire of the tribe to inflict such suffering passing into the general desire in the society of a civilized state to inflict suffering on the persons who act in a way prejudicial to the interests of the society, or which the society does not like. In this way, it may be said, a nexus between suffering and conduct condemned by the standards of the community came to be seen as something instinctively perceived, and the desire to establish the connexion in fact came to be the common emotion called righteous indignation, there being no such nexus in reality. Such a view naturally accompanies the belief that men's actions are determined by previous causes which they could not have made to be other than they were.

The man who is cruel to a child may be truly called unfortunate in that the molecules of his brain move in the way they do, but to suppose that you satisfy something called justice in the abstract by inflicting pain upon him in return is only inherited illusion. The emotion of righteous indignation is then one which we should suppress as irrational. This does not mean that it may not be reasonable to inflict suffering upon the person who acts against the interests of society, but you do so either simply to deter people in the future who may be disposed to act in that way, by bringing to bear the motive of fear, or you use certain means, which inflict something disagreeable, in order to effect a change in his character in the direction of what society would like it to be, as when you place criminals in a prison in which everything is directed to their reformation. We are thus brought to the theory of punishment, and the three grounds on which it has been based, the retributive, the deterrent, the reformatory, and the problem of the anger of God, as we shall see, is bound up with the question: What is the right theory of punishment? It is on this that the whole question before us in the present lecture and the following lecture really turns.

The view is common that while the two latter grounds, the deterrent and the reformatory, are valid grounds for punishment, the retributory ground must be repudiated as thoroughly wrong, a mere barbarous survival, at any rate quite incompatible with Christian humanity. And the first difficulty we notice in examining the question is that, as a matter of fact, the grounds in question are not conceived to determine action in most cases separately, in isolation, so that punishment would, for instance, be in one case simply for the sake of deterring others by fear, with no thought of reforming the criminal, and in another case simply for the sake of reforming the criminal

218

with no thought of being a deterrent. No, those who believe that deterrence and reformation are both valid grounds for punishment, but retribution not, almost always try to make the one punishment satisfy both requirements, serve as a deterrent for others who might be tempted and at the same time serve as a means of reforming the man who has already done wrong. Similarly those who believe that retribution is a valid ground do not in any particular punishment they may inflict, or desire to see inflicted, rest satisfied with its being retributive, but they try to inflict a punishment which will also serve as a deterrent and as a means of reformation.

Yet, though it is true that in nearly all actual cases punishment is intended to combine the deterrent and the reformatory purposes, still, where one only of the two purposes comes into consideration, because the other is ruled out by the circumstances, that single purpose by itself is held to be enough to justify the infliction of the punishment. Capital punishment obviously cannot be a means of reforming the criminal. Whenever capital punishment is supported by people who do not accept the retributive ground, it must be simply as a means of deterrence or as a means of getting rid of someone whose existence is an inconvenience to society. There are people who denounce the idea of retributive punishment as altogether wrong, and at the same time quite approve of those whose existence is a social nuisance being put to death. Even the mass executions which have characterized the Soviet régime in Russia seem to have their approval—not, of course, because there is any demerit in the victims which made them deserve to suffer, but because it is an admirably drastic and efficient mode of establishing a better social order.

I shall argue presently that most people's real feelings would not allow them to acquiesce in punishment as merely deterrent, that they do, as a matter of fact, acquiesce in it, whatever their professed theory may be, because they see it as following upon bad desert. But if they were right in justifying punishment on the sole ground of deterrence, in the case of capital punishment, they ought logically to admit that, for those who believe in the validity of the retributive ground, that one ground alone may similarly serve as a reason for punishment, where there can be no question of either of the other possible purposes of punishment being served. According to the Catholic doctrine of hell, the punishment cannot serve either a reformatory or a deterrent purpose. Of course, the threat of it, where it meets with belief, may be deterrent; but the punishment itself, removed as it is from the eyes of the living, cannot have a deterrent effect, and the punishment is held to be prolonged eternally after there have ceased to be any living men on the planet to be deterred. Catholics, however, believe in good and bad deserts and are therefore logical in justifying punishment, which can serve no other purpose, on the retributive ground alone. No doubt to a large number of Christians to-day, outside the Roman communion, this view of hell is abhorrent, and they are fain to believe that hell serves a reformatory purpose, as well as a retributive purpose —if they admit their belief in the retributive ground at all. Hell thus for them takes the place of Purgatory in the traditional Catholic system, and Hell, as conceived by Roman Catholics, is denied to exist. It would lie quite outside our field to discuss the merits of this controversy. There may be objections to the Catholic view of hell, especially in its popular and pictorial forms, which are insurmountable: all that it is relevant here to point out is that you cannot logically object on principle to the supposition of a punishment after death which has no deterrent or reformatory purpose if you believe that retribution is one of the valid grounds of punishment, and that, where neither of the other possible grounds can come into consideration, this ground alone is enough to justify punishment.

In practice, the attempt to make one single thing, or one single course of action, serve three, or two, wholly different purposes, commonly leads to its being unsatisfactory in its results, like the article of furniture in the story which professed to serve, if folded in one way, as a ladder and, if folded in another way, as a kitchen table. It was neither a satisfactory ladder, the story says, nor a satisfactory table. And this is largely the problem of punishment. Is it possible to find one treatment of the criminal which, while it is a thoroughly effective deterrent, can also serve to make him a better man? One may see how this essential factor in the problem is ignored in such a treatment of it as Galsworthy's *Justice*. The play shows in a very moving way the disastrous effect of the punishment upon someone who has fallen into crime through weakness of character: considered simply from the point of view of its power to reform this particular individual, imprisonment with its attendant shame has obviously an effect wholly harmful. Galsworthy, concentrating our attention upon the young forger, leaves us filled with pity for him. But outside the purview of the play there are the hundreds of other weak characters who may be tempted to forge; they too may surely claim our sympathy and consideration; for each of these at the critical moment it may turn the scale in the salutary direction that they have before them the fear of imprisonment and its attendant shame. For those many the quality of disagreeableness and shame attached to imprisonment may be an immense benefit; for the poor youth who has already forged and been convicted it may be ruinous. You seem obliged to sacrifice either the convicted criminal

221

to the tempted, or the tempted to the convicted criminal. For if in the interests of the convicted criminal you make prisons agreeable places, where moral influence of a gentle kind is brought to bear upon those enclosed in them, with no accompaniment of shame, you deprive all the tempted of the help which a motive of fear would give them at the critical moment. I do not know what the solution in practice of the problem is, but this at least should be clear: it is no good approaching the problem at all, until you see that it is a question of realizing two different purposes by one course of action, and we need not be surprised if that is difficult. The course followed to-day is a compromise, perhaps the best that can be found, but at any rate a compromise with the defects of a compromise.

Let us consider the reasons then for regarding the retributory idea of punishment as valid. One thing is plain to start with. If you study forms of punishment inflicted by the representatives of the community in organized societies as an anthropological phenomenon, it is certain that they arise out of what may be called the anger of the community directed against some kind of conduct which the community considers wrong. In societies despotically governed, like the ancient monarchies, it is the king who punishes the offender, and in whom the anger is displayed as a personal emotion, but when the offence which the king punishes is, as it very often is, an action regarded by the community generally as against its interests—a theft, for instance, or a murder —the king is supported by the general voice. Any king who did not have such support in the majority of his judgments would be considered an unjust king, and even in the despotic monarchies of the East, when injustice in the ruler is pushed too far, it is likely to bring about his assassination or a rebellion. Punishment is thus in its genesis an expression of the anger of the community against certain kinds of action. There is a general feeling that the man who acts in that way *deserves* to suffer, so that when suffering is inflicted by the authorities, the community as a whole receives satisfaction from seeing that kind of conduct and the appropriate suffering brought together in fact.

Someone may say: It is true, no doubt, as a matter of anthropological fact, that punishment in former times expressed anger; but that is no reason why we to-day, who have risen above the level of primitive man, should admit this irrational feeling. So far as we do to a criminal anything which he does not like, the only justification, apart from the purpose of reforming him, is that society acts in self-protection and is bound to deter others from acting in an anti-social way by attaching unpleasant consequences to their doing so. The idea of desert, of there being any mysterious nexus, on the score of justice, between anti-social action and suffering, is unworthy of a scientific age. If you call the criminal a bad man, you ought not to attach to such a term the feeling of indignant condemnation which our ancestors attached to it: you simply try to prevent his repeating his troublesome actions.

Now I believe that when we examine closely the language of those who put forward views like these, we always find that sooner or later, however much in theory they may deny reality to the idea of desert, of the nexus in justice, they admit it by implication, without realizing that they do so: they cannot really divest themselves of it. It is very much like the case of those who deny Free Will: they may show with apparent logic that the idea of free will is untenable, but the next moment they will be saying things which have no sense except on the supposition of Free Will. It has been pointed out by Westermarck who, as an anthropologist, is naturally moved by the connexion of punishment with indignation in primitive society, that if you rule out the idea of desert and retribution altogether, and leave only deterrence as a valid ground for punishing, there is no reason why you should confine yourself to inflicting pain upon the actual doer of the undesirable action, why you should not, for instance, inflict pain on his children. As a deterrent, preventing the wrongdoer from repeating his action and preventing other people who have children from doing similar things, that might serve quite effectually. Yet we know that any proposal to inflict pain on the innocent in order to deter the tempted would excite, even in our scientific age, a cry of horror. But why? How very hard, it would be said, that those who have done nothing to deserve it should be made to suffer! This implies that the nexus of appropriateness in justice between wrong conduct and suffering must be there as well in order to make us acquiesce in the deterrence. Why we do not mind a burglar or one who assaults little children being subjected to the inconvenience of imprisonment is that, whatever our professed theory of punishment may be, we feel that he deserves it. Capital punishment is maintained in those countries in which it is still used to-day because it is generally felt that the murderer is a person who deserves to be killed: otherwise capital punishment could not be tolerated.[1]

Even if we ruled out the idea of inflicting pain and inconvenience on anyone on the ground of desert, it would be impossible not to regard it as just that the doer

[1] Reference was made just now to the view which holds that while the idea of retributive punishment is quite wrong, it is right for the Russian Government to kill its opponents as a measure of social purgation. It is to be noted that the Russian Government itself evidently does not think that it can do the killing without exciting popular indignation against the persons killed as persons who *deserve* to be execrated.

of certain kinds of actions should at any rate forfeit the good which comes to those who follow an approved line of conduct. But if we admit no more than that the forfeiture of goods is appropriate to evil conduct, we are admitting the nexus in principle, apart from considerations of deterrence or reformation. Such a common exclamation as "Hard lines!" is altogether meaningless except on the supposition that there is such a thing as desert, that is, a nexus of appropriateness between wrongdoing and pain. It is where the pain is coupled in fact with conduct void of bad desert that our feeling instinctively vents itself in such a phrase as "Hard lines!" And I suspect that the philosopher most positive in asserting that bad desert is an illusion would be caught out sooner or later using that phrase or an equivalent.

One can say more. Not only would society find intolerable the infliction of pain upon particular individuals for simple deterrence, where there was no bad desert on the part of the sufferer, but the deterrence itself would be far less effective, if it were not combined with the idea of bad desert. No doubt people may be deterred from actions which they believe to be quite innocent by pains which others would inflict upon them, if they performed them. But mere fear of the pain of punishment is a very imperfect deterrent. In the vast majority of cases the tempted are deterred, not only by the prospective pain, but by the feeling that the punishment is an expression of the just anger of society. As anger, it is the general feeling that certain kinds of action create bad desert and that the nexus between such actions and pain ought to be realized in fact. In the vast majority of cases the tempted man himself recognizes this quality in the action, but his recognition is too weak to direct him against the strength of desire. There is a conflict within him, and that element in him which recognizes the bad quality of the action is reinforced by the thought of the anger of society expressed in the overhanging punishment. He himself feels "That is a beastly thing to do," but the voice within him which says so grows faint. Then he hears the innumerable voices representing society around him, declaring in unison: "Yes, it *is* a beastly thing to do: it is a thing which whosoever does deserves pain." If he thinks of society as angry, he thinks of it as feeling the nexus hotly, intensely, and his own wavering sense of the nexus gains helpful corroboration. It is the thought of punishment expressing an anger which he recognizes to be just that deters him, not the mere fear of pain.

Mr. Bernard Shaw has declared that retributive punishment can never make anyone better. "If you are to punish a man retributively," he says, "you must injure him. If you are to reform him you must improve him. And men are not improved by injuries." No one knows better than Mr. Shaw how to make play with catchy sophistries. The argument here depends entirely on the question-begging terms "injure," "injuries." If one made the statement "Men are never improved by the infliction of pain," it would be untrue as a matter of psychology. When the wrongdoer knows in his heart of hearts, as he very often does, that what he did was foul, the indignation of others which inflicts pain on him in many cases stirs that suppressed knowledge into activity. Certainly there have been bullies who were the better for a beating. It is equally true, of course, that in many cases wrongdoers have not been improved by pain inflicted upon them and have even been made worse, wrongdoers who might have been improved by some course of kindly moral encouragement. It all depends on the particular character of each wrongdoer, and one can no more argue that the infliction of pain is never reformatory from the fact that in some cases it has the opposite effect than one can infer

226

that a particular medicine never does good because in some cases it does harm.

These considerations show, I think, how false it is to regard righteous indignation and benevolence to one's neighbour as incompatible. If there are some kinds of actions which I am right in considering foul, and if I express indignation whenever I come across actions of that kind, I am adding my small weight, whatever it may be, to the general volume of social condemnation, and that general volume of condemnation, if it agrees with the testimony given by the conscience of the tempted or the wrongdoer, may help that testimony within him to prevalence over evil desire and so be of the greatest benefit to him. As one of those who have experienced temptation, I can say for myself that I feel only gratitude to those who would have expressed indignation if I had done things to which evil desire impelled.

Two common ideas, each true in its proper application, obscure, I think, the retributory principle in punishment. One idea is that the criminal is not necessarily a worse man, if all were known, than you or me. "There, but for the grace of God, goes John Bradford." Many a man of conduct externally respectable is in God's sight a worse man than the man who has committed what is legally a crime under the stress of some tremendous temptation, like the young forger in Galsworthy's play. Many of the sins which the State cannot think of punishing—pride, meanness, avarice, cold selfishness— may be worse in any true moral valuation than a large number of the offences which bring men to prison. To suppose then that punishments inflicted by the State are inflicted according to men's deserts or have their justification as measures of retribution for wrongdoing, it may be said, is absurd. No: they take account of offences simply in so far as they are actions inconvenient to society, which can be checked by fear: that is to say, their *raison d'être* is deterrence, and not retribution. I do not think that this argument really proves the idea of bad desert to be absent in regard to punishments inflicted by the State. It urges what is quite true, that there is a great deal of bad desert beside the bad desert which the State visits with pain, bad desert of which the State could not possibly take cognizance. The only cases of bad desert which the State punishes are those in which the punishment can also serve as a deterrent: but our feelings, as I have just indicated, would never allow the application of punishment as a deterrent unless we saw there some bad desert as well. If it is a law of justice that pain should be attached to bad desert, and if the universe is so constructed that what is required by justice is sooner or later realized in fact, then all the bad desert which the State cannot think of punishing, and which yet may be, as was contended, much worse in God's sight than the bad desert which the State does punish, must find its appropriate pain in another way, perhaps in another life on beyond, as most religions, not Christianity only, have believed.

But the admission just made, that there is a great deal of evil, which in God's sight (as we say) may be worse than the kinds of wrongdoing of which the State takes cognizance, shows, it might be argued, that the whole idea of righteous indignation is wrong. No man is himself sufficiently clear of bad desert for him to desire, in the case of others, that bad desert should be connected with pain. We may here be reminded of such sayings of Jesus as that about the mote and beam or "Let him that is without sin among you cast the first stone." What man of us, if he honestly looks within, has the right to feel indignation against his fellow sinner? It seems to me that light may be thrown on this question, if we think of the story of David and the prophet Nathan. When

228

Nathan tells David the story of the rich man who took away the poor man's ewe lamb, David's instant reaction is righteous indignation. It would perhaps be difficult to find a better example of righteous indignation. The rich man's action, as Nathan presented it, was one of peculiar meanness and beastliness: if any kind of action creates bad desert, such an action does: we might say that anyone who, if such an action were brought to his notice, did not feel anger, who did not desire that the rich man should suffer in consequence of what he had done, would be morally defective. And then Nathan drives home his thrust: "Thou art the man!" How are we to analyse David's state of mind after this discovery? Would he now feel that his former judgment about such an action as the imaginary rich man's had been wrong, that if in real life he came across such a rich man he ought to take a view of his action which divested it of any bad desert? Hardly. Such an action would seem to him as foul as ever, and the foulness would have all the greater horror that he recognized it in himself as well. The sense of his own bad desert might make him indeed feel: "I am not the person to impose upon my fellow-sinner the pain appropriate to his action," but he would not feel any the less that pain *was* appropriate in justice to such an action, and that any perfectly righteous being would have indignation both against his fellow-sinner and himself. So far as he cared for justice, it would not be good news to him to be told that, as the universe was constituted, action such as the rich man's and his own was not attended by any loss of happiness. He might cry out, like St. Paul, for some power to intervene which should deliver him from a self which he loathed and which yet clung to him and was his own self, and should deliver his fellow-sinners as well. If the Christian theory is true, that we all of us have so grave a load of bad desert as to need

229

the Divine forgiveness, the frame of mind of each one
of us ought to be, more or less, like David's in the story
after he had heard Nathan's "Thou art the man." We
shall not feel for that any more weakly that the evil
actions we witness around us are actions to which pain
is attached by the nexus of justice, and it may be our
duty to say so, yet it will be well that to ourselves all the
time we repeat: "Thou art the man."

THE WRATH OF GOD

(continued)

THERE is an interesting paper by Mr. Walter Moberly[1] devoted to the question of moral indignation. He agrees with the view I have been putting forward so far as to recognize that there is such a thing as moral indignation really different from selfishly vindictive anger, that this kind of indignation goes with fine human characters, and that it may supply the energy for noble struggles in the world against unrighteousness and oppression. "It is probably true," he says, "that if most of us became better men than we are, we should be righteously indignant much more often than we now are." And yet Mr. Moberly does not think righteous indignation compatible with quite the best type of character: he does not think it compatible with the Christian *ēthos*. He would put in the place of indignation "tender reproach" as the properly Christian reaction to all wrongdoing. He argues that "tender reproach" is superior to moral indignation on three grounds: (1) because righteous moral indignation so easily runs into hypocrisy, serving as a cloak for the baser kinds of vindictive anger, (2) because moral indignation accustoms

---

[1] Now (1937) Sir Walter Moberly. The paper was contributed to *The Forum of Education*, June 1923.

men to the idea of inflicting pain and so weakens the inhibition which in other cases would have restrained them from cruelty, (3) because it produces a pharisaical feeling of moral superiority.

I fully admit that indignation is beset with these dangers; what I have put forward about our continually reminding ourselves of our own bad desert implies that the dangers Mr. Moberly indicates have to be guarded against. But I do not think that Mr. Moberly's paper proves that righteous indignation, when free from selfish vindictiveness, has no place in the highest and most Christian type of character. We can hardly be more Christian than Christ, who is stated in our earliest Gospel on certain occasions to have displayed indignation. The reproaches he addressed to the Pharisees, if his words are rightly reported, were not exactly tender. Mr. Moberly might perhaps say that, since Christ had no bad desert, it was appropriate for him to be indignant, but it is not appropriate for us who have bad desert of our own. That, however, would not show that righteous indignation is in itself a wrong feeling: it would be to admit that it went with a perfect human character, and that it was only the defects of our own character which made it wrong for us to be indignant with our fellow-sinners. If indignation goes with human character as conceived in its perfection, the argument in this lecture would hold good—that there is really such a thing as bad desert, and that the ideally right reaction to it is indignation.

Perhaps, however, Mr. Moberly would hold that indignation is never the best attitude to wrongdoers, and that our account of Jesus cannot in this respect be trusted. His line of argument would rather suggest this, since he seems to think that desire that anyone should experience retributive pain is incompatible with good will towards him. He instances the attitude of the criminal's mother to the criminal. But here, I think, one may consider what he himself had pointed out a little before, that in some cases of indignation "the situation derives all its meaning and its poignancy from the contrast with an old intimacy of relation." "Moral indignation," he writes, "derives its character from the paradox that the person with whom we are indignant is at once an enemy and an ally; or rather is an enemy though an ally." There are none with whom people feel such indignation as those whom they love. When Mr. Moberly brings in the mother of the criminal, probably we think of the criminal as already suffering the penalty of his wrongdoing: if you imagine a mother both ideally loving and with an ideal care for righteousness, her concern at that stage of things might well be to mitigate her son's sufferings. But if you think of an earlier stage, when the mother sees her son doing something shameful and foul, and perfectly complacent and jaunty about it, I do not think love would exclude anger: she would feel greater indignation because it was her son who acted so than she would feel if it were a stranger in whom she was less interested. She would rather see her son brought by suffering from his present hideous self-complacency than see him as he is: she would desire most that he should suffer the particular pain of seeing the hideousness of his present self. Would the son be more likely to have his eyes opened to that "hideousness" if he encountered only the "tender reproach" of his mother and not her indignation and horror? One thinks of the Old Testament story of Eli and his sons. Eli did proceed, we are told, by the way of "tender reproach," with conspicuous failure. Of course, you may say, that is only an old story, and the Old Testament is not Christian, but, if you suppose the situation such as the story depicts, is it probable that "tender reproach" would be effectual?

If you are to have nothing but tender reproach, you fall, I think, between two stools. On the one hand, there is the view that desert is all illusion, because men's wills are wholly determined by causes other than themselves. Then, of course, anger is an irrational emotion and the idea of retribution absurd. But, in that case, the idea of "tender reproach" is no less irrational. You have no right to regard anyone's wrongdoing as his fault: you may feel pity for him, but not reproach. On the other hand, if there really is such a thing as desert, that is, an appropriateness in justice of pain to wrongdoing, then it seems unreasonable to hold that a vivid apprehension of it, and a desire that what is appropriate in justice should exist in fact (and that is the analysis of moral indignation), is wrong.

It is especially when one thinks of the proper attitude to one's own wrongdoing that a general substitution of tender reproach for indignation would appear unfortunate. We are all of us too prone, as it is, to regard our own sins with tender reproach. If we are to feel our own sins as really deserving pain, the fact that others feel intensely such actions to deserve pain will be a helpful corroboration. "Any indignation," Mr. Moberly says, "against other men must be wrong, which is more hostile and intense than what I can feel against myself." I agree, but the best way, it seems to me, of bringing about an assimilation between our attitude to other men's sins and our attitude to our own is not to extend to all wrongdoing the tender reproach we are so inclined to address to our own, but to extend to our own wrongdoing the keen sense of bad desert we have in regard to the wrongdoing of others.

There is one other thing to be noted. We saw that Mr. Moberly deprecates indignation as liable to produce in those who feel it three odious vices, selfish vindictiveness, cruelty and a sense of superiority. Now we should

234

all agree that tender reproach is not similarly beset with the danger of running into vindictiveness and cruelty, but I should question whether it was not just as liable as anger to go with a sense of superiority. The person who reproaches must feel that he is relatively free himself from the particular failing at any rate with which he reproaches someone else, and when tender reproach does go with a sense of superiority it may be more maddening to the person who is its object than downright honest anger. Where tender reproach is free from the sense of superiority, it may no doubt in many cases be more effectual than anger in making the wrongdoer sorry for what he has done; but I do not think this is true in all cases and I have tried to state why the contention that in the highest type of character tender reproach would *always* take the place of indignation does not seem to me true.

But one must recognize that we have not yet got to the bottom of Mr. Moberly's difficulty in regard to anger. Supposing in all cases where you desire that someone should suffer pain, the suffering of that pain would be the thing he would most desire himself, if he knew his true good, then it would be simple enough to show that your desire is compatible with benevolence. In many cases of moral indignation this may hold good. The pain which the mother, in Mr. Moberly's example, who has both an ideal love for her son and an ideal care for righteousness, would desire more than any other kind of pain that her son should suffer would be, as was said, the pain of self-condemnation, and we can see that to endure that kind of pain would be a greater good for him than to go on in his present jaunty self-complacency. But what Mr. Moberly no doubt feels is that in a great deal of indignation it is desired that the wrongdoer should suffer pain, not simply and solely in his own interest, but in the interest of something else which you call "justice" or "the moral order of the world." If the pain takes the form of self-condemnation and repentance, and so is the best thing for the wrongdoer himself, from the point of view of his own interests, that is all to the good: so far as the wrongdoer is your neighbour whom you love, that is what you desire for him; but even if the pain cannot procure any moral improvement for him, it is desired that he should suffer in the interest of the moral order, which makes pain appropriate to wrongdoing. In a concrete case, if you are indignant with the bully who has been brutal to someone weak and defenceless, and if the thrashing administered to him leads to his being ashamed of himself and becoming a better man—that is what you most desire, because in that case both the interests of justice and the interests of the wrongdoer have been served; but even if the thrashing leaves the bully just as bad a man as before, it is still a satisfaction to you to know that he has been thrashed.

Now what, I think, really troubles Mr. Moberly is the idea that pain should be inflicted upon anyone for any other reason than that it is in his own individual interest. As a Christian, he feels, he ought to love everybody, even the worst wrongdoer, and so his conduct towards the wrongdoer ought to be governed solely by the consideration: "How can I procure this man the good which is his own greatest interest?" If you once allow that there is such a thing as "justice," or "the moral order of the world," to which the interest of the individual ought to be subordinated, your action towards your neighbour may be different from what it would be if it were governed by the consideration of his individual interest alone, and this seems to Mr. Moberly a derogation from the love to your neighbour which Christianity requires. You have two interests to consider, instead of one, and the two may clash—or may appear to clash. Roman Catholic theology expressly recognizes that this clash does come in the case of God's judgment upon the impenitent. The wrongdoer suffers the pain of hell, in their view, in the interest of the moral order—or, in other words, because he deserves it—although there is no possibility of the pain making him better. According to St. Thomas to witness the sufferings of the damned adds to the felicity of the redeemed in heaven,[1] and an eminent Roman Catholic poet of the last generation, Coventry Patmore, thought it a defect in the men of his own time when they

[1] "Ut beatitudo sanctorum eis magis complaceat, et de ea uberiores gratias Deo agant, datur eis ut poenas impiorum perfecte videant" (*Summa Theologica*, Supp. Partis Tertiae, Quaestio 94, Art. I.).

The idea of the saints in glory deriving satisfaction from a sight of the punishment of the damned is found also in old Protestant theological works. The late Cyril Emmett described in the essay he contributed to *Immortality* (edited by B. H. Streeter, 1917) how shocked he was when he came across it in the writings of the Calvinist Jonathan Edwards: he seems to have supposed that it was something characteristically Calvinist, without realizing that it was just a bit of old Catholic doctrine. I may observe in this connexion that one often finds the conception of hell and its torments spoken of as "Calvinist." This is quite unfair. It is every bit as much Catholic. Indeed I doubt whether any Calvinist book gives such detailed descriptions of the torments of the damned, including damned little children, as some Roman Catholic books of devotion, approved by authority. An incredibly horrible example may be found in Lecky, *History of European Morals*, Chapter IV. It may be said that the Calvinist view, even if its conception of hell is no worse than the Catholic view, is worse in so far as it denies Free Will, and supposes that people go to hell because they have been predestined by God to perdition, whereas, if anyone goes to hell, in the Catholic view, it is his own fault, because he has freely and voluntarily chosen evil. This seeming advantage of the Catholic view, however, is neutralized if one looks closer. The pains of the damned are prolonged to eternity, not simply in punishment for the evil they chose in their brief earthly life: the disproportion between the punishment and the offence would in that case be too flagrant: the punishment continues because the evil will continues: it is therefore eternally appropriate. But it is quite impossible, according to Catholic teaching, for the damned sinner to repent. He could not change his evil will into a good will, except by the help of Divine Grace, which will never be given. But we do not feel that the choice of evil is culpable unless the person so choosing is able to choose good. Catholic doctrine allows Free Will to the sinner during his threescore years and ten on earth, but by denying him in effect Free Will during the ages of the ages after death, and prolonging the punishment because the evil will continues, Catholic doctrine, in regard to hell, comes in the end to very much the same as the Calvinist doctrine of predestination.

237

could not sympathize with Dante's pleasure in the Inferno, at the sight of thoroughly bad people getting their deserts.[1]

No doubt to us such a view of things is so horrible as to be grotesque, provoking a smile at the outworn absurdity of a past age. But in the case of a thinker such as St. Thomas, it may not be wise to treat any view as simply absurd: however inacceptable it is, it may be worth looking to see whether some principle which deserves serious consideration is not involved in it. And if we examine modern men's recoil in horror from the idea of the redeemed looking on with pleasure at the torments of the damned, we shall see, I think, that the recoil is not from the principle involved, but from this particular application of it. The principle simply is that for those predominantly interested in the moral order it is a satisfaction to know that a person who deserves pain has got what he deserves, even if the pain does not improve him. Our horror at the particular application arises from our feeling no proportion between the sufferings of hell, as traditionally depicted, and the bad

---

[1] "A wilful melancholy, and, the twin sign of corruption, a levity which acutely fears and sympathises with pains which are literally skin-deep, have been increasing upon us of late in a most portentous way. . . . It is, as we have said, a vulgar error to consider Dante a melancholy poet. . . . The *Inferno* is pervaded by the vigorous joy of the poet at beholding thoroughly bad people getting their deserts" (*Principle in Art*, etc. (1889), p. 33).

Of course, as a matter of fact, Dante's reactions to the pains of his *Inferno* differ signally according to the kind of sinner undergoing them. Virgil says indeed to him when he weeps at the distorted bodies of the soothsayers, "Art thou also one of the fools? Lo here is pity quickened, when it were well dead. Who is wickeder than the man who is moved to compassion by the Divine judgment?" (*Inferno*, xx. 27–30). Dante is gratified at the punishment of the brutally insolent (viii. 37–61) and of the traitors (xxxii. 76–111; xxxiii. 148–150), but he is overwhelmed with pity for the carnal sinners (Canto v.) and is sorry for his old master, Brunetto Latini, condemned to hell for sodomy (Canto xv.). Evidently while Dante accepted with notional assent the doctrine of Jesus and of the Church, that carnal sinners deserve the pains of hell, he did not *feel* that Paolo and Francesca deserved their punishment, as he felt that the brutally insolent Filippo Argenti and the traitor Bocca degli Abati deserved theirs.

deserts of the sufferers: we feel that no one deserves such sufferings, and so to imagine them inflicted on anybody is horrible and to imagine anyone gratified by witnessing them a monstrosity. But if you take a case in which we do feel a due proportion between the pain inflicted and the wrongdoing we are quite capable of taking pleasure in knowing that the pain is inflicted. If we are gratified at the bully being thrashed even though the thrashing does not improve him, we are giving our adherence to the principle involved in St. Thomas's view of the redeemed looking with pleasure at the sufferings of the damned. If we could conceive the redeemed having as vivid a sense of the appropriateness of the pain to the wrongdoing as we have in the case of the bully—a thing which it is impossible for us to conceive, though that is what St. Thomas supposed—then the difference between their pleasure in the pains of hell and our pleasure in the thrashing of the bully would disappear.

If we dismiss St. Thomas's application of the principle as unthinkable, the question still remains: Is there a moral order whose interests ought to prevail over those of persons considered individually? The question may be answered on two kinds of ground, the ground of general ethical considerations, and the ground of authority, the authority of Jesus or the authority of the New Testament. So far as the answer is based on authority, that is, on what purports to be a Divine revelation, a Gifford lecturer cannot take its validity for granted. While, however, it is not legitimate for a Gifford lecturer to put forward assertions of his own on the basis of the authority of Jesus or the authority of the New Testament, it may be permitted him to observe that those who do take this authority as decisive might have a difficulty in showing that it supported their view, if their view is that the individual good of my neighbour ought to be my supreme consideration. It may be noted that the commandment "Love thy neighbour" is put second, while the commandment "Love God" comes first, and, from a theistic point of view, God is especially represented by the moral order. Again, the commandment is "Love thy neighbour as thyself," and I certainly ought not to love myself more than the moral order. If we examine the question on general ethical grounds, it depends, I think, simply on the previous question whether we are going to allow that there is such a thing as desert or not. If we do—that is to say, if we allow that there is, according to the moral order, an appropriateness of pain to wrongdoing—then, if we wish that the nexus should not be realized in fact in the case of an individual neighbour, because pain is an evil from the point of view of his own individual interest, we are in effect wishing that the moral order should not exist. And that could hardly be justified on any theory of ethics.

It seems then we can hardly get out of allowing that in retributive punishment, whenever the punishment does not improve the wrongdoer, there really is a clash between his individual interest and that of the moral order, and the former is subordinated to the latter. All one can say in mitigation is that the clash is due to the wrongdoer's own action, to his own direction of will; if what the moral order imposes upon him is evil in the form of pain, that is only because all the time he is willing evil in the form of wrong. Though he does not will the pain he is in a sense imposing it on himself by willing that to which the pain is connected by a moral nexus. It is further to be noted that where a man is suffering pain in consequence of his past wrongdoing, and his will is turned from evil to good, then, though the pain does not, in most cases, immediately cease, the man's relation to the pain becomes something quite different. If he recognizes that he is suffering in the interest of the moral order, he may will the pain himself, as any free man may will to enter upon what is painful in the interest of a cause greater than himself. If it is really in the interest of society that a man who has done certain actions should undergo the pain of imprisonment for the sake of all others who are tempted, the man who undergoes that pain can, by recognizing it as pain borne for others, convert it from merely imposed pain into vicarious suffering willingly undergone, and so find, in the very sacrifice of his own individual interest to that of the community, an opportunity of being joined in spirit to the company of vicarious sufferers, the company which includes the noblest.

Another idea which may obscure the validity of the retributive ground for punishment is that wrongdoing or a wrong inner attitude is its own punishment. No adventitious punishment, it is said, is needed for vice: the punishment of a bad man is that he *is* a bad man; he can have no worse punishment than that. This maxim may seem to claim the authority of Plato. The odd thing is that people anxious to establish this doctrine habitually quote in support of it something which really makes dead against it, the well-known lines of a Latin poet who says, of those who choose evil,

Virtutem videant intabescantque relicta,

"Let them see what virtue is and pine in remorse that they have forsaken it."[1] So far from the poet asserting that it is sufficient punishment for vicious men to be vicious, he finds satisfaction in thinking of their being punished by the pain of remorse.

If it were true that to be vicious is in itself a sufficient punishment for the vicious man apart from any pain attached to viciousness, we ought to be perfectly content

[1] Persius, iii. 38.

241

to think of the vicious man continuing fully satisfied with himself and in the enjoyment of everything he desires in this life and, if there is any life beyond, in that life as well, the man, for instance, who has been cruel or mean, never sick or sorry, jubilant and triumphant to the end. Now no one, unless, in Aristotle's phrase, he is "guarding a thesis (θέσιν φυλάττων)" can maintain that he does contemplate as completely satisfying a permanent immunity of the cruel and the mean man from any kind of pain, on the ground that the man is having his punishment all the time by the mere fact of his being vicious, although the man himself does not mind that a bit, and it is only the looker-on who sees the viciousness as something hateful. And we may note, if the authority of Plato is adduced for the assertion that vice, apart from any attendant pain, is its own punishment, Plato himself certainly did not believe that, for he habitually insists upon the pain which those who choose evil will suffer after death.

We can now turn back to the problem of the anger of God. If it is true that apart from the use of punishment as a deterrent, and apart from its use as reformatory, there is a kind of appropriateness in justice, which attaches pain—or at any rate the forfeiture of good—to bad desert, if that is true, not simply as a feeling which happens to have been developed in man by the evolutionary process, but as an apprehension of Reality by the human spirit, of a value, justice, which is there, a constituent of the universe in its spiritual essence, then we must believe that this attachment of pain, or the forfeiture of good, to the evil will, is there for God, that it is real, as we say, in the eyes of God. God wills that the nexus which, according to justice, is something which ought to be, should in due time be realized as something which is.

Some people have suggested that the truth aimed at in the attribution of anger to God is capable of being expressed in a more precise, less symbolical, way. What is really meant by the wrath of God, they say, is simply the "law of consequences."[1] It is stern fact that conduct of certain kinds leads to unhappy consequences for the doer, consequences which issue by an inevitable natural process from that kind of willing. Such a view, one may note in passing, has to postulate a prolongation of the sinner's existence beyond death, because it is a patent fact of the world, as we see it, that, although certain kinds of vicious indulgence do naturally lead to pain and discomfort, people of persistent, quiet and judicious selfishness— people whom we may regard as far more detestable than many incontinent sinners—perhaps enjoy a more general level of self-contentment and freedom from troublesome emotions than any class of people, and often pass out of this life without ever apparently experiencing the unpleasant consequences which are inevitably attached, we are told, to the evil will.

But granted that it is a law of the universe that the evil will inevitably, by a natural process, sooner or later, in this life or in another one, issues in pain for the willer, can we say that that is all the wrath of God means? Surely not: to recognize such a law of consequences is simply to recognize that a connexion exists in fact between a particular kind of willing and pain; it is not to recognize that such a connexion ought to exist, that if it did not exist the universe would be an unjust universe. If the connexion is simply something which we discover to be a fact, there would be no reason why we should be dissatisfied with a universe in which pain happened to be connected with the *good* will: in such a universe we should still have a strict law of consequences: everything such as unselfishness, kindness, truthfulness, would inevitably in the end mean misery, and the selfish, the cruel, the

---

[1] Miss Lily Dougall, *The Lord of Thought* (1922), pp. 154 ff.

untruthful, would enjoy the greatest happiness. Of course, the people who say that the anger of God is simply the law of consequences would not acquiesce in such a universe. They do, in their hearts, regard the connexion of pain with the evil will not as something which happens, as a matter of fact, to exist, but as something which ought to exist, which is required by justice. It is this "oughtness" in the connexion, not the mere fact of the connexion, which is the mysterious thing, it is this which is discerned in human indignation, and if the human spirit is here analogous to the Divine Spirit, this must be meant by the wrath of God.

True, from the Christian point of view—indeed from the point of view of any of those theistic religions founded on the religion of the ancient Hebrews—Christianity, Judaism, Islam—the attitude of God to the sinner is not described in its most significant aspect by our speaking of God's wrath. God is conceived also as the God who forgives and loves, or (in Islam) as the Merciful and Compassionate. Unquestionably, we are confronted here with what has seemed to many people a hopeless contradiction. If, by the principle of justice, God wills that the doing of evil should issue in pain for the doer, how is God not unjust if, by forgiving, He wills that this nexus between sin and pain should be broken, that the sinner should be freed from the painful consequences of his sin?

It may be urged in reply that God's forgiveness does not mean that a man is freed from the consequences of his sin: he still has to bear those consequences, even if his relation to God has been changed from alienation to consciousness of being forgiven. But such an answer would not meet the case. No one who believes it possible for God to forgive thinks that the forgiven wrongdoer incurs *all* the painful consequences which he would incur if he were not forgiven. And if any of the consequences which by the nexus of justice are attached to the evil will are remitted because God forgives we have the difficulty that God apparently Himself breaks a nexus which He had willed as something that ought to be. It is no wonder that the idea of God's forgiving, breaking the nexus, should have been charged with being actually immoral. This charge has especially been made against Christianity by those who think that the Indian view of *karma* belongs to the right view of the universe. For *karma* is a law of consequences by which the amount of pain is precisely and inexorably measured to the amount of wrongdoing, throughout the series of reincarnations. No personal Divine Being would have any right to come in and confound this beautiful exactitude of adjustment by freeing individual sinners from the consequences of their actions. Of course, Hinduism itself includes forms of religion which take a very different view and insist upon the Divine Grace of a personal God who forgives sinners freely apart from any merit on their part,[1] but, from the standpoint of the strict Vedantist, the idea of *karma* being broken by Divine intervention is immoral.

The difficulty regarding the Christian view is that it includes both the apparently incompatible characters in one Divine Being. The idea of God's wrath is indeed different from the Indian view of *karma* in so far as *karma* is an impersonal law; but God's wrath is what the law of *karma* becomes if the nexus is regarded as willed by a personal God. For the law of *karma* is not simply that of a nexus which is discovered, or believed, to exist as a matter of fact. The Hindu too thinks of it as a nexus which exists because it ought to exist in justice. The idea of good and bad desert is so essentially rooted in the spirit of man that Indians can no more be without it than we can. And

[1] See the little book of Rudolf Otto, *India's Religion of Grace and Christianity.*

if there is a Divine Being who recognizes the "oughtness" in the nexus and wills it, the impersonal *karma* becomes the wrath of God. It is thus a problem for such a view as the Christian one how God can forgive without violating His character as willing the nexus, how God's forgiveness can be reconciled with His justice. This problem has been met in Christian theology by the various theories of atonement, of which, since they are professedly based upon what is believed to be a Divine revelation, a Gifford lecturer cannot speak. But on the more general question regarding forgiveness and the recognition of bad desert it may be pointed out that, so far from the idea of forgiveness being incompatible with the recognition of bad desert, forgiveness implies it and would be meaningless without it.

If the bad desert of men seems to constitute an obstacle to the realization of God's loving will, to bring about what would seem, from the imperfect human standpoint, a *conflict* within the Divine Will, it is precisely in overcoming this obstacle that the loving will of God manifests its wonder. We may put it in this way: there would be nothing wonderful in God's forgiveness, if there were nothing for God to forgive. And there would be nothing for God to forgive, if there were no bad desert. The theory that the painful consequences of wrongdoing are simply a law of the existing universe which we discover as a fact, without there being any requirement of justice that the connexion should be realized, does logically mean that there is no such thing as bad desert. If there is nothing for God to forgive, it is as absurd to say that God loves a man *although* he is a sinner, as it would be to say that a physician did his best for a man *although* he was ill. The word "although," implying an obstacle overcome, would be meaningless; there would be no reason why God should *not* love a sinner. Unless there is some reason why God should *not*, it is nothing remarkable that He does.

246

But because the idea of bad desert is involved in the idea of forgiveness, the question how forgiveness is compatible with justice, how God can both will the nexus and break it, is not thereby answered.

We may, I think, get light on this by examining what the deliverances of men's sense of justice really are. True, a universe so constituted that a mean or a cruel man enjoyed, in a protracted existence, jubilant happiness and self-satisfaction up to the end, would be felt to be an unjust universe: indignation at mean or cruel actions means that we want the doer of them somehow, some time, to suffer because of them; but at the same time this desire springing from the fundamental moral constitution of man is found, as a matter of fact, to be abolished when a certain thing happens—when the evil-doer recognizes the bad desert himself. It is a kind of paradox, but so it is: when the doer himself recognizes the nexus which in justice connects his former acts with pain, justice seems no longer to require that the nexus should be realized in fact. Recognition, of course, includes the evil-doer's now setting himself on the side of the adverse judgment, hating the self that did the act and adopting a volitional attitude such that, if he has any further opportunity of action, it issues in acts of the opposite kind. All this, of course, is comprised in the familiar religious term "repentance." It includes, as we are commonly told, "sorrow for sin." Such sorrow is the pain which cannot but be ours if we find a self we loathe to be actually our own self, or at any rate to have been our self in the past, a horror like that of the people whom Mezentius in Virgil tied up with corpses. An atheist may quite well have this bitter experience of loathing a past self: of course, in the case of a Christian, or a non-Christian Theist, there is a special quality of vileness in the evil action, because of the right relation to God which is violated by it. We need only appeal to the normal deliverances of our own moral sense, to know that however hot our indignation against a case of cruelty may be, it alters the position entirely, if the cruel man himself awakes to the horror and beastliness of what he has done and sees his action in the same light as we do.

If therefore, a theistic religion supposes God to will that this nexus shall be realized in the case of unrepentant evil-doers, but should not be realized in the case of repentant evil-doers, this supposition would not conflict with what man's own moral feeling delivers. In one way, indeed, the nexus is not broken in the forgiveness of a repentant evil-doer. Pain *has* followed the evil actions, only it is the pain of self-condemnation involved in repentance. On the theory of Christian or Judaic theism, the Divine forgiveness cannot be bestowed till this pain has been experienced. "High ordinance of God would be broken," Dante is told on the summit of the mountain of Purgatory, "if the river of Lethe were crossed"—the river which abolishes consciousness of sin—"and such a draught were tasted without some pain of repentance, which calls forth tears."[1]

But, while we are considering the normal moral judgments of mankind, we may notice at this point what seems to be a strange contrast. Whereas it is felt that justice would be unsatisfied if the nexus between definitely bad desert and pain were not somehow realized in fact, whether by pain imposed or by the pain of repentance, it is not felt that justice is violated by the bestowal of good on the undeserving—where, that is to say, there is not positive bad desert, but simply the absence of good desert, or at any rate of good desert proportionate to the good bestowed. Of course, according to Christian theology, there always is, in the case of every human indi-

[1] *Purgatorio,* xxx. 142–145.

vidual, a greater or less degree of bad desert, every individual being to that extent under the wrath of God, but if we suppose this bad desert cancelled on repentance, the bestowal of such good as, according to Christian belief, is bestowed by God upon members of the Divine Community is an act of Divine grace immeasurably in excess of any merits. There is necessarily an appearance of arbitrariness in God's choice of some individuals, apart from merits on their part, to bestow on them a richness of good which He does not bestow on others. This is the mystery of election; but while the idea of men being elected to undergo perpetual suffering has been rejected as intolerable by the moral feeling of nearly all Christians to-day, the idea of some men not being elected to receive good which other men receive is one which the obvious facts of the world, if given a theistic interpretation, seem to necessitate.

It is interesting, however, that the first great Christian theologian, Origen, felt this inequality in the good enjoyed by different conscious creatures of God to be incompatible with Divine justice, unless it were believed to be strictly proportionate to desert constituted by each creature's acts freely willed. He had therefore to suppose that in their original state in heaven all souls were absolutely equal, that by their individual defection they had fallen to be angels or men or devils or brute animals, and that by their own acts they could work their way up the ladder again, in a succession of lives, to their original state. According to this view, not only must suffering be strictly proportionate to bad desert, but good enjoyed must be strictly proportionate to good desert. God could not by an act of sovereign grace bestow good on one individual beyond his deserts which He did not bestow on all others with equivalent merits, or absence of merits: that would be unfair of God.

249

Is this a true construction of what our moral sense delivers? I do not think that Origen's feeling in this matter would be borne out by the general sense of men. We do not feel it unfair that some men are born poetical or artistic geniuses and we not. If it were unfair that some men should be born with gifts which others have not, it would be unfair that a pig should be born a pig and not a man. Origen would, as a matter of fact, have said that the inferiority of the pig's soul to the soul of the archangel Michael was entirely due to its wrong acts of free will in former lives: the two souls must have started equal, if the Creator was just. But there is a way, overlooked by Origen, in which the inequalities of endowment and vocation are redressed. It is not true that for a man to be in contact with someone much wiser or better than himself is necessarily a pain; it may be a joy. If his attitude to the other man is envy, it will be a pain; but if it is admiration it will be joy. Hero-worship involves an emotion in which the worshippers themselves feel lifted up. The passionate admiration which the followers of a great leader, a Napoleon or a Garibaldi, feel for him is something which gives them an exhilarating delight. When we consider men, not as isolated units, but as forming a society, the pre-eminent endowments of particular members of the society may in that way be shared by all. Coventry Patmore[1] speaks of the ordinary Christian thus sharing the peculiar endowments of the saint.

> Yea, if I lie
> Among vile shards, though born for silver wings,
> In the strong flight and feathers gold
> Of whatsoever heavenward mounts and sings
> I must by admiration so comply
> That there I should my own delight behold.

"Comply by admiration"! If we picture the Divine Society under the figure of a great temple or cathedral,

[1] *The Unknown Eros*, xxi. ("Faint yet Pursuing").

in which the individual stones are conscious of the whole, then I may be some quite plain unimportant stone in an inconspicuous place, nothing like the sculptured forms of pre-eminent beauty which dominate the aspect of the great building, but I may so rejoice in the glory of the whole, to which I make my small but requisite contribution, that the smallness of my contribution will not matter to me at all. All the beauty which those specially elect splendid forms contribute will by admiration, by my solidarity with the building, be mine. God's election of particular members of the Divine Society for pre-eminent endowment and glory thus gives no just grievance to the rest. Of course, to ask why He elected Michael, and not me, to be archangel, or Paul, and not me, to be Paul, or Dante, and not me, to be Dante, is to ask a foolish question. If our chief delight is in the Divine Order, "all things," as Saint Paul said, "are ours."

That is how Dante, at any rate, explained the attitude of souls in heaven who by their former wrong choices have permanently lost the higher grade they might have had. They recognize their lower grade to correspond with the Divine Order because of their inferior desert, and their joy in the Divine Order as a whole is so great, their will that it should be established, as it is, is so predominant, that it drowns any sorrow they might have for their personal loss. "His Will is our peace."[1]

The consideration of merits in regard to God's action towards men has led us some way from our proper subject, the wrath of God. It had to be made plain that to explain God's wrath as God's recognition of bad desert, as God's will that the nexus between sin and pain should be realized in fact, did not imply a belief that God's dealings with men were regulated only by men's deserts. It left it possible to regard the grace of God as rich in bestowing immeasurably beyond any possible human merits.

[1] *Paradiso,* iii. 70–87.

251

DISTINCTION OF LITERAL
AND SYMBOLICAL

ONE has good ground for believing that the language which men have used, in speaking of the unseen Beings whom they worshipped, was at first meant quite literally. There is no reason to doubt that there was a time when the ancestors of the Jews thought of Jehovah as really like a magnified man in the sky or on the top of Mount Sinai, perhaps a human shape of fiery substance, with actual face and hands and feet and back-parts, which, on one great occasion, He allowed Moses to see.[1] Later on, it was familiar doctrine with Jews that Jehovah was a spirit without any shape of which a visible similitude could be made. Similarly in regard to Jehovah's mental characteristics there was no doubt a time when the ancient Hebrews thought of these as closely resembling those of a man—Jehovah revolved different plans and went into rages and sometimes regretted His former decisions. Before Christianity came into the world, it had come to be familiar doctrine among educated Jews that all this kind of language was figurative, poetical metaphor; that Jehovah was not like a son of man that He should repent, that His purpose was unchangeable throughout the ages

[1] Exodus xxxiii. 23.

and His thoughts not as men's thoughts. It is impossible to say exactly when the grosser anthropomorphic ideas gave place to more spiritual ones, because the old language continued in general use long after the ideas it covered had undergone essential change. Even to-day we commonly speak of the eyes of God or the hand of God. The ideas changed by a subtle and gradual process under the uniform language, and it is often impossible to say in regard to the documents of a particular time how far expressions relating to God or the unseen world were understood literally by those who used them, how far only as symbols.

What happened among the Jews happened also among other people. In India, some seven or eight centuries before the Christian era, the idea of the supreme God as a magnified man was superseded for wide circles of people by the idea of God as One immaterial Reality behind the manifold appearances of the world, the Reality which a man who dived into the innermost of his own being might find to be identical with himself. Among the Hindus generally, one need hardly say, the most gross and anthropomorphic ideas of deity have continued to this day; for Indian culture is like a tree which, when it puts forth new leaves, does not shed the old ones, so that advanced mystical speculation and intellectual subtlety are to be found side by side with the grossest and most degraded barbarism. Among the Greeks and Romans, the Platonic school at any rate regarded the traditional conception of an anthropomorphic deity as symbolical of a Reality which could be apprehended only by the higher mind, the *nous*, and had no characteristics perceivable by the senses. The Stoics too insisted on the allegorical character of the old mythology, and, even if the Reality to which they believed it pointed was hardly spiritual, since their God was a material fiery gas, in His complete being a material globe of subtle fire, His form was at any rate far from being the human one. Thus Christianity, when it came into the world, had not to insist that God had no human form and was an omnipresent Spirit: it found this idea already established among Jews and philosophic pagans.

It has therefore long been a problem, not for Christianity only, but for any form of theistic belief, where you are to stop in freeing the idea of God from anthropomorphic elements. Thought, already at the beginning of the Christian era, had not stopped simply at rejecting those connected with the material human form: it had already reached the point of recognizing that many characteristics of the human mind could not be attributed to God: it was recognized that the life of God was something which no experience of man could enable him to imagine. Yet if you could not attribute to God a mind like man's, what you did attribute to God—wisdom, love, justice, will—were still bits of the human mind, thought of as raised to a supreme degree of perfection. If you went on with the process and removed from the ideal of God everything which you knew as a characteristic or constituent of human personality, you would have nothing left at all. God would be for you a complete blank. It would not be worth while your saying that you believed in the existence of God at all, any more than that you believed in the existence of x.

We have at this point to consider what seems at first a strange contradiction in the attitude of many people to-day to the interpretation of religious belief as symbolic. On the one hand, it is a commonplace accepted by all present-day thinkers who have any belief in God—Catholic, Protestant, or vaguely Theist—that any ideas which man may have of God must come infinitely short of the Reality. All our terms in speaking of God are figures which stand for a Reality we cannot imagine. Roman Scholastic theology indeed, as will be pointed out, goes as far as any Theism can go in denying resemblance between our ideas of God and the Reality. Yet the very people who say this about our ideas of God, and the terms in which we speak of Him, sometimes declare the view that religious ideas are all symbols to be destructive of the very basis of the Christian faith. It was a main maxim of the Modernists whom Rome crushed in the first decade of this century that the dogmas of Christianity were symbols only, and it was a maxim which Rome held to contain all their heresy in germ. The very word 'symbol' came to have, for the theologians of the Roman Church, a bad sound. How are we to explain this?

We may find an expression of the view of Christianity which Rome repudiated in a little work, *Profession de foi du Vicaire savoyard*, by one of the precursors of the Modernist movement in the Roman Church, the priest Marcel Hébert, who ultimately severed his connexion with the Church, though at his death in 1916 he attested his belief in the future life and charged a Protestant pastor to declare at his cremation that he had died "believing and hopeful." When Marcel Hébert was still trying to combine the exercise of his priestly office with his new philosophy, he did so by "taking refuge," as a Roman Catholic historian puts it, "in symbolism":[1]

I believe in the objective value of the idea of God, of an absolute and perfect ideal, distinct, though not separated, from the world which He draws and directs towards the greater good, One and Three, because He can be called infinite activity, infinite mind, infinite love. And I believe in Him in whom there was realized in an exceptional or unique degree the union of the divine with human nature, Jesus Christ, whose luminous superiority, impressing simple hearts, is for them symbolized by the idea of a Virgin Birth, whose powerful action after His death caused in the mind of the apostles and disciples the visions and appearances narrated

[1] Jean Rivière, *Le Modernisme dans l'Eglise*, p. 143.

in the Gospels, and is symbolized by the myth of a descent to Hell and an ascension to the upper regions of the sky. I believe in the Spirit of love (one of the aspects of the threefold Ideal) who [or which] quickens our souls, gives them an attraction, an impulse to everything that is true and beautiful and good. . . . I believe in the holy church universal, as the visible expression of the ideal communion of all beings. . . . I believe in the survival of that which constitutes our moral personality, in the eternal life which is already present in every soul leading a higher life, and which popular imagination has symbolized in the ideas of the Resurrection of the body and of eternal felicity.

How, we may ask, can a Church at the same time admit that all its ideas of God have only analogical truth, and at the same time denounce, as destructive of the essence of faith, a symbolical interpretation of religion like that just described? The problem is indeed not one which concerns the Roman Church alone, or indeed the Christian Church alone, but all who have any theistic view of the universe. For while it is obvious that any ideas we can have of God must be figures, it is true that there is a mode of dissolving religious beliefs into symbols which is really destructive of their truth. No doubt when those of us who are not Roman Catholics consider the action of the Roman Church in putting down Modernist doctrine, we should hold that a number of the particular beliefs which the Modernists were condemned for regarding as merely symbolical were either untrue altogether, or really had only symbolical, and not literal, truth. But it is quite impossible to see the issue between Rome and the Modernists truly unless one realizes that there was a real menace to religious belief in the theory of symbolism carried as far as the Modernists carried it.

I think that the first thing to see is that, in respect of the correspondence between symbols and truth, religious symbols fall into two distinct classes. There are the symbols behind which we can see and the symbols behind which we cannot see. By the symbols behind which we can see I mean those which represent an idea which we seem to discern in a way enabling us to express it in other terms more truly. When, for instance, Marcel Hébert said, in the passage I have quoted, that for simple minds the luminous superiority of the union of the divine with human nature in Jesus Christ was symbolized by the idea of a Virgin Birth, he obviously meant that he could see the truth intended behind the picture of the Nativity presented to the imagination in the Bible story, and the truth he saw he could express more truly than the symbol expressed it by using such phrases as "the superiority of this particular union of the divine with human nature." He might still perhaps allow the symbol to occupy his imagination in order to stimulate feeling, but when he wanted to express what he believed to be the real truth he could do so in the phrase given. Being able to contemplate both the symbolic picture and the reality behind it, he could compare one with the other and definitely see how the symbol was *only* a symbol, that is, how it was *unlike* the reality.

The other class of symbols are those behind which we cannot see, such as many ideas we use to represent the life of God, if, as we are told, they have only analogical, and not literal, truth. When we speak of the love of God or the will of God, we know that we are speaking of something different from any love or any will we can know in men, and the idea "love of God," "will of God" may, in that sense, be regarded as an element in the life of man taken to symbolize something unimaginable in the life of God. We cannot see behind the symbol: we cannot have any discernment of the reality better and truer than the symbolical idea, and we cannot compare the symbol with the reality as it is more truly apprehended and see how they differ. The symbol is the nearest we can get to the Reality.

These two classes of symbols are not sharply distinguished, inasmuch as there are an indefinite number of degrees of clearness with which the reality behind the symbol can be apprehended. In some cases the reality is apprehended with the same clearness with which any event in the natural world of which we have knowledge is apprehended: at the other extreme our apprehension of the Reality may be so shadowy and vague that the symbol in question is hardly distinguishable from one of those behind which we cannot see at all. If, for instance, Christians speak of the Church as the Bride of Christ, they have a relatively clear idea of the Reality. They conceive an innumerable multitude of men and women throughout the centuries, characterized by the series of personalities who have been dominant figures in the life of the Christian society, from the beginning till to-day— St. Peter, St. Paul, Augustine, St. Francis of Assisi, Luther, Ignatius Loyola, and so on. They can compare with the symbolical figure of a woman this conception of the great multitude which they know as a fact in the history of the world. On the other hand, when Marcel Hébert said, in the passage quoted, that for him the Resurrection of the Body was "a symbol created by popular imagination for the survival of that which constitutes our moral personality," although he felt no doubt that he could in a way see behind the symbol, that when he expressed what he saw behind it as "the survival of that which constitutes our moral personality" he was indicating the reality more truly than was done by people who imagined a number of re-animated bodies rising into the air out of their graves, he would, nevertheless, himself probably have allowed that he had only a very vague conception of what "the survival of that which constitutes our moral personality" meant. He would hardly have claimed to be able to imagine what the experiences of a

258

person after death were. A conception of a kind he certainly had of that life, in so far as he believed that it would satisfy the exigence he felt for the continuance of his personality as one apprehending moral values. He could say that much about the future life, and because he could say that much, he felt that the supposition of its involving a re-animation of the old body must be incompatible with the Reality. Yet this seems the case of a symbol in which the apprehension of the Reality behind it is so vague that it almost falls into the same class with the symbols behind which we cannot see at all.

When we have before us the distinction between symbols of the two classes it is evident that the trouble arises in regard to the symbols behind which men think that they can see.

Even in the case of many symbols used to express things in the life or activity of God we may be said to see behind the symbol. Take such a figure as the Hand of God. If we say that in a certain event we can see the Hand of God, we mean that the event appears to us to have come about in order to realize some particular value—Justice or the good of mankind or an exhibition of beauty—for which we think of God as caring, and the event appears to us to have been brought about by the Will of God as the efficient cause, either directly or working through the natural order. If we put our belief in that way we should be convinced that we were stating things much more as they really are than when we talk of God as having a hand, though in such a case as this the figure of the Hand may have a truth for the feeling greater than the truth in the other, intellectually more correct, statement. The figure of the Hand makes us feel God's action as the simple direct act of an almighty Person more vividly, and this emotional realization may be an apprehension of the truth more perfect than one gets by the other concatenation of more

259

abstract intellectual notions. However, we must, I think, admit that in the case of such a symbol as the Hand of God, we do see behind the symbol, and so can contrast the symbol with a truer view.

We can now, I think, see how it is that a religious community which admits that a large number of its conceptions are only images representing by analogy an unimaginable Reality can at the same time complain, of theories put forward, that they dissolve beliefs into symbols. All the cases concerned are cases in which a claim is made to see behind the traditional belief a reality which can be better expressed or understood in other terms. There are many cases in which the affirmation on which the system of belief of some community rests refer to events in the time-process, and if these are symbolical the reality behind them would be much more within the compass of our imagination. Here then anyone who says that they *are* symbols may think he has a relatively clear view of the reality behind them, a reality differing from the symbol, if understood literally. And it is to these beliefs put forward as substitutes for the traditional affirmations that objection is raised. Those Christians, for instance, who hold it to be of great religious importance to believe in the literal Resurrection of the body of Jesus do not find themselves confronted with the view that the Resurrection is a symbol behind which no one can see, the truest statement of the reality possible in human language: they are confronted with the belief that the reality was something wholly imaginable, and quite different from the presentation of the story in Christian tradition; it was the natural corruption of the crucified Body in some unknown grave or common pit for the corpses of criminals, followed indeed by a remarkable influence of Jesus upon the minds of his disciples, and subsequent generations of men, through the memory and

260

record of what he said and did. That is a clear and imaginable conception. If it is true, the traditional story of the Resurrection is fiction, though, since it was fiction which arose in the minds of men because they were keenly conscious of the continued influence of Jesus, it may be taken to typify, stand for, symbolize that influence. If Christians have good ground for regarding such a substitute offered for the traditional belief as unacceptable, their objection is not adequately stated, if you say merely they object to the view that the narrative of the Resurrection is symbolical; what they object to is the imagined sequence of events put in its place.

The fact which to-day makes the difficulty acute, which largely explains the appearance of such a movement as Modernism in the Roman Church and analogous movements which have freer course in other religious communities, is that it is admitted by every one that the increase of knowledge in recent times regarding nature, regarding the past history of man on the planet, regarding the origins of the planet itself, has made a new intellectual atmosphere in which certain traditional beliefs have become impossible. The story of the six days of creation, of the Garden of Eden and the talking snake were taken by most Christians, both Catholic and Protestant, even in the days of our grandfathers, to be a literal account of events which took place about four thousand years B.C. It may be questioned now whether any educated Christian, Catholic or Protestant, thinks that the first three chapters of Genesis are a literal description of past events on the planet. Even those who believe that the writer of these documents was divinely guided consider indeed that the story in some way stands for truth about the world and about man, but that its truth is symbolical, not literal. They think that our present knowledge enables us to see behind this symbol and to state the reality more precisely in other terms. If, for instance, the truth symbolized by Genesis i. were said to be that through all the processes of the Universe there was the working of a Divine Will and that the process had gone by orderly stages from a condition of the material universe in which life was impossible to a condition in which, on our planet at any rate, life appeared at first in low forms and then passed through the various phases of animal development to its consummation in man, the old story would be the picture of a process of which we believe that we can to-day give an account much closer to what actually happened. The poetical pageant made to pass before our imagination in Genesis i. and the actual process as we conceive it would have this in common, that the process is marked by an order leading by stages up to man, and, if so, we may recognize a truth impressed upon ancient Hebrew man by the mythical story.

But when once it had come to be commonly acknowledged that a part of the traditional religious narrative, which former generations had believed to be a literal account of past events, was to be given symbolical value only, it was inevitable that there should be people who asked whether the same principle of interpretation might not be extended much further in regard to the traditional narratives. Wherever those narratives contained things which seemed incompatible with modern Rationalism, it was an expedient which naturally suggested itself to say that the narrative was symbolical, not literally true. And "symbolical" meant in this case, as in the case of the cosmogony in Genesis, that they were symbols behind which one could discern a reality different from the story —a reality, for instance, which, according to one view, included the natural decomposition of the body of Jesus behind the Gospel narrative of the Resurrection. Such an extension of the principle of symbolical interpretation at once called forth protest and condemnation in religious communities which were quite prepared to accept a symbolical interpretation of the Mosaic cosmogony. It was held vital to believe that certain events spoken of in the Gospel narrative had taken place literally, just as they were narrated: those particular events must not be touched. And what made it worse was that the Modernists put forward the principle of symbolical interpretation as the right way of understanding religious beliefs in general, and that there remained no event at all in the time-process, amongst those which had hitherto been believed to be vital for each religious view of the universe, which on this principle was not liable to be removed to the sphere of symbolical myth, while on the plane of history quite a different conception was substituted for it. It was thus a very much larger question than determining simply whether some particular event, such as the Virgin Birth of Jesus or the literal re-animation of his body, must be believed to have occurred. It was quite possible for some-one to think that the tradition regarding those two particular events might be interpreted symbolically—that it did not, for instance, really matter for Christianity whether the material body of Jesus was resuscitated or not, so long as Jesus continued to be active in the fullness of his personal life—and still shrink from the theory which extended the principle of symbolical interpretation to the whole range of religious belief. At that rate, not only the question, what exactly was the nature of the Resurrection, became of no religious importance, but even the question whether there ever was such a person as Jesus at all.

If however you admitted that a certain part of tradi-tional belief, such as the Mosaic cosmogony, might be interpreted symbolically, and at the same time asserted that certain events declared by the religious tradition to have taken place on the earth must be believed to have taken place in the literal sense, the task was obviously one of drawing a line, of determining which events might be regarded as symbolical, and which must be believed in literally. And, as a matter of fact, the position that part of traditional belief might be interpreted symbolically and part must be understood literally was the position held by educated Christians generally at the opening of the twentieth century, in all communities, even in the Roman Church. When it comes to drawing the line there are, of course, great differences of opinion. The Roman Church would insist upon a literal understanding of some events in regard to which a symbolical interpretation is allowed in the Anglican Church; events in which a literal belief is still required in the Anglican Church may be regarded as symbols in some other Reformed communities. All this shows that the question of the range of the symbolical in religion is a very living issue in Christendom to-day and that the issue has not been raised by the Modernists through any sudden caprice. It arises inevitably out of the growth of modern scientific and historical knowledge. An analogous problem must confront any non-Christian religion which attaches religious importance to any past events in the time-process or any personal figure who has appeared in the time-process: it must be a problem for any Buddhist who has modern knowledge what historical facts about the Buddha are religiously important, or for a Moslem what historical facts about Mohammed.

What value or importance for religion can belong to particular events in the time-process, or particular persons who have appeared in time as compared with general truths about the spiritual life? To say that all religious beliefs about events in the time-process are to be understood as symbols is really to assign value to the general, as against the particular. For whenever anyone says of any

264

part of the traditional religious narrative that he takes it as a symbol, on the plane of history he substitutes for it, as we have just seen, the conception of a different series of events. He thinks he has a notion of what did actually, as a matter of fact, occur at that moment of the time-process, and this, the real series of events, is relatively unimportant for religion. What is important for religion, what the tradition symbolizes by a narrative of particular events, is a general truth about the spiritual life. When, for instance, Marcel Hébert said "I believe in the holy church universal as the visible expression of the ideal communion of all beings," he meant that the story of events by which a particular religious community, the Christian Church, was established at a moment in the past, the story of the events as the Roman Church believes them to have actually and literally occurred, is of relatively small religious importance. Supposing you think that the actual events which happened in the first century A.D. were really quite different, that need not much matter. What is important is the general religious truth that all beings are always in ideal communion. If you say you regard the belief that Jesus gave himself voluntarily as a sacrifice upon the Cross as a symbol only, what you mean is that whether any real man ever did do what Jesus is alleged to have done is relatively unimportant for religion: what is important is the general obligation of men to sacrifice themselves for other men, the general beauty of such self-immolation.

Of course, such questions as these lead to the very large philosophical question about the relation of value and existence. And here I perhaps hardly need to remind my hearers of what Professor Taylor has, I think, admirably stated—that "value always involves some kind of reference to the activities of persons."[1] The process of human

---

[1] *The Faith of a Moralist*, I. p. 47.

life on the earth is not ruled by disembodied values but by the personalities and doings and sayings of unique individual men and women.

From the point of view of Greek philosophy and modern Natural Science, a fact gets its value, not from what is individual and unique in it, but so far as it exemplifies a general type or law. To understand it you have to eliminate its peculiar individual quality, its opaque, not-to-be-rationalized, actuality. From the point of view of history and religion, it is just the unique quality of each person or set of persons or event which is important. Each person and event has his or her or its value, not because it exemplifies a general type, but because it occupies a special place in a continuous process whose course as a whole is, to a greater or lesser extent, characterized by it, just as a note in a bar of music gets its value from its individual quality, though it would not have that value if it were not a note in a series. And when it is asked how an historical event, an event long past, can have supreme value for religion, the answer is that the significance of an event cannot be seen if you look at it simply as an event in isolation. By their effects persons who lived long ago, things done long ago, reach through the process and touch us to-day—in that way, at any rate, remain present for us. Caesar's crossing the Rubicon was not simply something that happened 49 B.C., but so far as it brought about the imperial system of the Roman Empire, and the life and thoughts of each one of us to-day are what they are through the consequences of the Roman Empire, the reality with which we are in contact gets some of its character, some of its worth and unworth, from the particular act of the individual person, Caesar. If religion means a relation between each individual spirit and other spirits it can no more be enough for religion to apprehend values in general than it is enough for a man to apprehend the general value of parenthood and have unsatisfactory relations with his own individual father and mother. The world-process in which we find ourselves is a unique process made by unique persons and acts, yet those persons and acts have the value they have only because they are not isolated, but are factors in the process. One constituent of the universe our relation to which obviously characterizes our religious attitude to the universe as a whole is the Christian Church. There it is, not simply the idea of a Church, but that particular society, that unique solid fact. So far as the Church remains a durable fact the personality and actions and sayings of Jesus, through which the Church came into being, are not simply historical events belonging to the past. You may recognize this so far as true, even if you think that Jesus was only a man like other men and that his personal existence came to an end on the Cross. He would, even in that case, have value for religion according to whatever value may belong to the lives of Christians throughout the centuries. It would still be true that all these lives, as bits of reality, were not created by the general idea of the beauty of self-sacrifice, but by the personality and acts of a particular man. But, of course, for anyone who accepts the Christian faith, the truth would go far beyond this, and Jesus would be present not simply by the effects of what he said and did 1900 years ago, but as a personal Spirit in living communication with the spirits of men now.

It is from such considerations, I think, that we can see where, on principle, the line must be drawn between figures and stories which may be regarded as mythical, as symbolical of certain general values, and figures and stories which it is vital for religion to accept as literally true. The question is "How far does our communication with other personal spirits here and now involve a belief that lives lived and acts done by particular personal spirits in the past were real events?" If our communication with other personal spirits here and now would not be essentially different, even if certain figures or events in the religious tradition never actually existed or occurred, there seems no reason why we should mind regarding them as mythical symbols, supposing historical inquiry makes their historicity improbable. There seem indeed to be a number of figures and events occupying an intermediate position between figures and events which can be regarded as mythical without making any difference to religion, and figures and events which are so important to religion that if they were proved to be mythical, the religion would be altogether destroyed.

I am thinking of such a case as that of Abraham, whose call by God has been represented in the tradition both of Judaism and of Christianity as the beginning in time of the special vocation of the Israelite people. It is the opinion, I think, of most Old Testament scholars that Abraham is a purely mythical figure.[1] That view is accepted by Liberal Jews and by many Christians, who feel that the vital value of the Jewish Community or of the Christian Church as a fact in the world is not destroyed by it. If you believe that the story of Abraham, as given in the book of Genesis, is historically true, it must have a special religious interest inasmuch as the Israelite people and its offspring, the Christian Church, are facts constituent of reality; and if they embody the religious values they do in consequence of Abraham's relation to God, the Jew or Christian must have an interest in Abraham which he cannot have if Abraham is simply a myth symbolizing an ideal of the ancient

[1] Not of all: I remember that very vigorous critic, the late Canon R. H. Charles, once expressing strongly to me what nonsense he thought it to dissolve Abraham and similar great figures of religious legend into myths.

Israelites. Many orthodox Jews would no doubt feel that it was a great religious loss, supposing it were proved that Father Abraham was a myth. Yet it is obviously possible to believe that Abraham is a myth and still hold that the Jewish community or the Christian Church embodies higher religious values than any other society of men.

The life of Mohammed belongs to so comparatively recent a period that no one, so far as I know, has ever put forward the theory that Mohammed never lived. But if we ask whether, apart from that, the belief that Mohammed really lived is necessary to the Moslem religion, it would certainly be hard to imagine Islam surviving after Mohammed had been shown to be a merely symbolical figure. This is so, although Moslems do not believe themselves now to be in living communication with the spirit of Mohammed, as Christians believe themselves to be in living communication with Christ. Yet there would seem no reason why a modified form of Islam should not continue, if the importance of Mohammed was not in his person, but in the truths he is said to have proclaimed. The truths would remain valid, supposing the person who had actually proclaimed them were concealed behind a mythical figure.

In the case of those Jews and Christians who believe that Abraham is a myth, it is important here to note of what they believe him to be a symbol—not of a merely disembodied ideal, but of a kind of life which was actually lived by individuals in the past and so created a religious tradition still working to-day in the Jewish community and the Christian Church. As facts of the world, these two communities do owe the impulse which carries them on in part to actual unknown persons long ago whose lives were characterized by faith in God. Thus it is possible for Jews and Christians to see Abraham resolved into a myth without losing their vital connexion with the

269

progenitors of their communities, because in the dim background, behind the mythical figure, they see those real men and women long ago, whoever they may have been, in whom the valuable traits of the mythical figure must be believed to have been actual.

Perhaps it would be as well to emphasize that, when one speaks of modern Jews and Christians taking figures and actions described in the sacred narratives as symbols, one does not mean anything at all like the ancient theory of Philo and the allegorists—that wise men of old deliberately hid moral or religious teaching in symbolical types. For the Hebrews of long ago who wrote the story of Abraham, as we have it in the book of Genesis, he was doubtless not a symbol, but an actual person who had lived in the past. But when they wanted to describe him as they felt a man of God should be, they drew their ideas from a kind of life which they knew as having actually been lived more or less consistently by particular individuals in the Israelite community. It was lives like that in former generations which had established certain ideals in the tradition of the community. No ideal comes into being simply out of the blue; every ideal must have been formed in the first instance under the suggestion got from the lives of people who have turned their efforts and aspirations in that direction.

Thus, if it is true that the spiritual ideals which came to be formed in Israel had a special value which distinguished them from the ideals prevalent in other ancient peoples, and if it is true that these ideals were those in Israel, because real individuals in former generations of Israelites had lived lives marked by faith in God, and if it is true, in the third place, that every development in history carries out a Divine Purpose running through history as a whole, then we can see how all these three truths may for us modern men, looking back, be symbolized by the mythical figure of a progenitor of the Hebrew people who received a special call from Jehovah and exhibited in his life spiritual characteristics which distinguished the religion of Israel. Because those three things are true, the myth may present them vividly to our minds, may 'stand for' them, as we say a symbol does for the things we apprehend by means of it.

And in this connexion we may see how it is that ideals all the world over—religious ideals, of course, but not religious only—express themselves in myth, in stories how particular imagined individuals once upon a time did certain things. Behind the mythopoeic tendency is the perfectly true apprehension of the importance of individual actions—the love of a story, because men and actions are real and create reality. And it is true that all that primitive man had of value did come to him from the actions of individuals in the past. So that when he had forgotten who those individuals had been his imagination made mythical individuals to take their place. For the ancient Hebrews those men in the past who had first lived by faith in the God of Israel had left no record, and so the ideals which must have come down from real individual lives get attached in tradition to the name of Abraham, which some critics have conjectured to have been the name of a local God, though others, I think, to-day would admit that it may quite well have belonged to some actual leader of the tribe in its wanderings long before.

But neither the case of Abraham nor the case of Mohammed can be put in the same category as that of Christ, with whom, as was said, Christians believe themselves to be in communication to-day. Supposing all men were convinced that Christ was only a symbol, then if anything called Christianity survived, the name would cover a wholly different thing. But even here, in the present-day situation, the question is not so simple as this

271

might make it appear. For it is plain that to-day there are many Christians who, while quite convinced that they are in communication with a real unseen Person, nevertheless give only mythical or symbolical value to different elements in the story of Jesus as told in the early Christian documents—such as his birth from a Virgin and the disappearance of his dead Body from the sepulchre. On the other hand, there are many Christians who maintain that to regard these elements as not literally true would be destructive of the Christian faith. It is outside our province to discuss a controversy within the Christian Church. We can take note of it only in so far as it shows a problem which must come up in any form of religion, according to which men believe themselves to be in communication with an actual Person or actual persons. A real person can never be only a symbol; but if, at the same time, certain ideas connected with the Person are admitted to be symbolical only, it becomes a vital question what beliefs about the Person it is essential to hold as literally true.

But that for a religion which does not involve any belief in present (or future) communication with the Person or persons who are central for it, this Person or those persons may be resolved into myth and symbol without that particular type of religion suffering vital injury, may be seen by certain forms of religion to-day which would call themselves Christian, but regard Jesus simply as someone who lived long ago, not as someone with whom men remain in communication. Rudolf Bultmann, for instance, one of the most prominent New Testament critics in Germany to-day, says in his little book, *Jesus*, that he is doubtful whether any part of the story of Jesus told in the Gospels is historical. He thinks we may be pretty sure that Jesus was really crucified, but that is about the only fact we *can* be sure of. To try to say what manner of man he was is quite idle. Bultmann is particularly scornful of the attempts made in some modern Liberal theology to describe the psychology of Jesus or the mode of his self-consciousness. Nevertheless there the words attributed to him are. Some of them he no doubt did utter himself, though a great many took shape in the primitive Christian community which was stimulated by the few authentic words remembered to multiply more of the same kind. The words sound through the ages with a demand for personal decision, as no other words do with such power. The value of Jesus, in fact, is not that of a Person, but of a megaphone, or loud-speaker; it is the words themselves which are God speaking to men. Plainly for Christianity of such a type Jesus might be resolved altogether into a myth without much loss. How long such a Christianity could survive in the world as a distinct religion is of course another question.[1]

Whether you stand outside the Christian Church or within it, you can, I think, recognize that this problem of drawing the line between the literal and the symbolical affects Christianity to-day just in so far as Christianity asserts that Jesus is a Person still active, not only through the memory of his past life, but in the reality of his present life, in intercourse with the souls of men. Whether that is true or not, it does not fall within the range of these lectures to discuss. But so much every one, I think, must

---

[1] In this connexion it may be important for those interested in the theology of Karl Barth to note that Bultmann has ranged himself with the Barthians. His affinity with them can be easily seen. The Barthian theology lays its emphasis on the authority inherent in the utterance recognized as the voice of God apart from the personality of the speaker or the personality of the hearer. Its tendency is to eliminate the part of man altogether. Bultmann carries out this tendency by eliminating the man Jesus and leaving only the words resounding in the air by themselves. People who have regarded Barthianism as a return from Rationalist Criticism to a faith somewhat like the old Evangelical one should carefully note the way it works out in Bultmann.

[Since this was written I have been told that Bultmann has gone back from the extreme scepticism of his little book *Jesus*. 1937.]

recognize: if it is true, then plainly the Christian Church could not allow that all Christian dogma is merely symbolical without self-destruction. An actual person with whom we are in intercourse cannot be a mere symbol. This vital issue is obscured by a great deal of the discourse one hears or reads, because the influence of Jesus upon men is taken to consist simply in the impression which is made by his personality as shown in the record of his sayings and doings 1900 years ago. The crucial question which all such talk overlooks is, *What has happened to Jesus since?* Has he ceased now to exist, just as much as the old horse we may have seen last year in a neighbouring field? Or does his spirit still exist, but only as one among a crowd of discarnate spirits in the unseen world? As long as the answer to such questions is left hazy, you obviously cannot discuss, with any hope of a conclusion, the questions raised in this lecture.

SYMBOLS WITHOUT CONCEPTUAL MEANING

WE are now to consider symbols which have no conceptual meaning. So far as something seems to represent or stand for some reality other than itself, it may be counted as a symbol. Yet there are cases in which there is no distinct conception in the mind of that reality behind, nothing expressible in words or even visually imagined. William James describes how some mad people see the things around them charged with a meaning which is sinister and terrifying. They have no idea what they are afraid of, but as they look at a table or a door, they are horribly afraid. They see the thing there as a sign; it has a peculiar expression; it means something tremendous, something altogether frightful. The reality they think they apprehend behind the visible thing is characterized purely by the emotion it produces; they know nothing about it except that its effect is overmastering fear. Such a case of morbid psychology seems analogous to the way in the normal life of men certain things seem to stand for some vague vast reality characterized only by the emotion it produces. There are three main kinds of emotion called forth in this way by visible objects—the feeling of the beautiful, the sexual feeling, and the germinal feeling of religious awe, what Rudolf Otto has made it the fashion to call the numinous.

If we analyse the feeling called up by intense admiration for the beautiful it certainly contains something beside mere pleasant sensation. It contains something akin to intellectual apprehension; you seem to take knowledge of some world of reality there behind the object, or spreading out like a halo from the object. But it is not intellectual apprehension; you have no definite concept what the beautiful object stands for: you only know that it means something, means something real and wonderful, introduces you into a fairyland. The only account one can give of this reality is that it is characterized by the feeling of a peculiar kind it excites in us, the feeling which we cannot analyse, which we could not explain to anyone else who had never had it, what we indicate when we call something "beautiful." By the absence of any intellectual content this sense of weighty meaning in the ecstasy aroused by the beautiful is very like the feeling of terror aroused in madmen by a table or a door. It differs simply because the feeling aroused is of a different quality. Many natural objects—a sunset, a summer meadow at evening, a graceful or finely coloured animal, a human face or hand, may give us this sense that it *means* some vast reality. But to give this sense is the special purpose of art. And it is, I think, noteworthy that we seem sometimes to get the feeling simply by the fact that what we see reminds us of something else. It is odd to inquire why in modern houses people often like to have brick floors, a lowish ceiling with oak beams showing across it and a large fireplace opening. It looks picturesque, we say; that is, it suggests old cottages which belong in our thought to a time long ago. We call the modern house æsthetically pleasing in such a case because it reminds us of an old house. But if we saw an old house with its brick floors,

276

oak beams and large fireplaces for the first time, if we brought no associations in our mind of a past world which went with that kind of thing, I do not think that the brick floor, oak beams and large fireplaces would give us the feeling they do.

So that even the old house we admire because it reminds us of something beyond itself: we have not yet got to the original beautiful thing which we admire simply for itself not for anything of which it reminds us. It may be very hard to say when we have reached something which we admire simply in virtue of itself, without any suggestion of something else, the thought of which it evokes, clearly or dimly. And there seems a reason why the feeling for the beautiful should so often be connected with the object reminding us of something else. In all feeling for the beautiful, as I have suggested, there is the sense of a world of reality for which the beautiful thing stands. Where we admire something beautiful, apart from any associations, the world of reality it stands for must be one without any definite concept attached to it, characterized simply by the emotion it excites, and by nothing else. But it seems that the artist can sometimes secure that the object has that halo of association which constitutes beauty by making it remind us of something more or less definite other than itself. If we do not attend to that other thing, or that other world of things, which the object suggests, still the fact in itself that the object does suggest something other than itself may give us the sense that we are apprehending a world other than our ordinary everyday world—an ideal world, a dream world.

One can see how the principle holds good, not only by the work of art suggesting to us something other than itself, but by natural objects in turn suggesting to us works of art. All our admiration of nature is now mixed up with reminiscences of innumerable paintings and drawings we bring to the contemplation of landscapes and figures. We use the term picturesque, and truly. It is in this way that when a new school of art begins to represent things in nature which had not been represented before, men come to see those things in a new way, they instinctively imagine natural scenes as pictures of that particular kind. I remember once at Oxford, at the Ashmolean, looking through, not very carefully, a series of water-colours by Turner of Oxford, and when I went out again from the Museum into the Oxford streets, it all looked different; there were new lights on trees and houses; it all looked like a painted picture by Turner. That happens to everybody on an extensive scale; all the pictures we have seen, ancient and modern, leave a general residuum of association in our minds and we are continually getting pleasure because something we see, although we may not analyse our feeling, looks like a picture.

No doubt there must be some kind of beauty inherent in the things of which the object we see reminds us, because the being reminded of something æsthetically displeasing may work the other way. I know people for whom the beauty of Switzerland has been largely destroyed because it now all looks to them like a crudely coloured picture postcard. Yet it is not simply the beauty of an otherwise known object of which the object before our eyes reminds us; what we see gets a new power by the very fact of its being a reflexion. Sometimes a natural object may remind us of pictures for which we did not so very much care when we saw them, and yet the reflexion of those pictures by association in the object we see may succeed in exciting the essential feeling: the objects we see stand for a vaguely imagined world other than the world of every day. It may be objected that the theory which makes the appeal of beautiful works largely depend

278

on their reminding us of something other than themselves is refuted by the fact that modern art has struck out a wholly new line, which reminds one of nothing, and yet is warmly admired by the young, or those who aspire to be young.

But it is certainly true that modern art owes a good part of its appeal to its reminding people of other art. The sculpture of Epstein, for instance, quite professedly sets out to remind us of negro art. The gross disproportions and thick limbs of the figures in the Rima bas-relief in Kensington Gardens have excited in many observers anger and disgust, but no doubt really do give æsthetic pleasure to many people of trained judgment. I am sure it would be wrong to doubt that many practised judges of art really get the pleasure they tell us they do from these modern works. And one can, I think, see how it is that such works give the suggestion of a dream-world other than this, a suggestion which is the essence of artistic beauty. The dream-world in this case is the primitive world revealed in the rude strangeness of savage art. We can feel *that* to be a world in which some of the more primitive impulses and emotions have freer play than in civilized society, and to have such a world suggested to us is therefore to find an escape from the uniformities of our every-day life. Psychologically, therefore, there is a close analogy between this modern art which suggests the primitive world of savage peoples and what seems to us the affected archaism of some of the later Greek art in the Roman Empire; only in that case it was not the childishness of savage art which the sculptor wanted to suggest, but the early Greek art of some six or seven centuries before, when Greek art was still immature and stiff. This later archaistic art, as is well known, even exaggerates the stiffness and unnaturalness of figures and drapery. But there was the same reason for that affectation as for the

279

disproportions of modern art. The world of primitive Athens was for the Greeks of the Roman Empire a dream-world which contrasted with the oppressive present, and the art which suggested that dream-world gave to a later generation the feeling which art is meant to give.

In different periods the imagined paradise into which art, whether painting or poetry, transported the spirit has differed in character. In the eighteenth century, for instance, it was an imagined classical world, an idealization based on the remains of Graeco-Roman antiquity. Little classical temples in their landscapes, or poetry full of nymphs and lyres, in metrical forms and vocabulary which corresponded, all that may seem to us intolerably frigid, pompous and dull to-day, because that imagined classical paradise is no longer our paradise. Later on, of course, after the Romantic Movement, the imagined paradise came to be medieval, not classical, and by suggestions of the Middle Ages, of knights and ladies and ballad poetry, much art and poetry in the days of our youth excited the feeling of a lovelier world than that of every day. It was Swinburne's great discovery in poetry how strong suggestion could be got from the use of language which sounded like the Old Testament. You could produce a cumulative effect by piling up Old Testament forms of speech, when to pile up classical forms of speech, Latin in complexion, would sound simply turgid. Language of Old Testament character, cadences reminiscent of the poetical books in the English Version, suggested another world more primitive than ours, with a speech to express great emotion which had not become cheapened and vulgarized like the speech we use for our everyday concerns. When Swinburne likes to make the past participle of the verb 'to help,' not 'helped' but 'holpen,' that is because 'holpen' suggests the Old

Testament and the Old Testament suggests that ideal world.

In modern art the imagined paradise, so far as the world suggested can be defined in clear intellectual notions, is a world in which the basic impulses and emotions of man's animal life have freer play. To express such impulses and emotions by a direct brutality, which throws off all the conventions and concealments which civilization has imposed upon the raw stuff of human nature, also provides an escape from our ordinary life into another mode of existence. That, I suppose, is the explanation of such a work as Epstein's Genesis. The brutality of the forms, the obvious not-minding if the effect you produce goes against all traditional ideas of beauty, intimates perhaps the strong will which in that imagined primitive world goes straight to its purpose and tramples down whatever stands in the way. No doubt, in actual fact, the life of savages is more tied and bound by convention and tribal custom than the life of civilized man: the kind of imagined primitive world of unfettered crude impulse may be as unlike the real primitive world as the classical paradise of the eighteenth century was unlike the real Graeco-Roman world: that does not matter so long as the work of art suggests a world which has an ideal existence in man's imagination. In a great deal of modern architecture, which discards classical or medieval traditions, there is plainly the suggestion of primitive strength shown in piling great block upon great block, careless of adornment, or you seem to be getting back to something older than Greek elegance, to something Babylonian or Egyptian, in its bare geometrically-ruled extension, the kind of building which the children of men might have put up when they first built great cities upon the earth in the land of Shinar.

In all these cases, eighteenth-century classicism,

Romantic medievalism, present-day straining after the primitive, you can have a more or less definite conception of the ideal world of which art, in each case, reminds. But in many cases art, whether painting or sculpture or poetry, may give us the feeling that it stands for a dream-world other than the world of everyday, without our being able to have any intellectual concept of that world, beyond its being a world which excites in us the feeling which we call "sense of the beautiful." It may not be possible to say why one particular sequence of sounds, and not another, in poetry or music, one particular arrangement of forms and colours, and not another, in painting or sculpture, should excite in us this feeling that they stand for a world of reality other than our ordinary world, a world which we seem to have known in forgotten dreams. But we find that they do, though, of course, while there are certain sequences of sound and arrangements of form and colour which give the feeling to the great majority of people, there are some which give the feeling to only a minority, who may on that account regard themselves as an *élite* with finer perceptions than the common herd, and some again which may give the feeling to the would-be poet or artist himself, but to no one else. In this latter case he is called a bad poet or artist. A poet or artist called good may be defined as one whose reaction to particular sounds or forms and colours happens to correspond so closely with that of people generally, or with that of some special literary or artistic *clique*, that the sounds or arrangements of form and colour which he chooses as awaking the feeling in himself awake the feeling in those others also.

It is of course exceedingly difficult to say how much, when we are affected by the beautiful, is due to a beauty inherent in the object admired, how much to its containing a reminiscence of something else we have known.

It is all the more difficult because the memory awoken by the object may remain in the subconsciousness. To disentangle that which is original and immediate in our perceptions of beauty from that which is the result of latent associations may be almost impossible. We do not, as I said, know how we should be affected by different landscapes, if we had never seen the landscape-painting of the last two centuries: we cannot now empty our minds of that residual mass of associations and know how things would look to us without it. In the charm of poetry it would probably be true to say that the sounds and cadences affect us mainly by their inherent virtue, and the words mainly by their associations. But whether the feeling we have that the thing which affects us as beautiful stands for a world of beauty different from our ordinary world because of some magic in particular collocations of form or sound, or because it reminds us more or less distinctly of other beautiful things we have known, in either case it is this sense of the beautiful thing standing for an ideal world which gives a peculiar quality to our feeling.

The fact that this ideal world may be one of which we have a feeling only, without any intellectual concept, has given rise to some of the theories and experiments which have marked the art of the last generation. We have seen an intense depreciation of the logical, intellectual element in favour of vague suggestiveness. Some modern pictures have become a mere arrangement of shapes and colours and we are told that it is a mistake to ask what they mean or what they represent; we ought simply to get a certain feeling by looking at them. Similarly, a certain amount of modern poetry is deliberate nonsense, if you try to understand it as having a logical meaning; but it is supposed to stir certain feelings which lie deeper than the logical intellect. The stream of feeling and emotion goes on, it is explained, with its own inner connexions quite different from those of logical thought, below the activity of our intellect; it is something more fundamental, nearer to the basis of animal life; and it is this stream which poetry of the kind in question sets out to affect. The logical intellect really gets in the way; the stream of feeling and emotion can be better quickened into the activity desired if you avoid calling the intellect into play: one writer on the theory of modern poetry or imaginative prose explains that the aim is actually to produce the mode in which a madman's "magnificently disordered" mind works.[1]

There are no doubt many things which can be urged against a view which goes to these extremes. It is not true that in any picture it is simply the pattern of forms and colours which has beauty for us apart from the natural objects which the picture recalls to imagination. If an artist is painting, say, the picture of an expanse of still water in an evening light, it is not simply a pattern of certain colours on the canvas which moves us: it is the recall of feelings we have had when we looked at water in the evening light more or less like that, and, in order to awake that reminiscence, the picture has to be sufficiently like the real object, according to the old manner of painting, to enable us to feel we are actually looking at the scene represented. Similarly, it is absurd to overlook the extent to which in poetry the effect depends on the logical meaning as well as on the sounds or the emotional suggestions of individual words. Beauty may belong to an intellectual concept as well as to an object of sense.

> But such a tide as, moving, seems asleep,
> Too full for sound or foam,
> When that which drew from out the boundless deep
> Turns again home.[2]

[1] H. Barranger, quoted by J. Sparrow, *Sense and Poetry*, p. 31.

[2] An intimate friend of A. E. Housman's once told me that Housman had cited these four lines to him as an example of what he understood by poetry in its perfection.

284

Certainly in such lines as these the effect is partly due to sound and rhythmical cadence, but they would be nothing without the concept they embody. Anybody who knew the meaning of individual words—'asleep,' 'foam,' 'boundless deep,' 'home'—and for whom these words had all separately the emotional suggestion which they had got from their previous use in English speech, would still fail altogether to understand the beauty of the lines unless they had, presented to their minds, the idea of the soul going back to the deep whence it came; and that idea is an intellectual concept, logically expressed by the poet. It is to that idea, as well as to the sounds, the cadences and individual words, that beauty attaches.

Yet, while the anti-intellectualist theory of poetry, driven to the extreme it is in the modern theory, is absurd, it goes upon something true. The charm of poetry, as that of other fine art, implies the suggestion of a world other than the world of everyday, and that suggestion may be void of any clear intellectual concept and the world suggested may be characterized simply by the feeling which is aroused.

Here, then, in the feeling aroused by the beautiful, whether beautiful things in nature, or beautiful things made by man, there is something which shows analogy to the sense of meaning without definite intellectual content which is seen in the horrible significance felt in one form of madness. The sexual excitement shows, as I noted just now, another analogy. For while good food may excite desire for a particular bodily gratification, that and nothing more, and similarly a comfortable sofa or a warm bath may excite desire for that and nothing more, desire for *bodily* gratification is by no means the whole of sexual excitement. This implies also a sense of immense *meaning* in the object that attracts. It may express itself in an ecstasy of contemplation of the face or hand of the

285

person loved. When a lover looks at the bodily forms of his lady, he may feel that those particular forms have an overpowering interest because they stand for some tremendous world of reality. He has no intellectual concept of that world: his mind is just as much a blank in regard to it as the mind of the madman in regard to the terrifying significance of a table or a door; but he feels that this reality is there, close to him, pressing upon him. The only characteristic it has for him is that which it gets from the peculiar sexual stimulus: he could no more describe that reality than anyone could describe what a sense of the beautiful was to anyone who had never had it. Both senses are senses of significance, of meaning, which cannot be defined. They are obviously not the same: in most cases where we have a sense of what we call the beautiful, the sexual sense of significance is quite absent: or, on the other hand, there may be a strong sexual sense of significance without any sense of the beautiful. But, of course, they easily go together and may fuse in a single feeling in which the two constituents are no longer possible to distinguish. The lover ordinarily sees his lady as beautiful; and beauty in a person has a natural tendency to excite love. The lover's contemplation of his lady's face will then imply a joy whose intensity comes from the fusion of two great interests in one.

All these analogies, however, lead up to the consideration of that sense of significance which specially concerns us in these lectures. Certain objects or experiences or actions have from the most primitive times aroused in man a sense of meaning *sui generis*, that which we describe as the divine or the religious or, in Otto's word, the numinous. Like other cases we have looked at, it may be a sense of tremendous meaning with little intellectual content; the sense of a reality characterized only by the special kind of awe man feels in the neighbourhood of the

286

divine. Like those other special feelings it could not be described adequately to those who have not felt it, but can only be indicated to those who have. As a sense of meaning, the religious experience in its most rudimentary form is more than mere emotion. A sense of meaning is akin to cognition; it seems to be the making acquaintance with something really there, to be an objective apprehension, not a purely subjective feeling. This was true of the other kinds of meaning we were considering just now. Each of them involved the quasi-cognitive element as well as the emotion. Yet it cannot be properly cognitive whenever the apprehension is a blank so far as any content goes expressible in intellectual conceptions.

Of course, Otto says, at a very early stage man began to embody this feeling of the numinous in definite intellectual conceptions. The vague sense of something there to which the necessary reaction was a kind of awe or dread got clear articulation in the idea of an anthropomorphic deity whose anger was terrible. And, as time went on, there came the successive rationalizations of the numinous feeling seen in the polytheisms of the ancient civilizations and the theistic beliefs of Judaism and Christianity. No doubt this theory of the genesis of religion is highly conjectural, inasmuch as the supposed passage from a vague feeling of the numinous to the conception of an anthropomorphic deity must lie further back than any phase of religion of which we have actual acquaintance. The most primitive savages, as Father Wilhelm Schmidt has shown, conceive of their God distinctly as a Person. And the vague feeling of something numinous is perhaps more common in advanced civilizations such as our own, where many men have come to disbelieve in the traditional religion, and yet retain a conviction that the religious feeling is the reaction to something real. It may be regarded rather as the emotional relic of an abandoned system of belief than as the raw material of religion. And it is in such times that the desire to retain the religious feeling, while rejecting the intellectual conceptions which had been associated with it, gets formulated in the common demand for an "undogmatic religion."

A purely undogmatic religion would be a religion in which no conceptual idea of God at all, or of any Reality beyond the sensible world, was entertained, but only the sense of a numinous meaning attached to particular things in this world—the starry sky, or a piece of music, or a revelation of human character—or the universe contemplated as a whole. These things would still be felt as symbols of a Reality beyond; it would be felt that they stood for something truly there; religion would so far for those who had the sense, not be a mere emotion; but what that something was, regarding *that* there would be in the mind no conception which could be expressed in any statement. That such a conception of religion is not an impossible one, may, I think, be fairly urged by pointing to the other cases we have surveyed in which a meaning strongly felt but without intellectual content is attached to constituents of the universe. On the other hand, the parallel with those other cases would not be altogether favourable to the value of the numinous feeling. The first case we noticed belonged definitely to mental disease— the madman's sense of the horrible significance of a chair or a door. Most people, other than those who had this sense, would pronounce it unhesitatingly to be a mere delusion, of which it would be good to get rid. And for people who crave undogmatic religion it must be discouraging to think how close an analogy such religion offers to those phenomena of the madhouse. Most people, again, would hold that the sense of tremendous meaning attached to sexual attraction was a delusion, though in

288

this case not a pathological delusion, but one developed in normal man because it furthers the propagation of the species. The sense of beauty is certainly of a different character. Most, if not all, of those who believe the Ground of the Universe to be spiritual would hold that the sense of the beautiful was not a mere human emotion, but the apprehension of the Reality there in God. This sense of the beautiful thing being the symbol of a world of Reality beyond itself would then be veridical —a communication of the Divine Spirit to the spirit of man.

But, notice, this view of the beautiful could hardly be held by anyone who did not for other reasons believe in God, believe that the Ground of the Universe was spiritual. The sense of the beautiful, taken by itself, would hardly carry in it any assurance of its being more veridical than the insane sense of meaning or the sexual sense of meaning. For those people who believe that the development of man on the planet was due to a chance concurrence of material circumstances, wholly apart from any spiritual purpose, the sense of beauty in developed man must, of course, be there as a fact. They may even assign value to it as an emotion because it gives those who feel it a peculiar kind of pleasure. But the *meaning* attached to the beautiful thing, as was indicated in a former lecture,[1] will be as much an illusion as the meaning felt by the madman or the meaning felt in sexual interest. It will just be a mode of emotional reaction to certain sense-stimuli which happened by the chances of the evolutionary struggle to be developed in man generally. There is no world of spiritual Reality of which the beautiful thing is a veridical symbol. It might be more difficult to say how such a mode of emotional reaction came to be developed than it was to say how the sexual sense of meaning came to be

[1] Pages 145, 146.

developed. There does not appear to be anything in the sense of beauty which would specially favour any particular species in the struggle for survival. But so far as both the sexual sense of meaning and the sense of beauty were illusory feelings, in seeming to symbolize a Reality beyond the objects to which they were attached, they would be on a par.

If the numinous feeling is combined with any belief in the real existence of a Divine Being whom the feeling apprehends, the resulting religion cannot be purely undogmatic, the belief implies a dogma in McTaggart's sense, "a proposition having metaphysical significance."[1] If you go no further than the bare proposition that a Divine Being of some sort exists, that the sense of the *numen* is to that extent veridical, you already have dogma. To have undogmatic religion really pure the meaning which the numinous sense seems to attach to particular objects must be as void of conceptual content as those other senses of meaning. And since you have ruled out even the belief that the Ground of the Universe is spiritual —for that would be a dogma—you cannot regard the apparent meaning indicated in the sense of the beautiful as other than illusory. When, from the point of view of pure undogmatic religion, all cases of the sense of meaning other than the religious are held to be illusory, that must make it hard for the upholder of "undogmatic religion" to maintain that his own numinous sense of meaning is any less illusory.

Probably what conceals this difficulty from many people who talk about undogmatic religion is that religion, as they imagine it, is not completely undogmatic. They mean only that it is not to include particular traditional beliefs which they dislike: it is to beliefs which they do not share that they apply the term "dogma": any belief

1 J. M. E. McTaggart, *Some Dogmas of Religion.*

290

they hold themselves they do not call a dogma, though such a belief would be equally a dogma to others who do not share it. There seem, nevertheless, to be some people to-day who do go the whole way of excluding all conceptual beliefs from religion, and still put a value upon the numinous feeling aroused by certain objects or the contemplation of the universe as a whole. Any statement about the character of the Reality to which the numinous feeling seems to point interposes something unwelcome. Religion is a mass of symbols whose meaning is purely in the feeling connected with them, a mode of emotional reaction to the universe, or to parts of the universe: it spoils it to try to put into it any intellectual content. I remember once hearing a man describe in conversation an experience of his, when he was visiting an English cathedral. Service had not yet begun, but the organ, if I remember right, was already playing. He described how the ancient building around him, the half-light, the waves of music, as he wandered about, gave him a rich sense of the numinous; and then he described the fearful fall into bathos, into dreary tedium, when the music ceased and he suddenly heard a voice proclaiming through the aisles, "To the Lord our God belong mercies and forgivenesses, though we have rebelled against Him." The proposition that the character of God is such that you can see it specially typified in the act by which a man who has received great wrongs forgives the person by whom they were inflicted is a proposition which to some people would be good news indeed, if they could believe it. If any statements can be made about God, not characterized by dry theological technicality, that statement, one would think, would be one. But to the man in question any statement about God would have been equally disagreeable, a fall into bathos. He could only enjoy his sense of the numinous when no intellectual content of any kind

291

was imported into it, when it was a sense of meaning characterized by the specific emotion alone.

It will be seen how closely analogous such a view of religion is to that modern theory about art and poetry we were considering a little while ago, that theory which asserts (to quote a recent writer in the Literary Supplement of *The Times*) that "the reasoning mind is an intruder in the realm of poetry, and poetic content varies in inverse proportion to intellectual content."[1] Yet to apply such a theory to religion is a very different matter from applying it to poetry and art. For in religion the question whether the peculiar sense of meaning is veridical or not is important in a way in which it is not in poetry and art. The sense of meaning in poetry and art can be held to have its main value unimpaired, even if there is really no world of being other than the symbols contemplated to which the symbols point. The feeling that they point to such a world of being, even if quite illusory, may be worth having simply because of the peculiar pleasure it involves. But it is a question whether anyone could go on feeling the religious sense of meaning attached to the universe, or to parts of the universe, worth having simply for the thrill of it, if he did not believe that there was some kind of Reality beyond to which it pointed, that, when he said the objects in question were symbols, they really did stand for something not themselves. For at the very heart of all that can be properly called religion is the conviction that what is apprehended is an immense Reality.

Such considerations would make it impossible to regard a peculiar sense of meaning, a peculiar emotional reaction, without conceptual content, as making the whole of religion. If it is true that religion is throughout a matter of symbols, that God and the world beyond our sensible

[1] *The Times Literary Supplement,* "The Essay on Man," August 10, 1933.

experience cannot be conceived except by means of symbols, religion in practice amongst men has always involved as well the attempt to get a knowledge of God and the spiritual world which, so far as it went, could be expressed in human language in definite propositions. A religion void of this constituent of real knowledge, consisting simply in numinous feeling aroused by a sacred building or a piece of music or the universe as a whole, could hardly exist; if it may seem to exist in the case of certain individuals to-day, that is probably only because religion of a completer kind exists in their social environment and they live, as it were, upon its aroma. An aroma cannot continue for long when the thing from which it is thrown off has been removed. But while all this is true, it must be recognized that the conception of religion as a sense of meaning, attached to certain things which seem to symbolize a world of being which cannot be apprehended intellectually, is not so much false, as partial. A durable religion must involve dogma (in McTaggart's sense) as well as numinous feeling; but so far as all the dogmas are recognized as a wholly inadequate expression of the Reality aimed at, they have a halo of meaning spreading beyond them which can be felt to be there, but which the mind of man cannot grasp.

Even more than to the dogmas of religion this applies to the sacred acts and sacred objects of a religion. Certainly a sacramental act, to be effective, must have some explanation of its meaning attached to it, which can be expressed in words. But when the best verbal expression has been found, it is felt that this does not exhaust the significance of the sacrament. As an act it can have a meaning that seems to reach further than that of any verbal statement can, just because the significance of an act may include an indefinite range of suggestion, felt not formulated. Even in those forms of religion in which

293

the sacramental element seems least this principle can be found at work. The periods of silence, for instance, at a Quaker meeting may convey a sense of meaning felt to extend beyond that of the most able exposition of truth in words. And this incapacity of words and intellectual concepts to embody the whole meaning of religion is not a mere failure of human power. It corresponds with that craving of the human spirit for the boundless. It is akin to the suggestive halo in poetry, which seems to tell of some dream-land more beautiful than the world we see, some lost paradise we knew in another sphere. A religion whose dogmas and sacraments had not this halo of indefinite suggestion beyond all verbal statements would be quite unsatisfying. Of any heaven which could be described to us in words we should feel, if we took that to be a literal description: Is that all? Is heaven no more than that? Any attainment of man's spirit in intellectual conception or visual imagination, if taken as final and complete, would bring terrible flatness and disappointment, any limit reached beyond which there was no further to go.

One can hardly speak of this without thinking of Plato's mythical expression of it in his doctrine of *anamnesis*. Whether we think it true or not that the soul which finds joy in the contemplation of some earthly beauty is dimly remembering a world of eternal ideas it knew before birth, Plato is truly describing what the admiration of beauty feels like; it seems to have this reference to a world of being we have known somewhere, somewhen. All artists, in language or in material, know how often the suggestion of something not expressed is far more powerful than any distinct expression could be. The clear expression brings the mind up to a bound or limit, whereas the suggestion incites the mind to reach out as far as its power goes without check. It is thus

294

essential, if religion is to meet this exigence of the spirit, that the expressions of it in word or action or sensible object should never be taken as complete, that they should all be symbols standing for something which can never be expressed.

A religion which consists simply in the enjoyment of numinous feelings without any effort to grasp the Reality by intellectual conceptions, criticized and corrected, is a very poor affair. But one may say with equal truth that a religion which thinks that it has enclosed the whole Truth of God in a set of dogmatic formulas is a poor affair. Thus dogma seems to be one of those things which exist in order to be transcended and negated, which yet must be there in order that the act of transcending and negating can take place. In this respect dogma would be analogous to duality in love. The more two people love each other, the more the duality seems to be transcended and negated in union. Yet suppose the duality ceased, the love would cease too, for love is just the transcending of a duality or plurality, which must always be there in order to be transcended. This may illustrate what is the case with intellectual concepts of the Divine. Just as it is a mistake to found on the true observation that an increase of love means a progressive transcending of duality or plurality the supposition that the perfecting of love would mean an abolition of duality or plurality altogether, so it is a mistake to found on the true observation that apprehension of the Divine Reality means a transcending of the best intellectual concepts we can have the supposition that the attempt to get the best intellectual concepts is effort misdirected.

So far as the intellectual concept stands for a Reality which differs from it, it is a symbol only. So far as it corresponds with the Reality, it is not a symbol, but the actual truth. All our effort to think true thoughts about

God is an effort to get rid of the symbolical character of our conceptions, to change them from symbols into precise apprehensions. And if there has been any progress in thought about God between the primitive level and that of a twentieth-century philosopher, progress has consisted in freeing conceptions from symbolical imagery. No one to-day in a civilized country who believes in God at all could deny that the process has been in large part successful: no one could now hold a view of God anthropomorphic in the same way in which the primitive conception was anthropomorphic. A Theist to-day would hold that his conception of God was less symbolic than that of the primitive man who thought of God as literally a person in human form living in the sky. But an intelligent Theist would also hold that this process of superseding symbols by precise apprehensions can never be complete. Any conception of God which man can reach must always be, more or less, a symbol still. And yet we must always go on trying to make our conceptions less symbolic, more precisely correspondent with the Reality. Only we must beware, when we do so, of supposing that we have got the truth behind a symbol because we substitute for the symbol a philosophic formula; such a formula may be less true than the symbol, as will be urged in a lecture following.

PRAGMATISM AND ANALOGY

THE question whether, or how far, any religious conceptions are true raises the more fundamental question, what is meant by Truth. The plain man understands by truth the correspondence between the belief in someone's mind and a fact outside his mind, existing or happening independent of his belief. This is called the correspondence theory of truth, and it has been strongly attacked by certain idealist philosophers, notably by Bradley, and by Professor Joachim, in his youthful work *The Nature of Truth*, written under Bradley's influence. The theory set up in opposition to the correspondence theory is the coherence theory. A belief is true when it coheres logically with the whole system of experience which constitutes the universe. When we strive for truth, we strive to make all our beliefs a logical harmony. Another theory of truth is offered by the Pragmatist school. "Truth is what works." If, in practice, to act on a belief is found to give the results desired, that belief is so far true. If another belief is found to work better, the former belief is pronounced to be so far untrue. When the Pragmatist theory is applied to religious belief, it means that certain feelings, a certain direction of the will, are held to have value in themsleves, and if a particular belief nourishes those feelings or confirms that set of the will better than any other belief, it

K*   297

may be taken as having all the truth a religious belief need have. It meets human needs; it is justified by results.

The view that in religion symbols are useful simply because, when men act and feel *as if* they were true, they act and feel with the best practical result, even if the symbols are not true in the sense of corresponding with any independent reality, may derive some plausibility from the fact that an analogous view has been maintained in recent times in regard to scientific truth. A truth in science is a hypothesis which works, we are told, in practice. As man pursues his inquiry into nature, he does not reach any apprehension of the Reality as it is in itself. His picture of the constitution of matter, for instance, is simply a convenient symbol because, if he proceeds in practice as if it were true, he can so arrange material objects that the effect he desires to secure comes about. All that we call 'laws of nature' are simply hypotheses which we find to be practically useful.

There are two things which appear to me obvious in regard to such theories. One is that any theory which tells you to act *as if* something were true, does, by very implication, assert the importance of truth of fact in regard to practice. It implies that if such and such a thing *were* true —true in the sense of fact independent of the mind discovering it—a certain line of conduct would follow as appropriate. Supposing matter really did consist of a set of mathematical formulas, or whatever it may be, taken by science as its hypothesis for practice, that constitution of matter would determine a particular course of action. The rightness of conduct would depend directly on the truth of fact, which would be fact apart from the discovering mind. Only, the theory goes on to assert, a right course of conduct—a course of conduct, that is, which leads to the attainment of human purpose—may sometimes be followed on a supposition regarding fact which is not

298

really true. Nobody can deny that this is so. There may be a large number of different sets of facts all of which would determine the same course of conduct. According to some theories, for instance, there is something in the material constitution of alcohol which makes it deleterious to the human body: according to another theory, God inspired Mohammed to forbid men to drink alcohol. The material constitution of alcohol, as discovered by modern scientific research, and its effect upon human organs are quite a different set of facts from the alleged communication of God to Mohammed. But they both determine the same course of conduct, abstinence from alcohol. Supposing it is true that alcohol is deleterious to the human body, and supposing it is not true that God inspired Mohammed to forbid wine, then a man who knew nothing of what modern Science may have to say about alcohol, but who abstained from it because he believed that God through Mohammed had forbidden it, would pursue a right course of conduct, of conduct which would promote his bodily health, but on a supposition regarding fact which was false. But this would not show that conduct is independent of truth of fact: it would only show that the supposition on which a man acts may be false and his action may nevertheless lead to the result he desires.

When, therefore, some modern philosophers say that a certain hypothesis about the Ground of the Universe is not really true, in the sense of being fact independent of the discovering mind, but that we shall find in practice our purposes best realized by our acting *as if* it were true, they are not saying anything incredible. Only it is quite clear that they are not, as Pragmatists have supposed, implying that truth is only what works in practice. They are implying most distinctly that knowledge of what is fact independent of the mind dictates a particular course. If we knew what the Ground of the Universe really is, that knowledge would dictate the conduct by which we could best realize our purposes. Only we do not know and cannot know, they say, what the Ground of the Universe really is. In this case therefore we have to act on a supposition which is probably not true, as a *pis aller*. Experience shows us that if we take this supposition as a working hypothesis, acting *as if* it were true, we attain our purposes better than in any other way. The fact that we attain our purposes does not prove that the supposition on which we act is true, since a right course of conduct may follow on a false supposition. But when it is impossible for you to know what the facts are, then you may adopt the hypothesis which leads to the best results in practice as a *pis aller*.

The other observation which seems to me obvious, in regard to the pragmatic theory of truth, is that it is taken wholly from men's dealings with inanimate nature. When it talks of truth, it has always in mind theories in the field of Physics. It seems to me unfortunate that the problem of truth in the field of Spirit is not seen to be something quite different from the problem of truth in regard to inanimate nature. It may be that everything which has been said to show the unsatisfactoriness of the correspondence theory of truth, the contention that any idea which Science forms of the ultimate constitution of the material world is not to be supposed to correspond with a reality existing apart from the human mind, but to be merely a hypothesis for practice, which turns out according to expectation when we act as if the hypothesis were true—it may be that all this holds good in regard to inanimate nature. But the moment one comes to the world of conscious Spirit, every theory of truth except the correspondence theory becomes absurd. If one thinks of the anxiety of the lover to know whether the person he aspires to win really loves him, it is precisely the question whether an idea in his mind, the image of the other person's state of mind, really corresponds with fact existing independently of his mind which torments him. What would the lover say if we told him not to be so concerned about reality apart from his mind; it would be enough for him to act as if the person in question loved him? Should such an hypothesis lead to the material results which he desires, or should such an hypothesis best give logical harmony to his system of thought, that will be all the truth he needs. But does she really—really, apart from anything I may think—care for me? What really are her thoughts in themselves, her way of regarding me in itself?—that is his insistent cry. My belief about another human spirit, about what that spirit now thinks or feels or has experienced in the past is essentially belief about a reality existing apart from my own mind. And the desire to know the truth in this sense is raised to its greatest intensity in love. But it is the characteristics of love between human beings which must be our best guide to belief about the Reality which reaches beyond man, if the Reality surrounding man is spiritual.

This is why a religious man must feel it wholly inadequate if you tell him to act *as if* there were a God who cared for goodness, who loved and judged him. He cannot be satisfied unless he believes that there really is a God who cares for goodness, who loves and judges him. It is a wholly different case from that of telling a man of science to act as if the ultimate constitution of matter were such and such mathematical formulas. For in regard to inanimate nature it is the results of action that we really care about. If the results of an hypothesis are good, we really do not mind much, if the hypothesis does not correspond with any reality outside the mind. The chief trouble about a false hypothesis is that, sooner or later, it is likely to mislead us in action. But if we could be sure, about any hypothesis regarding the ultimate constitution of matter, that we should always attain the results we expected, supposing we acted as if it were true, I do not think it would trouble us much to think that the ground of the material world, apart from the human mind, might really be something quite different. But in regard to other spirits it is not the results we mainly care about: it is the truth as it is, independently of our knowledge.

There have indeed been philosophical theories which suppose that nothing is really inanimate, that the material world itself is ultimately a multitude of individual consciousnesses, inaccessible to us but making, by their action in the mass, the laws of the physical world. If such a theory—or any theory which supposes conscious spirit to be behind material phenomena—is accepted, then, of course even in regard to what we call inanimate nature, truth which is merely a working hypothesis, is merely 'As if,' would not be satisfactory. We should have true knowledge only when we were able to have in our minds an image of what was in those other consciousnesses, an image corresponding with the independent reality. Supposing we believe that such consciousnesses are there, but for ever in this life inaccessible to us, we must reconcile ourselves, of course, to registering their action in the mass as a statistical uniformity which gives us a relatively trustworthy rule for conduct and which we treat as a law of inanimate nature. But that offers only a *pis aller* to our desire to know what is. That which, all the time, really *is*, is the conscious life of all those innumerable entities which we can never know because the minuteness of the range of each consciousness in the material field makes communication between us and them for ever impossible. This theory, however, that the ultimate constitution of matter consists of innumerable individual consciousnesses, that there is nothing really inanimate at all in the universe, is still to-day a somewhat eccentric opinion, and we may without hesitation provisionally speak of the processes of the natural world, other than those of organic bodies, as inanimate. And, if they are inanimate our concern is to know the results to which the processes lead, not what they are within, apart from the mind of the human observer—if indeed an inanimate process can be said to have any 'within.'

But religion is concerned with Spirit, conceived as extending beyond the world we feel and see, extending, according to Christian theology, infinitely beyond it; it is concerned with the relation of my individual spirit to that all-encompassing Spirit and to the other human spirits included, with me, in His embrace. And perhaps one ought not to limit the other finite spirits with whom religion brings us into right relations to human spirits. Even if the established philosophy of the Roman communion teaches that the animals inferior to men have no rights, it seems incredible that, if God is at all what Christian theology believes Him to be, the infliction of unnecessary pain upon any of His sentient creatures is not an offence to Him.

If again there are invisible finite spirits in the universe, other than human spirits, between whom and man there can be interaction—as the traditional belief of the Jewish and Christian Churches affirms—religion may include a right relation between man on earth and those other invisible spirits—or some of them. The practice in the Roman and Orthodox Churches of asking the intercession of angels implies the view that this is so, and even old-fashioned Protestants believe that religious men in the past have been sometimes visited by angels and that a proper attitude to these messengers belonged to religion. No doubt belief in the existence of non-human invisible spirits is at a low ebb in the modern world, and perhaps no educated person would question that a great deal in the old stories of angelic appearances is the work of mythopoeic imagination. But to rule out the existence of non-human intelligences, good and evil, in the unseen world with which man is in spiritual contact, as something in itself incredible, while belief is retained in the continued existence of human spirits after death—the common Modernist view to-day—seems to me a half-way-house Rationalism, which has no logical ground. Why, if the unseen world contains spirits of any kind, should those spirits necessarily all be human ones? With what possible show of reason can we, whose knowledge of a little bit of the universe is so imperfect, set limits to the creative activity of God in those reaches of the universe which we cannot see? If one is going the whole way of Rationalism and pronouncing all belief in anything inaccessible to the human senses to be fabulous, very well: then of course angels and devils are fabulous, but then the continued existence of the spirits of dead men now in the unseen world is fabulous too. I do not wish to put forward any theory regarding the truth there may be in the old belief that man upon earth is in contact with non-human spirits; I am only led into this digression in order to indicate that a conception of religion which limits the spiritual relations of a man to his relations with God and with other human spirits *may* involve too poor a conception of the universe.

In any case, the relations of a man with God and with other human spirits would be those mainly to be considered. In all forms of Christianity the human spirits taken account of would include, not only those of living men with whom each individual on earth is in contact, but spirits of men who have died—at any rate, certain particular spirits. Catholic Christianity, of course, gives the invocation of saints in the unseen world a prominent place in its religious life and worship, though it strongly condemns all attempts to communicate with the spirits of the dead on the lines of Spiritualism. Protestant Christianity, generally speaking, condemns both the invocation of saints and Spiritualism, though, even in regard to Protestant Christianity, it would be true to say that religion includes relations with the spirits of the dead. For the ultimate consummation to which all Christians look forward is the union of all redeemed spirits in the perfected community, and so far as the Protestant's religion includes an assurance that spirits he has known upon earth still exist in the unseen world and the hope of renewing relations with them beyond death, it means that a relationship with the spirits other than those of men now living is part of his religious concern.

It is not Christianity only, it is all religion, which purports to bring each man into the right relation with Spirit extending beyond the phenomenal world, with God or with gods, and consequently into a particular relation with his fellow men, or with a group of his fellow men. In the most primitive forms of religion the feeling of the worshipper towards the god, and the conduct which follows upon that feeling, is based on a belief that certain feelings of anger or goodwill, similar to feelings which the man knows in himself, are actually there in the god's mind. His truth, if it is truth at all, is the truth of correspondence between ideas in his own mind and a reality existing independently. So far as, in his worship of the god, he is concerned only for his advantage, he no doubt thinks more of the possible effects of the god's anger than of the anger itself, and he seeks to propitiate the god, not so much because it is a pain to him to think that the god is angry, but because he is afraid of what the god will do to him, if the god goes on being angry. This is something different from the love of God found in Hebrew and

Christian religion, and in some forms of Hinduism, in which the worshipper is directly concerned with what the Spirit he worships is in Himself, apart from consequences to his own advantage or disadvantage. Yet, even in ancient polytheism, such as we find it among the Greeks, it would no doubt be a mistake to think that the relation of deity and worshipper was purely mercenary, that the will of the worshipper was simply to induce the deity by prayers and sacrifice to do what he wanted, and nothing more. It is pretty clear that where a deity was thought of as having affection or goodwill for a particular group or city, such as Athene was believed to have for Athens, there was a correspondent feeling of warm affection and pride on the part of the worshippers. The relation was felt to be a personal one. Supposing an Athenian had been brought to believe that there was no real person corresponding with his idea of Athene, but that by acting *as if* there were —by offering sacrifice, for instance—he secured the prosperity of his business and agriculture in consequence of some inscrutable inanimate process in nature, it would not have been the same thing at all. The essence of his religion would have gone. It could not be religion unless he believed that there was a real personal being somewhere who had feelings of the special kind imagined in Athene towards the people of Athens.

This is much more so when you come to religions such as Judaism and Christianity, in which the love of God Himself is central. God has come to be conceived in these religions as much less like a human being than the Athenian thought his Athene to be, but so far from this meaning that the worshippers can now be better satisfied with a theory of religion which makes it simply a matter of acting 'as if,' the Jew or Christian can be much less satisfied—just because in these religions a personal relation to God of a particular kind is made much more an end in itself, is regarded much less as a mere means to secure the attainment of the worshipper's desires than relation to Athene was for the ancient Athenian. If God is Spirit in any sense, He has a conscious life in Himself and I attain truth about God only so far as I attain a conception of God corresponding with the Reality outside myself. We need not in this connexion raise the question how far it is right to speak of the life of God as outside myself, whether God is to be regarded as the *ganz Andere*, or whether my own spirit is part of God. Even if you adopt the view which identifies the human self with God, God extends at any rate infinitely beyond any individual finite spirit, and truth about God would be a conception which corresponded with the Reality beyond myself, a conception of that Spirit extending beyond my own, even if it included my own.

But religion cannot be concerned with the relations of my own soul and God exclusively: to some extent it must require truth about the finite spirits other than myself in the universe. Some religions, as we noted just now, have regarded the other finite spirits with which each individual man on earth comes into contact as including non-human spirits in the unseen world, angels or evil spirits, but we may for our present purpose leave such a supposition out of account. Religion in any case requires truth about other human spirits, beside truth about God.

The extent to which this is so would differ according as a religion lays greater or less stress on events in the time-process. In a former lecture of this course we were considering how far it is possible for a religion to allow the persons who, according to the tradition, were important for the religion in the past to be reduced to myths and symbols. We may note again here that for Judaism and Christianity certain events in the time-process, certain human individuals who have lived at a particular

307

moment on earth, are of central importance; for Hindu religion or ancient Greek philosophical religion, it is true, no events in the time-process, no persons who have lived on earth, have the same importance, since religion consists in the apprehension of a static Reality outside time. Yet popular Hinduism attaches importance to particular incarnations, such as Krishna, or to a personal being such as Siva; and Buddhism, although the doctrine of the Buddha is declared to be more important than his person, certainly attaches considerable importance to the experiences of the man Gautama.

An event in past time before our own birth is a moment in the experience of other human spirits. Events in some sense no doubt happened in the formation of the solar system before there was any conscious life that we know of; but since, when we try to imagine those events, we inevitably think of ourselves as witnessing them from a particular standpoint, our experience of them being, in part at any rate, made up of sense impressions which would have been got by any human spectator looking on at them from that standpoint, it opens difficult philosophical questions to ask what the truth of the events was, apart from any spectator. But it is certainly true to say of the events which have formed the history of man on this planet, that they were moments in the conscious life of spirits. And if any events are religiously important, if the conscious life on earth of any spirits is religiously important, then truth about those events, about those spirits, is not any 'as if' which is found to lead to desirable results in practice, but the correspondence between our conception and what those spirits actually experienced.

The question how far the truth of our conceptions means their correspondence with an independent reality is different, we must admit, when it refers to conceptions about God and when it refers to conceptions about the experience in time of other human spirits. In regard to the latter it seems easy enough to show that the correspondence theory of truth is the only tenable one. But it is a different matter when you ask in what sense our conceptions of God can be true, if you have affirmed that the life of God is wholly unimaginable by us. In the philosophy of St. Thomas, now endorsed by the authorities of the Roman Church, a systematic effort was made to meet the difficulties of this question—an effort the more notable that it was made under the influence, on the one side, of the Neo-Platonic doctrine represented by the false Dionysius and the influence, on the other side, of the Hebraic-Christian tradition.

How to combine Neo-Platonic doctrine about the Supreme *One* with Christian doctrine about God was obviously a very grave problem. According to Neo-Platonism the Supreme was so perfectly *One* that there could be no plurality at all in that Unity. It could have no attributes or qualities because a quality would imply a duality composed of the quality which inhered and the substance in which it inhered. The Supreme must be simple in such a degree that there could be in It no distinction between being and wisdom and goodness. Strictly, you could not even attribute being or existence to it because it was above being and existence. You could express its transcendence only by thinking first of the extreme superlative in every mode of praise used by men and then denying that this was true of the Supreme because the Supreme was far beyond that. Such a doctrine of the Supreme had to be combined with the Christian doctrine of God which ascribed to Him very positive attributes—goodness, love, wisdom, justice—and which declared that the innermost essence of the Unity included a plurality of "Persons."

It is not to be wondered at that inconsistencies can be found in the Thomistic theology as it oscillates between these two traditions. But even apart from the influence of Neo-Platonism, the problem for Christian thought would have been there from the moment that the Ground of the Universe was declared to be incomprehensible. This implied that any ideas which men could form of it, and any language in which men expressed those ideas, must be inadequate. If you laid such stress on the incomprehensibility as Neo-Platonism did, if you said that you could know only what God was not, but could never know what He was, you were soon landed in something indistinguishable from agnosticism. God was simply the great Unknown—the Cause of the world in so far as the world somehow existed because of Him—or It—and continuously depended upon Him—or It—for its process, but a Cause of which you could say nothing positive. If on the other hand you laid stress upon the attributes ascribed to God in the Christian religion—goodness, love, wisdom, justice—you easily fell into an excessive anthropomorphism, thinking of God as like a good man, a wise man, and so on. Yet any Theism which says that conceptions by which men think of God are not literally true, has to answer the question how then God can be known at all. There are many believers in God to-day who do not much mind the charge of anthropomorphism. They would say that the charge was unintelligent. If they were blamed for believing in any kind of God at all, that might be reasonable on an atheistic theory of the universe; but to allow people to believe in a God of some kind, and then blame them because they attached to him notions derived from human personality, was merely silly. It is to be noted that Catholic theologians have been much more afraid than this of anthropomorphism: they have felt it as a pitfall into which it is only too easy to tumble. And yet if there

310

is a pit of anthropomorphism on one side of the road there is a pit of agnosticism on the other. Is it possible to find a narrow path between them on which feet can tread safely?

The Scholastic teaching, which has the approval of the present ruling authority in the Roman Catholic Church, affirms that you can. The safe way between Anthropomorphism and Agnosticism is found, this teaching says, by the principle of Analogy, and it is claimed as a signal merit of this theory that it supplies a path between the two pitfalls just named which otherwise it would be impossible to find. It is to be noted that the theory of Analogy is carefully distinguished from the theory of Symbolism. They may look very much alike, but the theory of Symbolism is a deadly error and the theory of Analogy is wholesome doctrine. The theory of Symbolism is said to be erroneous because it is really only Agnosticism in disguise. The terms by which God is represented— wise, loving, just—are adopted, according to the symbolic view, we are told, simply to satisfy certain human cravings, as useful fictions, helping to produce desirable modes of conduct or sentiment. But there is nothing in the Reality, on this view, apart from human fancy, to correspond with them. Some people regard it as quite legitimate to satisfy human cravings in this way, and since there is nothing in the great Unknown Reality to which these symbols correspond, any symbol which satisfies human craving, or produces desirable conduct, serves the purpose, and the Symbolist theory can thus extend a general blessing to all contradictory varieties which human religion shows according to differences of time or race. This at least is how the Dominican philosopher, Father Sertillanges, describes what he calls the Symbolist view.

In these lectures we have been using the word 'symbol' in a larger sense. Who exactly would be Symbolists such as Father Sertillanges describes I am not sure, but certainly the view of people in France like Dr. Couchoud, who, while he disbelieves that Jesus ever existed, has a tender admiration for Christianity, would seem to correspond closely with the description just given.

There was a time [Dr. Couchoud writes] when, in the presence of the sacred texts, Rationalist criticism thought it the proper thing to adopt a tone of supercilious mockery. This tone concealed a secret fear. We to-day no longer have this fear, which is really itself a superstition. We know that man invents religion out of his own deeper self and draws forth God from his own inner substance. The sacred texts proceed from man: that is what makes them venerable and precious. . . . Jesus is a composite being. It is just such beings which are properly called gods. How many gods has humanity created all over the globe, and throughout the centuries for companionship on its hard journey! . . . Jesus is perhaps the highest god who has ever issued from the thought of man. How many theologians, poets, artists have collaborated to construct that figure! Down from the time when the first circles of Messianic believers gazed at the sky, frantically calling him to come, he has lived in the hearts of the faithful by a continuous creation which even to-day is far from being exhausted.[1]

If Symbolism means this we can well understand that no form of Catholic theology can have much good to say of it.[2]

---

[1] *Le Problème de Jésus*, 1932, pp. 77 and 138.

[2] While, however, it seems the regular thing in Catholic schools to insist that the doctrine of Analogy is something quite different from Symbolism, there does not appear to be agreement on the question of what Symbolism means. We have just seen what Father Sertillanges understands by that term. But another Dominican teacher, Professor in the University of Louvain, Father de Munnynck, according to an article he contributed to the *Revue Néo-Scholastique* in 1923, understands something quite different. He applies the term Symbolism to the theory that earthly appearances generally are symbols of things belonging to a higher unseen world which they do really resemble. He refers to the literature commonly called "Symbolist" which proceeds on the belief in a mysterious concordance between visible things and invisible—incense smoke rising in the air has a real resemblance of a kind to prayer, and so on. Professor de Munnynck does not at all condemn Symbolism in this sense: he thinks it may be useful within limits, though too much a matter of subjective fancy. But the chief fault he finds with it is the opposite fault to that which Father Sertillanges found with what *he* calls Symbolism. The fault of that

When Roman theologians expound the theory of Analogy, two terms of the Aristotelian logic come a great deal into the discussion. Are such attributes as 'being,' 'wisdom,' 'goodness' properly ascribed both to God and man, it is asked, *univoce* or *aequivoce*. One must explain what these terms mean. When one word is used of two different things *univoce* the word has the same meaning in each case: *animality*, for instance, is used *univoce* both of a man and a dog: although in many respects a man and a dog differ, in respect of their possessing certain physical characteristics which belong to all animals, as such, they are similar: 'animality' in the two cases means the same thing. When a word is used *aequivoce* of two things, it means in each case something different: the word 'bull' for instance may mean a particular kind of animal or the centre of a target. Supposing then you speak of 'being' or 'wisdom' in regard to God and in regard to a man *univoce* you mean that God exists in the same sense as man exists, or that God is wise in the same sense in which a man is wise, though of course in an infinitely greater degree. On the other hand, if you say that God is wise and a man is wise *aequivoce*, you mean something totally different by 'wisdom' in the case of God and in the case of a man. Now the Roman doctrine is that you cannot properly call God 'wise' either purely *univoce* or purely *aequivoce*: the theory of Analogy steers in a wonderful way in between. If you were to call God wise *univoce*, that is, in the same sense in which a man is wise, you would fall into the pit of anthropomorphism: if you were to call God wise *aequivoce*, that is to say, if by wisdom in the case of God you mean an unknown something not parallel in any

was that there was believed to be no unseen Reality with which the symbols corresponded, and that Symbolism was therefore veiled Agnosticism. The fault which Professor Munnynck finds with his kind of Symbolism is that it is too naïvely realist in believing a resemblance to exist between the visible symbol and the unseen Reality.

313

respect with what is ordinarily understood by 'wisdom,' you fall into the pit of agnosticism. There is a real resemblance between God and man, the theory goes on to assert: but it is a resemblance of "proportionality." You cannot say what "wisdom" means in the case of God, but you can say that there is something which is to God what wisdom, when a man has it, is to the being of a man, that there is something which is to God what being or existence is to a man, something which is to God what goodness is to a man; and so on. Yet since God is perfectly simple, He can have no real plurality of attributes. His "wisdom" is therefore identical with His "goodness" and both are identical with His "being." There is nothing but the one Reality, God. You can call that Reality at one time wisdom, and at another time justice, and at another time love, but that at which all those different words are thrown out is One inconceivable Something without distinctions.

The words are not used wholly *aequivoce*: they point to something which is in God, as the logical terms express it, *formally*, not only *virtually*. Here again we must explain. There was a theory, said to be that of the Jewish philosopher Maimonides, which held that God could be said to have goodness only *virtually*; that meant that He was the cause of goodness in others but was not really "good" Himself: all goodness in created beings could be traced to Him as its source: in that sense you could call Him good, but you could not properly ascribe goodness to Him as something belonging to His own nature. When St. Thomas, on the other hand, maintained that goodness was in God *formally*, this meant that it did belong to God Himself, that it was involved in His own nature. This goodness was not a quality different from His being or His justice: only somehow there was a real resemblance between what God's being is to Himself, what God is to

314

God, and what a man's goodness is to a man, or a man's justice to a man, or a man's wisdom to a man. Because of this real resemblance in "proportionality" you can hold that goodness, justice and wisdom, whatever the words may mean in this case, are in God not only virtually, but also formally.

I cannot profess myself able to make sense of this explanation.[1] But there are two things to be noted. One is that Catholic theologians themselves have not found it easy to understand. The great doctor of the generation following St. Thomas, Duns Scotus, definitely rejected some of the assertions with which it is built up. He maintained that we did ascribe such attributes as "wisdom" or "goodness" or "justice" to God *univoce*. That is to say, there was no sense in saying that God was *wise* or *good*, unless you meant by wisdom and goodness what you meant when you said a man was *wise* or *good*. God's wisdom and goodness were infinitely greater than man's in degree but by "wisdom" you meant one definite quality belonging in different degrees to God and man, and so with "goodness" and so with "justice." But if this is so, there must be in God Himself a distinction between "goodness" and "wisdom" and "justice": God was both "good" and "just," but His "goodness" could not be precisely the same thing as His "justice." It would be absurd, Scotus thought, to say: "God punishes because He is merciful and forgives because He is just." From the point of view of the Thomist School, Duns Scotus thus slid into the pit of anthropomorphism, while from the point of view of the Scotist School the Thomists tried to escape from anthropomorphism by using words without meaning.

But even in the Thomist school itself, the school

---

[1] Nor apparently can the French thinker who has now found his home in the Roman communion, Gabriel Marcel. See his second *Journal Metaphysique*.

recommended still to-day on Papal authority to the faithful, there is disagreement how the very delicate lines of this difficult theory of Analogy are to be drawn. This is made plain in the recent book of the Dominican, Father Garrigou-Lagrange, who occupies a chair of theology in the Academy of St. Thomas in Rome: "*Dieu, son existence et sa nature.*" He is very loth, he says, to expose the controversies between Roman Catholic theologians, when Catholics have enough to do to-day with their common adversaries. But there the disagreements are, and to those outside the Roman communion it may even serve to recommend a study of the theory of Analogy, that more than one way of understanding it is allowed in the Roman Catholic theological schools themselves. Father Garrigou-Lagrange does not find the statement of the theory of Analogy by his fellow-Dominican, Father Sertillanges, Professor of Philosophy in the Catholic Institute of Paris, satisfactory. Sertillanges seems to him to lurch dangerously over the pit of agnosticism (p. 508 note). Obviously it is in great part a matter of emphasis. If you lay as great stress as Sertillanges does on the essential difference between any attribute ascribed to God and that which the same word connotes when applied to man, you do go perilously near implying that we cannot really know anything about God at all.

In his volume *Les grandes thèses de la philosophie thomiste*, Sertillanges, after setting forth the theory of Analogy as he understands it, writes:

Quite a negative position, it will be seen, so far as any real definition goes. You learn nothing at all about God, considered in Himself. You refuse to refuse anything to the Prime Cause: you affirm at the same time that everything which implies perfection in His work must be allowed Him. You recite the names. But in doing so you are aware that the recital is faulty. You know quite well that the derivative affirmation adds nothing to the original negation. This exigence is nothing but the refusal in a positive form: the truth remains: "We know not what God is: we know only what He is not, and what relation everything else bears to Him." In regard to God, the question "Does He exist?" marks the ultimate point beyond which one cannot go (p. 73).

In view of such utterances of an official exponent of Roman teaching, rehearsing what is claimed to have been current doctrine in the schools for at least six hundred years, it is curious to find people to-day supposing that it is only very modern, relatively enlightened, thinkers in the Christian Church who are at last beginning to shed the traditional anthropomorphism.[1] One would think that such a view as that of Sertillanges goes as far as it is possible to go away from the anthropomorphic pitfall without tumbling over into the agnostic pitfall on the other side. And in the judgment of Father Garrigou-Lagrange, as we have just seen, Sertillanges does go, with one foot at any rate, over the edge.

It would be quite a mistake to suppose that these discussions are of interest only to Roman Catholic theologians. The problem with which they grapple is a problem which must confront any modern thinker who believes in any God at all. For no one supposes that we can imagine, even faintly, what it is like to be God. We should all agree that all human terms used of God— wisdom, love, justice—are to some extent figurative modes by which we think of a Reality we cannot, except in the poorest and most fragmentary way, conceive. Well, then, just how much truth have these terms, drawn from the spirit of man, when applied to that Reality?

[1] See, for instance, Julian Huxley, *What I Dare to Think*, pp. 228, 229.

MANSEL AND PRAGMATISM

In our last lecture we were considering the way attempted in the philosophy of St. Thomas to secure, on the one side, a recognition that any ideas of God we might have could *not* show what God in Himself is, and, on the other side, a recognition that the ideas conveyed in the Christian tradition had a true correspondence with the transcendent Reality. To-day we shall begin by considering how a theologian of the Anglican Communion, a hundred years ago, Dean Mansel in his Bampton Lectures, famous in their day, attacked the same problem and gave an answer parallel in some respects to that of St. Thomas, as interpreted by Father Sertillanges to-day. If you took the representations of God in Christian theology, Mansel also said, to be literally true, when used of the Infinite, and argued on that supposition you were soon landed in absurdities. We could have no imagination at all of the Divine Reality. So far a Thomist and Dean Mansel would agree. But Dean Mansel seems to go further in speculative agnosticism. He is indeed presented to us as one of the actual progenitors of the Spencerian Agnosticism in the nineteenth century.

When one compares Thomism with Mansel's view, one sees that Thomism is not really as agnostic as its phrase: "You cannot know what God is; you can only know what He is not" might seem to suggest. It might, of course, be questioned whether it is really possible to separate knowledge of what a thing is not from knowledge of what it is. You can hardly deny with any assurance that something is compatible with the Divine Nature unless you have some positive notion, though it may be only a dim one, of what the Divine Nature is. And we see that Thomism, for all its repeated declarations that nothing positive can be known of God, does make affirmations which imply a claim to know something of what God is. Its theory of Analogy is built up, we have seen, on the affirmations that God is perfectly simple in such a way that there can be in Him no plurality of attributes, and that His being, His wisdom and His justice are all only different names for the self-same one inconceivable Reality. It makes these affirmations, partly as conclusions to which you are driven by the laws of thought if the conception of God is to correspond with the demand that you think of God as wholly perfect, as that than which nothing greater can be conceived, partly on the authority of the Neo-Platonic tradition. But the laws of thought, according to a thinker of the calibre of Duns Scotus, do not carry you to the Thomist conclusion about the Divine simplicity, and the person through whom the Neo-Platonic tradition mainly became authoritative in the Church was an impostor. Those fundamental affirmations therefore about the Divine Nature are not so self-evident as to be accepted by everybody without question.

Dean Mansel would presumably have denied that you had any right to declare that God was perfectly simple in the Thomist sense, or that God's wisdom was the same thing as His justice. He would have said that in making such assertions about God you were going far outside the limits prescribed by God for the human mind. He would have ranged himself neither with Thomas nor with

319

Scotus, but have said that both were talking about something of which they could know nothing.

As a matter of fact, so far as I can see, while it is obvious that God, if He is what we mean by God, must be perfectly simple in the sense of being wholly self-explanatory, it is an altogether adventurous affirmation that He must be simple in the sense of excluding a plurality of attributes. It is true that if there were anything in God whose presence needed something outside God to explain it, God would not be ultimate, and would therefore not be God. But simplicity in this sense does not exclude a plurality of attributes. We may say in the case of a triangle that nothing is needed beyond the nature of the triangle itself to explain its three inner angles being equal to two right angles. As soon as you see that this is necessarily involved in triangularity, you cannot ask how it comes about that the inner angles happen to be equal to two right angles. A triangle in regard to its possession of this attribute is self-explanatory, in that sense simple, pellucid. But if it is an equilateral triangle it has another attribute, namely, that any one of its inner angles is equal to either of the other two, and for this attribute too no explanation is required outside the triangle itself. We can see that, granted the triangle is equilateral, the equality of its inner angles is as necessary as that twice three are six. The equilateral triangle is thus perfectly self-explanatory in regard to either of these attributes. But the two attributes remain two different attributes: the equality of each of the three angles with either of the other two is not the same thing as their being all together equal to two right angles. If anyone could know all that God is—which, of course, no one can, except God Himself—there would appear nothing in God which was not necessarily involved in His Deity; nothing about which "Why?" could possibly be asked. But I do not see that it follows from this that there is no difference between His wisdom and His goodness.

An argument sometimes brought forward to prove that His attributes must all be identical, is that each of them is conceived as infinite: but if there were a difference between them there would be a dividing line, a limit, which marked off one attribute from another, and they would not in that case be infinite. It seems to me that the term infinite in such an argument is improperly used. It is used as if it meant "everything that exists." Of course, if it meant this, then infinite wisdom, let us say, would mean that nothing at all existed, whether as a substance or as an attribute, except wisdom, nothing from which it could be distinguished by any difference. But in the proper sense of infinite, two or more infinites can exist together without their being identical. If space is infinite and time is infinite it does not follow that space and time are the same thing. If the whole of infinite space were filled with a substance which was both luminous and hot, one could say that light was infinite and that heat was infinite; but they would not therefore be the same thing. Where two infinites differ in kind they do not trench upon each other or put any limit to each other's extension. If we speak of their difference from each other by a spatial figure borrowed from the case of two co-terminous areas marked off from each other by a dividing line, which limits their extension, that is only a metaphor, which misleads, if applied to specific difference. I do not put these considerations forward to prove that Duns Scotus was right in holding that there was a difference between God's wisdom and God's justice: my purport is only to show that the contrary assertion, that there is no difference, does not follow by a necessity from belief in God as infinite and perfect and self-explanatory. Whether wisdom, in whatever degree of eminence, remains always something different from goodness and justice and will, or whether all these terms are only human modes of diversely presenting the inconceivable undifferentiated unity of the Divine being are questions about the life of God which, Dean Mansel would say, it is absurd for men to ask. Similarly, in regard to the assertion which had become a commonplace of Platonizing Christian theology, from Augustine onwards, that in the existence of God there is no distinction of past, present, and future, Mansel said that we had no means of ascertaining whether the assertion was true or false (p. 57).

When the medieval Scholastics made these affirmations, it was at a time when men had a much greater confidence of possessing exact knowledge about the supersensible world. St. Thomas, building on the assertions of the false Dionysius, carefully discussed the psychology of angels, the mode in which they cognized. It belonged to the same confidence that men were ready to make assertions about the attributes of God. Just, however, because Mansel is agnostic where St. Thomas affirms, he is much less shy than Thomas is of the traditional anthropomorphic imagery. He would have us adjust our thought and our will to the anthropomorphic representation of God in the Hebrew and Christian scriptures as the best mode possible for men to think about God. He speaks of "that morbid horror of what they are pleased to call Anthropomorphism, which poisons the speculations of so many modern philosophers" (p. 12). Of course, he said, it was all human imagery and the inconceivable Reality was immensely different. But it was a mistake to suppose that you could get to anything more literally true than the anthropomorphic imagery. People who tried to do so, who put out what seemed more philosophical statements about God, statements such as those of St. Thomas or Duns Scotus or any modern Rationalist philosopher, were under

322

an illusion. They did not realize that these would-be philosophical notions were just as much marked by the essential limitations of the human mind as the anthropomorphic imagery. "Downright idolatry is better than this *rational* worship of a fragment of humanity" (p. 13). The high-brow philosophical notions were more likely to impose upon people, by pretending to yield statements literally true, than the imagery which was quite obviously a figurative representation. "We dishonour God far more by identifying Him with the feeble and negative impotence of thought which we are pleased to style the Infinite than by remaining content with those limits which He for His own good purposes has imposed upon us" (pp. 60, 61). This imagery had, Mansel said, been given us by God Himself in the Scripture as the way in which we, with our little human minds, could best think about Him, and those who took it with child-like simplicity, who prayed to the Father in heaven and tried to be obedient to His will in the old *naïf* way, apprehended the Reality much better than the people who tried to understand God by metaphysical categories.[1]

The clinging to anthropomorphic imagery may thus not be the *naïveté* of the man who has never perceived its philosophical inadequacy, but the result of a scepticism pushed far enough to feel the inadequacy of all philosophical formulas offered as a substitute. We can see how, if Mansel is right, rational argument about God or the presentation of God's action in the documents of religion may be completely fallacious. Not because the Reality is

[1] Since this was written a charming instance of what Mansel protested against has come my way. Dr. Reinhold Niebuhr tells us in his book, *An Interpretation of Christian Ethics* (p. 223), that we ought to love our fellow-man, because God loves him, "in other words . . . from the transcendent unity of essential reality." The ingenuous writer seems to have no suspicion that some of his readers might feel "the transcendent unity of essential reality" to be not quite the same thing as the love of God. For him, it is just an immaterial variation of phrase!

itself irrational; we may believe that if God and the actions of God could be known to finite minds they would exhibit reason in its ultimate perfection, and yet believe that reasonings about God or His actions are fallacious. If all our notions of God are merely images which stand for an inconceivable Reality—counters, as it were, which more or less misrepresent that Reality—our reasonings are no more than the manipulation of such counters and the result we arrive at may be remote from the truth. We may have conducted the process of reasoning with flawless logical consistency all through, but we are operating all the time only with counters, not with the realities themselves.

Mansel's insistence upon the utter inability of man to raise himself by thought to apprehension of God above the figurative mode in which it had pleased God, Mansel believed, to reveal something of Himself to man in the Scriptures reminds one sometimes of the movement in our own day connected with the name of Karl Barth. The Christian doctrine, Mansel says in one place (p. 127), "must be unconditionally received, not as reasonable, nor as unreasonable, but as scriptural." "We have no right to say that we will be Christians as far as it pleases us, and no further; that we will accept or reject, according as our understanding is satisfied or perplexed" (p. 186). He quotes a passage from Lord Bacon as giving his own contention. "Out of the contemplation of nature, or ground of human knowledge, to induce any verity or persuasion concerning the points of faith is in my judgment not safe. For the heathens themselves conclude as much in that excellent and divine fable of the golden chain: That men and gods were not able to draw Jupiter down to the earth; but contrariwise Jupiter was able to draw them up to heaven" (p. 88). One might almost fancy one was listening to a Barthian preacher. The affinity is shown also in the strong dislike of mysticism common to Mansel and the Barthian School. The mystic's claim to apprehend God in an elevation above the ordinary level of human consciousness, to have direct experience of God, is for the Barthians presumptuous impiety. Similarly, Mansel talks about the "diseased ecstasies of mysticism." "We cannot," he says, "be directly conscious of the Absolute or the Infinite, as such" (p. 81).

On the other hand, Mansel felt much more than Karl Barth apparently feels the need for a man's having some reason why he should believe the statements of Scripture to be inspired by God. Barth seems to regard any *apologia* for, any defence of, Christian faith, as a mistake, a presumption of the human mind undertaking to justify at its own tribunal God's sovereign word. You hear God speaking to you through the written Scriptures or by some other vehicle of His word, and there is an end of it. Or even to admit so much human share in the matter as is implied in hearing seems sometimes to Barth to allow too much to man. He insists in one place that in man's recognition of God's word, God must be thought of not only as the speaker, but as the hearer, too[1]—whatever in Barth's rhetorical mode of utterance that may mean.

Here Mansel is quite different. When once you are convinced that the Scriptures are the inspired word of God, then indeed, according to Mansel, you must accept the anthropomorphic representation of God in these Scriptures as the best way in which the incomprehensible Reality could be expressed to the human mind, and you must not presume to adjust to any human philosophical

---

[1] "Durch den Geist wird die Offenbarung von dem Zeugen und ihr Zeugnis von uns as solches vernommen. Durch den Geist, ich wiederhole: durch Gott selber. Der in dieser Sache allein Zuständige spricht *und* hört." *Das Schriftprinzip*, p. 241; *Zwischen d. Zeiten*, III Jahrgang, Heft 3 (quoted by H. W. Schmidt, *Zeit und Ewigkeit*, 1927, p. 36: I have not myself seen the writing of Barth referred to).

theory those things in the representation which may seem to you absurd: the human intellect must humble itself to accept God's mode of expressing the truth as the proper mode for man; but before making this submission to the statements of Scripture, Mansel thought it right that the human mind should examine the grounds for believing these statements to be inspired. In regard to this we find him taking a position which is likely to appear strangely old-fashioned as we look back across the intervening century. Mansel laid great stress on the argument from miracles and from the literal fulfilment of Old Testament prophecies. Already in his day he heard people round him beginning to say that "the doctrine must prove the miracles, and not the miracles the doctrine" (p. 164). Mansel thought this a deplorable aberration. "The crying evil of the present day in religious controversy," he says, "is the neglect or contempt of the *external* evidences of Christianity" (p. 165).

But what gives interest to his defence of his Christian belief is that he put forward other grounds as well, grounds which anticipate strikingly modes of thought which belong to our own time. In some passages he puts forward what sounds curiously like some modern utterances of a Pragmatic philosophy. "Action, and not knowledge," he says, "is man's destiny and duty in this life; and his highest principles, both in philosophy and in religion, have reference to this end" (p. 105). The anthropomorphic representations of the Bible are not to be judged apparently by the extent to which they satisfy metaphysical speculation, but by the degree in which the conduct of those who act in accordance with them is superior to other kinds of conduct. They are not meant to satisfy man's desire to understand the universe intellectually but to supply rules for practice. In Mansel's own way of expressing it, "the highest principles of

326

thought and action to which we can attain are *regulative*, not *speculative*—they do not serve to satisfy the reason, but to guide the conduct: they do not tell us what things are in themselves, but how we must conduct ourselves in relation to them" (p. 100). The distinction between the "speculative" and the "regulative" Mansel of course derived from Kant. For instance, God is sometimes represented as governing the universe by General Law, sometimes as specially intervening by miracles which break the uniformity. "If the condition of Time," Mansel writes, "is inseparable from all human conceptions of Divine Nature, what advantage do we gain, even in philosophy, by substituting the supposition of immutable order in time for that of special interposition in time? Both of these representations are doubtless *speculatively* imperfect; both depict the Infinite God under finite symbols. But for the *regulative* purposes of human conduct in this life, each is equally necessary: and who may dare, from the depths of his own ignorance, to say that each may not have its prototype in the ineffable Being of God?" (p. 132).

The last sentence shows how in one respect Mansel's theory is less agnostic than that of St. Thomas (at any rate as understood by Sertillanges). As we saw, Mansel was more agnostic than St. Thomas in so far as St. Thomas was prepared to assert that God's wisdom, whatever it is, is identical with His being, and that God's being has a relation to Him analogous to that which a man's wisdom has to the man. Mansel would not here admit that we had ground for the assertions. Yet Mansel was the less agnostic of the two in so far as, while St. Thomas denied any resemblance except that of "proportion" between God's attributes and the things which were called by the same names in man—wisdom, love, justice, will—Mansel was prepared to believe that there *was* a resemblance, though you could not know in what way. What reality was pointed to, for instance, by such a phrase as the love of God, was utterly unimaginable: only you might believe that there was in the ineffable Being of God something which was the prototype of what we know as love in man.

If the latter element in Mansel's view is emphasized, I would submit that it does offer us a better way between the two pitfalls of anthropomorphism and agnosticism than the Scholastic theory of Analogy. It seems to me that the strongest position which any Theism can hold to-day is a position for which Mansel in such utterances has indicated the general lines. That all our conceptions of God are absurdly inadequate to the Reality, all our imaginative representations are figures only by which we think of the utterly unimaginable, would be accepted by any Theist as a commonplace. And if this is so, Mansel is reasonable in contending that anthropomorphic imagery may give us the essence of the Reality better than an abstract metaphysical formula which will be just as much beset by the limitations of the human mind and may deceive by its pretence to superior knowledge. But if this meant that we were to take every anthropomorphic representation of God offered us in every religious tradition indiscriminately as giving the best approximation to the truth possible for human minds, or as having the highest regulative value for practice, we should be delivered over to a welter of contradictory superstitions.

Mansel would seem to have been right in teaching that we must have some ground, of which we can give a rational statement, for accepting one particular set of anthropomorphic representations and rejecting another set. Few people to-day would be able indeed to follow Mansel in regard to his criterion determining which anthropomorphic imagery is to be taken as regulative, so far as his criterion is based on the belief that the Hebrew and Christian scriptures are documents, every statement of which is dictated by God, documents whose infallible inspiration is proved by miracles performed in Old Testament and New Testament times and by the literal fulfilment of a number of detailed Old Testament predictions. This belief has ceased for most educated people to-day to be a possible one, though there may be a sense (which we cannot discuss now) in which the writings of the Old and New Testament must rightly continue to have a peculiar value as a norm for Christians of all later ages.

But Mansel did not, as we saw, confine himself to the argument from miracles and fulfilled prophecy, as grounds for accepting the statements of Scripture. He also indicated a ground like the Pragmatic one: conduct regulated by these beliefs had a special quality. With regard to belief in God's existence, since that obviously must have a ground other than statements of Scripture, Mansel held that this was a necessary deliverance of "the religious sentiment" or "the religious consciousness": "we are compelled by this," he says, "to believe that a personal God exists" (p. 87). Since there are many people who do not believe that a personal God exists, Mansel cannot have meant that a man could no more help believing in a personal God than he could help believing in his own existence: he must have meant that, for himself and many other people, belief in God's existence was a conviction which something in themselves made it impossible for them to question, and that everyone ought to have the same feeling, even if they did not have it now.

But while the religious consciousness, Mansel held, necessitated for himself and others belief in God's existence, the religious consciousness told you nothing of God's nature. You could know anything about that solely through the disclosure of Himself God was pleased to make in the anthropomorphic imagery of Scripture. This shows a parallel, though no doubt not quite a precise one, to the doctrine of the Roman Catholic schools, that reason by itself can yield proof of God's existence, but that no one, except by revelation, could have had any notion of the Trinity. But so far as Mansel assigned a Pragmatic ground for accepting the scriptures in their entirety as a revelation, that ground is one which may still be held a valid ground to-day, not indeed for regarding every statement in the Christian scriptures as infallible, but for believing that the general body of ideas belonging to some particular religious tradition—it may be the Christian one or some special stream of the Christian tradition, Catholic or Protestant—gives in anthropomorphic imagery the best conception of the Divine Reality which it is possible for men to have. Such a belief would, of course, rest upon what seems to those holding the belief to be the direct perception of a certain quality in a particular kind of life, a quality which commands their reverence or admiration and implies an obligation for them to attempt to follow it.

And in saying that any belief is recommended on a Pragmatic ground we may think, not only of the conduct which flows from it, but of the degree to which it satisfies certain exigences of the human spirit, which, we hold, ought to be satisfied, if the universe is reasonable. Mansel would seem to have held that Christian beliefs did this, and that their doing so was a reason for accepting them. It is noteworthy that he would not include among the exigences which ought to be satisfied that of the speculative intellect for knowledge of God, other than in the scriptural symbols. That craving was a vain desire on man's part to reach beyond the ordained limits of life on earth. But he thought apparently that it was right to ground acceptance of the Christian revelation on the extent to which it met man's other spiritual needs. The contents of the revelation are not to be "judged by their conformity to the supposed nature and purposes of God," but "by their adaption to the actual circumstances and wants of men" (p. 163).

So far as the acceptance of any belief is grounded on its practical consequences, whether the character of the conduct flowing from it or its effect upon temper and feeling, the ground is Pragmatic. But if you have mere Pragmatism, and nothing more, it is enough that the consequences of a belief are desirable and you are indifferent to the question whether the belief is true. An agnostic might hold the philosophy labelled "*Als Ob*," after the writings of Vaihinger, in regard to any body of religious belief, might consider, that is, that it was desirable that men should act as if it were true. We have considered this theory elsewhere. If Mansel had only meant that to accept the anthropological imagery of Scripture as if it were true issued in desirable conduct or gave people desirable feelings, and that it had no other kind of truth, his position would have been fundamentally agnostic. But he plainly did hold that, apart from its effects in conduct and feeling, the imagery had a truth in regard to the real Being of God. No man indeed could discern what in the imagery resembled the reality and what was only symbolic vesture. "It is going beyond the limits of a just reserve in speaking of divine mysteries, to assume that the one is merely the symbol, and the other the interpretation" (p. 181). You have to take the representation in its entirety as offered. But while you are aware that a great deal in it could not possibly correspond with the Reality, you may believe that the essential thing in it does in some way, we cannot tell how, resemble the Reality. Not only is there "a religious influence to be imparted to us by the thought of God's Anger, no less

331

than by that of His punishments; by the thought of His Love, no less than by that of His benefits"—that would not take us beyond "*Als Ob*"—but we may believe that both conceptions, "inadequate and human as they are, yet dimly indicate some corresponding reality in the Divine Nature" (p. 181). "We may believe, and ought to believe, that intellectually, as well as morally, our present life is a state of discipline and preparation for another; and that the conceptions which we are compelled to adopt, as the guides of our thoughts and actions now, may indeed, in the sight of a higher Intelligence, be but partial truth, but cannot be total falsehood" (p. 103).

Mansel's philosophy then comes to this: When we think of God as just or as loving, we attribute to Him something which we know as a manifestation of the spirit of man. But whereas we have an imaginative realization of what love means when we think of it in our human friend, we can have no such imaginative realization of what love is in the life of God. Yet we must believe that to think of God as loving is not only the best way of making our conduct and temper what they ought to be, but is also the nearest approximation to the *truth* of which the human mind is capable, a much nearer approximation than to think of God, for instance, as the Infinite or the Absolute. If we *could* know the life of God we should see in it something which human love really resembled, so that to call it love would be the best way of saying what it is in human language. Thus conduct which flows from the belief that God is love is not only the best kind of conduct, judged by the scale of human ethical values, but is also the kind of conduct which corresponds best with Reality. If you are unable to imagine what the Reality is, you can know at any rate that it is of such a character that the right reaction to it in conduct and feeling is the

332

reaction which follows upon your thinking of the Ground of the Universe as a loving God.

If this truly describes Mansel's fundamental position, it seems to me one which that of any philosophical Theism must closely resemble. We must perhaps allow that Mansel assigned too little value to the speculative exigence. If the Christian faith is to be recommended on the ground that it meets the spiritual needs of men, there is, I think, no reason to exclude from these needs the desire to have an intellectual understanding of reality, no reason to regard that as a vanity which ought to be suppressed. I should say that while Mansel is right in saying that no intellectual conceptions attainable by man are more than figurative approximations to the Reality, and that therefore an idea of God which commands our allegiance by some immediate perception of its authority or its worth is not to be discarded because we cannot fit it into the system of concepts which represent only our provisional and imperfect intellectual apprehension of the universe, nevertheless the continual attempt to make our intellectual apprehension less imperfect is not a vain effort, but one which has an important part in the spiritual life. A religious apprehension of God may owe little of its positive content to the critical intellect, but unless critical thought has played upon it and searched what weak elements there may be in it, it is not likely to be strong and healthy.

What created a certain odium in regard to Mansel's philosophy of religion, especially among theologians of the Broad Church School such as F. D. Maurice, was Mansel's incorporation in it—an incorporation which may appear to us unnecessary—of the belief that every representation of God in the Hebrew and Christian Scriptures must be taken as dictated by God Himself and that therefore, however incompatible any of them might

333

seem with our standards of moral goodness, we must accept the representation as the best figurative approximation to the truth possible for man, and the best conception for the regulation of our conduct. It was especially Mansel's application of this view to the doctrine of everlasting punishment which excited indignation. If the Bible said that the wicked were to be punished everlastingly after death, we must not presume, Mansel said, to arraign God's justice by our own imperfect human conceptions of what is just. Mansel did not indeed hold, as St. Thomas apparently did, that the word "justice" when used of God meant something different than when that word was used of men, but he did hold that many things which are really just might appear unjust to men. It was not the *connotation* of the term "justice" which differed in the case of God and in the case of man, but the *denotation*; the particular things which God saw to be just did not coincide with the particular things which men supposed to be just.

Nevertheless, when this view was used by Mansel to justify belief in everlasting punishment, it was easy for those to whom the idea of everlasting punishment was abhorrent to understand Mansel as asserting that "justice" actually meant something different in the case of God. It was this which provoked John Stuart Mill to his famous outbreak in his criticism of Mansel's philosophy —that he refused to call God just, if "just" in God's case did not mean what "just" meant in the case of men, and if God sent him to hell for his refusal to misapply the term—"to hell I will go!"[1] But, as I have just urged, Mansel's general philosophy does not stand or fall by the rightness of his belief that the Hebrew and Christian scriptures gave a representation of God every element in which had to be accepted without question, as dictated by

[1] *An Examination of Sir William Hamilton's Philosophy*, Chapter VII.

334

God. The conceptions of God which command our allegiance may seem to us to rest on another ground than simply that they are presented in a particular collection of ancient writings. Yet whatever our conceptions may be, we cannot refuse to admit that they are only more or less figurative representations of an unimaginable Reality, as Mansel insisted, and that we give them our allegiance because they meet the exigences of the human spirit and issue in the mode of action and feeling we perceive to be the best, and that further, because they do this, we believe them to be in their essence true.

There is thus a view of religious belief which, if stated, sounds at first as if it meant very much the same as the Pragmatic view, and which I should wish to put forward as the true view. While our best conceptions of God remain symbols of a Reality we cannot imagine, it is because these conceptions, when acted on, produce a life of a certain quality, as compared with other conceptions of the universe, that the man who believes in God gains assurance that he does right in believing. How does this differ from the Pragmatic view? It differs because in religious faith there is an enduring reference all through to a Reality believed to exist in absolute independence. The worth of the conception does not lie only in its effects in experience, but in the measure of its correspondence with that Reality. As merely symbolic, it is to that extent unlike, but this does not rule out its being in some respects like the Reality. Let us take the conception of God as a loving Father. Obviously such an idea of God is symbolic. But the Theist or Christian does not merely say: "Act as if there were a God who is a loving Father, and you will find certain desirable results follow" (that is Pragmatism): he says: "Act as if there were God who is a loving Father, and you will, in so doing, be making the right response to that which God really is. God is really of such a character that, if any of us could know Him as He is (which we cannot do) and then had to describe in human language to men upon earth what he saw, he would have to say: 'What I see is undescribable, but if you think of God as a loving Father, I cannot put the Reality to you in a better way than that: that is the nearest you can get.' "

I may quote in this connexion the remarks of a French writer, Jean Guitton, in a recent book *Le Temps et l'Eternité chez Plotin et Saint Augustin* (p. 155). He has been pointing out that in the Neo-Platonic idea of the procession of the world from God, after the analogy of the processes of the human intellect, there is a latent anthropomorphism "more subtle and more insidious" than "the seemingly more childish idea which Saint Augustine had of creation."

Now since man cannot anyway [Guitton goes on] escape from the snares of metaphor, is it not well to have recourse to the homelier metaphors (*aux plus grossières*)? Mythical imagery, used by a thinker who can subordinate it to his purpose, has in this respect an advantage. In the first place, it can furnish instruction, telling and explicit, for the common man. Wisely used by the "prophet," it can put people on their guard against dualism, polytheism, the vague pantheism of primitive thought, which have always had unfortunate consequences for conduct. And is there any real danger of its leading the wise man astray? The crying disproportion between the image and the reality it represents warns him that the words are only expedients and makeshifts. Their very poverty helps him to realize that God is beyond every possible conception, every possible image. God's creative causality is by its essence inexpressible. One is always compelled to present it treacherously under an image drawn from that which is in man. Whether we represent it after the analogy of a material manufacture or of a mental process, anthropomorphic we shall always be. And which of these two treacheries is the more dangerous? We shall never surmount the limits by which nature has circumscribed us. But while the mental anthropomorphism in assimilating the Divine mode of working to the measure of the human spirit is liable to lead astray, the material anthropomorphism is its own safeguard against its miserable inadequacy: the inadequacy is too obvious.

An objection to such a way of thinking immediately presents itself. If—it may be said—you are going to be content with any conception of God and the spiritual world, however philosophically absurd, however crudely primitive, so long as it calls forth a kind of emotional and volitional response which you consider desirable, are you not practically giving free course to every gross form of superstition? There is none which cannot be justified on these lines. As a matter of fact, the defence which some pagans made against the criticisms of the early Christians closely resembled the argument just put forward. You may find an example in the little dialogue of Minucius Felix, entitled *Octavius*. The advocate for the old religion, Caecilius, admits in effect that the beliefs it involves may seem philosophically unwarranted, but he takes his stand on the essential limits of the human mind; it cannot hope to understand the universe: the universe must always remain an enigma, for philosophers as much as for common men. How much better then to acquiesce in the old religion with its mass of traditional associations and its value for life! How foolish of these new subversive renegades to try to overthrow it—a religion *"tam vetustam, tam utilem, tam salubrem,"* "so venerable, so useful, so wholesome." Some years ago, when Pragmatism was very much in vogue, and the late Canon J. N. Figgis put forward an eloquent defence of the Christian religion on the lines that its doctrines should be judged, not so much by their satisfactoriness to the intellect, as by the conduct and feeling they promoted, *The Gospel and Human Needs*, I remember hearing that Indians of European education were putting forth on similar lines a defence of the multi-form superstitions of Hinduism against criticism from the Christian side.

All rational argument proceeds upon the primary Laws of Thought, which rule out everything involving a logical

337

contradiction. Nothing can both be and not be at the same time in the same sense. But if we say that a logical contradiction between two factors in our conception of God, does not matter because it is only a contradiction in the symbolical imagery, not in the Reality, what possibility of rational criticism do we leave? Any contradiction which such criticism exposes may be declared to be one of those which do not matter, and we may go on with our conception of God unaffected.

What, I think, such objections bring home to us is that the issue is really thrown upon the positive ground which anyone may have for holding a particular conception of God. It is really that which is decisive. When the believer, for instance, in face of the rational argument which proves that the characteristics of personality, as personality is seen in man, cannot belong to God, retreats into an unimaginable something where criticism cannot follow, that may seem a dishonest shift, in order to go on holding a conception which cannot be defended against criticism. But the question is: Why did the believer ever think of God as personal? What positive ground had he for that conception of God, symbolical let it be? This is what it all turns on. If the ground on which he thought of God as personal was valid, the demonstration that God could not be a person of the same kind as a human individual, left that positive ground still there. His belief in something unimaginable was not an arbitrary expedient to enable him to go on holding, in some sense, a concept which there was no ground for holding; it was the necessary consequence of two different kinds of consideration bearing upon him both together, one, the positive consideration that the Reality must be of a kind to satisfy certain exigences, two, the critical consideration that God could not be personal in the same way in which a man is personal.

338

But we have further to consider that conceptions of God get rejected, not only because something in them is shown by rational criticism to be incompatible with our general beliefs about the universe, but because they are displaced by some other positive conception which meets the spiritual exigence better than the previous one. This was the case with the pagan conception of deity for which Caecilius was spokesman in the Dialogue *Octavius* already referred to. Mere negative criticism in religious history has had comparatively small effect in the displacement of existing conceptions; they have generally passed into extinction because they were superseded by conceptions more religiously satisfying. At the period to which the Dialogue refers it was a case of competition between the pagan idea of deity and the Christian idea. The Christian idea of God prevalent to-day will never be destroyed by merely Rationalist criticism: it will become obsolete only when the world is confronted with a rival idea of God which meets its religious exigences better. Supposing in the days of Caecilius the pagan conception of deity had been the one which met the religious exigence best, the argument of Caecilius, based on a consideration of the limits of the human mind, the argument that because men could not hope to attain an adequate knowledge of the Reality it was best to think of it in the symbols consecrated by the worship of past generations, would have had considerable strength. The trouble was that there was another conception of deity in the field, against which the old pagan conception could not stand.

From all these considerations one can, I think, see how precipitate it would be to go from the true affirmation that all ideas of God we can possibly have are symbolical, that we can have no precise imagination of what God is, to the inference that we can therefore take any idea of God which happens to come to us by tradition or otherwise, as

339

a symbol as good as any other. We see that, even if all ideas of God are symbolical, there is a scope for criticism and purgation. Some factors in men's conceptions of God have had to be discarded altogether as simply misrepresenting the Reality, such as the conception that God has corporeal magnitude; other factors, once taken as precisely true, have had to be recognized as symbols standing for something unimaginable. And to say that a conception has symbolical *truth* does not only mean that it promotes a certain kind of emotion and will; it implies a belief that God, although unimaginable, is really such that a response of that kind is the appropriate response to Him. It means that the symbolic expression is the best possible way the truth could be expressed in terms of human ideas. All this, however, still leaves open the question why we should believe that there *is* any Reality of this character.

RATIONALISM AND MYSTICISM

IN our previous lectures we had before our minds the fact that the ideas associated with the various religions of men are declared to be largely symbols or analogies of unseen Reality. We have seen, further, that the question whether there is truly an independent Reality with which these ideas correspond is one which cannot be put aside as unimportant, either by assigning value to their vague suggestion of meaning apart from intellectual content or by a Pragmatism which is satisfied so long as they promote a certain type of conduct. That the idea of God embodied in the Christian tradition follows by a necessity of thought if you once grant that there is really a Being in whom every moral and aesthetic value apprehended by men is united in one personal life, free from any kind of imperfection or dependence upon any other being, a Being such as is signified by the term God, can hardly be disputed. If you once grant that—but why should you grant it?

It may be questioned whether anyone believes in God because he has been confronted, as a disbeliever, with a rational demonstration of the existence of God, and been changed into a believer by giving his mind to it. The things which determine a man's belief in God, just as the things which determine a man's disbelief in God, are

341

much more complex than that. They include an innumerable number of impressions he has received from his contact with men and things from childhood, which have all worked together in a way impossible to trace, and have left certain convictions in his mind as their total result. So that if any one tries to give an account of the reasons for which he believes in God or does not believe in God, he can do so only very imperfectly, and many things which may have been most important in determining his belief may lie so far back in his mental history that they are outside the range of his present consciousness. That, of course, is one of the reasons why the arguments which a man puts forward for his belief or disbelief may seem so weak to someone else and yet be felt so convincing by the man himself. For the verbal statement of each consideration does not show all it means to the man himself—how it is reinforced in his own mind by a whole mass of particular experiences gathered obscurely in the background, of which he is only partially aware. Does this mean that the application of rational consideration, of rational argument, in this field is wholly vain, that everybody must just hold to the conviction which he finds there in his mind, according as he has chanced in his course through life to "knock up against" one set of things or another set of things—ὅτῳ προσέκυρσεν ἕκαστος, as the old poet Empedocles put it long ago? That would be an excessive view. Although it is true that rational argument or demonstration does not account wholly by itself for anyone's beliefs or disbeliefs, attention to rational argument may certainly modify a man's beliefs to a very large extent.

Reason does not, of course, by itself tell us anything about the actual universe, but is only the demand that the beliefs which we draw from our experience should be logically coherent. Rational argument applied to the existing aggregate of a man's beliefs, applied by himself in reflection, or by others, can thus cause him to modify any part of them only by making it plain that there is a logical contradiction, of which he has not been aware, between one of his beliefs and another. He will then, as a rational being, feel an urgency to modify or reject one or both of these beliefs so that the logical contradiction will no longer trouble him. But in most cases the modification of a man's beliefs is not due merely to a rational criticism of those beliefs he held at a particular moment, but to an extension of his experience, introducing a new belief which is incompatible with some part of his previous aggregate of beliefs, and so sets rational criticism at work.

This, of course, is what has happened in the case of very many people whose aggregate of religious beliefs acquired in childhood has been upset by their coming into contact with the up-to-date results of Natural Science. Rationalism here upsets religion, not simply by showing a logical incoherence in traditional beliefs, but by bringing forward new concrete facts, involving new beliefs which a man has somehow to reconcile with what he believes on other grounds. It is improbable, however, that the effect of rational argument on the beliefs of men generally can be seen by observing the impact of a particular argument on a particular occasion. It is seldom that the fabric of a man's beliefs is shattered in a moment—though it happens sometimes. Mostly rational argument acts upon a man's previous beliefs only in so far as a certain mode of discourse becomes generally current in his social environment: gradually the repeated ideas soak in and beliefs which he once had are dissolved. The result is that to-day, while nobody's beliefs can be regarded as the conclusions of pure rational argument operating on data of general experience recognized as trustworthy, while every man's beliefs are determined in some measure by his individual

343

intellectual and spiritual temper and peculiar acquaintances, his beliefs will also in no small measure have been modified and shaped by rational considerations.

People differ very much from each other in the degree to which they feel an exigence to make their aggregate of beliefs a rational system: some people are content to go mainly by what is commonly called instinct, and, if they find a conviction in themselves, not to bother much how it came to be there. Even a philosopher may in certain cases accept, as his guide, convictions whose validity he cannot prove. But if the philosopher does so, he will, unless he is untrue to the philosophic character, fit these convictions into some logical system of thought, and, if he cannot give a ground for his acceptance of them, he will have at any rate some theory why, in this case, it is reasonable to follow an unproved conviction. He will be aware what he is about, when he does so. The philosopher is a type of the person who cannot rest till he has applied rational criticism to the aggregate of his beliefs and removed, by rejection or modification, any contradiction there may be between one belief and another. Reason, I repeat, by itself tells us nothing, but only reason working on the data of experience. And it is plain that the data upon which what is commonly called "Rationalism" works must be data of *general* experience—facts of the universe which all normal men can recognize apart from their individual peculiarities of temper or experience.

It is conceivable that someone believes in God with good ground on the basis of some experience quite peculiar to himself. But if so, he cannot make such an experience a datum in a rational argument which will be cogent generally. Rationalism means a body of beliefs provable by arguments which are cogent generally, and it can therefore go only upon such data as are verifiable by everybody. The data verifiable by everybody do, as a matter of fact,

344

form a very large part of every individual's experience. Rationalism is thus fully justified in pressing them upon the attention of those who hold any form of religion. If a man says that his belief in God is derived from personal experiences which are not data of common experience, he will have at any rate, if he aspires to be rational, to adjust that belief in God to the results of reason working upon the data of common experience, and he cannot therefore treat the conclusions of the Rationalist as something that does not concern him.

But even if a man's religious beliefs rest in large measure upon personal experiences which Rationalism cannot touch, the need to make his body of beliefs, as a whole, coherent compels him to find some reconciliation between these beliefs and beliefs drawn from the common field. He may, in doing so, have to modify the beliefs which he had at first drawn from his individual experience, discovering that he had to some extent misconstrued the meaning of that experience. In this way Rationalist criticism may constitute a useful check and control upon all religious belief, help to purge it of illusions which had been incidental to the first immature construing of special experiences. And a man, as was pointed out just now, is likely to be less affected by Rationalist criticism as embodied in one particular argument than by Rationalist criticism generally current in his social surroundings, by Rationalism in the air.

Rationalism appears as a poor sort of thing only in so far as it claims to extend to the whole field of reality. It is reason drawing its data from the field of common experience only, and so leaves out of account the data of peculiar personal experience which count for so much, not only in religion, but in all the higher activities of the human spirit, in art and poetry and conduct and the appreciation of life. It is when Rationalism pretends to be co-extensive with life that it deserves epithets such as jejune, arid, dull.

But one has to observe at this point that the contrast which we have been making between data of common experience and data of peculiar personal experience does not properly represent the actual state of things. In between the data which are peculiar to one individual and the data which are common to all normal people, there are the data which belong to the experience of groups or classes of people, but not to the experience of everybody. An instance, not of religious character, would be a musical ear. You cannot call a sense of the meaning of music a datum of universal experience, because there seem to be many people wholly destitute of it, people who know that "God save the King" is being played only when they see other people stand up. Now many of the data most important for religion are of this intermediate kind—the experience, for instance, which is commonly called "mystical." Since one answer to the question: "How do you know that your religious ideas, which you admit to be only symbolical or analogical, correspond with any independent Reality at all?" is the answer of the mystic: "I know because I have apprehended that Reality myself directly," and since there are other people whose faith is built on the testimony of mystics, we must devote a little time to considering this peculiar experience.

And we may observe first that the people capable of the mystical experience in the full sense are a very much smaller group than those who have a musical ear. Even among religious people mystics are only a small minority. They do not belong to any one religion; they were found amongst ancient Neo-Platonists and have appeared amongst Moslems and Hindus, as well as amongst Christians. Nor perhaps is mysticism necessarily connected with any definite religion at all. Some experiences

346

which seem similar have been described apart from any distinctive religious belief. It is, I believe, a great mistake to regard mysticism amongst Christians as Christianity in its highest and purest form. There is a notable absence of any description of a distinctively mystical experience in the documents of Hebrew religion which the Christian Church has always regarded as containing the purest revelation of God before the coming of Jesus; there is an equally notable absence of such descriptions in the documents recording the life and sayings of Jesus himself. Only perhaps in the experience described by St. Paul, when he seemed to be carried up into the third heaven, do we find in the New Testament something of distinctively mystical character. And, although later on there was a rich development of mysticism in Christianity, its origins in the Christian Church were not altogether creditable. The main fountainhead of the Catholic mystical tradition is to be found in the writings of the fifth-century impostor who pretended to be Dionysius the Areopagite, an immediate disciple of St. Paul, and whose teachings were taken over wholesale from the pagan Neo-Platonist Proclus. It seems to me idle to defend the imposture by saying that it accorded with the ethical principles of the time. Professor Dodds in his recent edition of Proclus's *Elements of Theology* calls the writings of the pseudo-Dionysius outright a "fraud," and adds in a footnote: "It is for some reason customary to use a kinder term; but it is quite clear that the deception was deliberate" (p. xxvii). Considering the high place which the Roman Catholic Church has given to its "Mystical Theology," this taint of fraud in its origins is unfortunate.

It is strange to think what an immense influence has been exerted upon Catholic doctrine in two different fields by two bodies of writing which were definite impostures. The Catholic doctrine regarding the temporal rights of

347

the Sovereign Pontiff rested largely for many centuries upon the forged Decretals—a forgery which the Roman Church has now long recognized as such, and repudiated. It is perhaps unfortunate that it has not yet repudiated with equal decision the other imposture, whose influence has been no less in the field of metaphysical theology than that of the forged Decretals was in the field of the Pontiff's temporal claims—the works of the false Dionysius. It is true, of course, that the immense majority of Roman Catholic scholars admit that the writings in question are not really by the first-century Christian by whom they pretend to have been written, but are products of the fifth century. Yet the fraudulent author is still regarded with respect as a Doctor of the Church, and some elements in the Catholic tradition which St. Thomas took over from him, in the ingenuous belief that they were warranted by the authority of an immediate disciple of St. Paul, remain there in the tradition of the Catholic schools undisturbed.

One can sympathize with those few Catholic theologians—Professor Dodds tells us that they exist—who still, even to-day, in the face of overwhelming evidence to the contrary, cling to the belief that the writings in question are genuine writings of the first-century Christian, Dionysius the Areopagite, mentioned in the Acts.

Yet this taint does not prove that the mystical tradition in Christianity is without value. Christian mystics did not depend upon literary suggestion only; they went also upon fresh experiences of their own. Their account of their inner life agrees to a remarkable extent with the utterances of mystics outside Christianity. Not, of course, entirely. So far as Christian mystics combined mysticism with the main stream of Christian life, Christian mysticism has had a distinctive note. And even in regard to

348

mysticism outside Christianity, Rudolf Otto has warned us against talking as if it were all of one pattern.[1]

He distinguishes the two great divisions of mysticism according as the Supreme Reality which the mystic apprehends (or believes that he apprehends) is thought of primarily as the Being whom the mystic finds by sinking to the centre of his own self—the way of *Selbstversenkung*, or the One behind the many phenomena of the world, the way of *Einheitsschau*. Yet, in spite of its varieties Christian or non-Christian, there is something common to all mysticism, something which justifies us in embracing all these varieties under a single name. Probably that general characteristic might be defined by saying that in the mystical experience a man's ordinary consciousness of temporal sequence is suspended and he seems to apprehend by direct contact, or even by identification, some tremendous Reality which is above, or below, or behind, the multiplicity of things or psychical events, a Reality which reduces this multiplicity of things to an unreal appearance. It involves an apprehension which seems knowledge in a supreme degree, even if it is knowledge without any conceptual content.

It seems as if in the mystical experience one might have a vivid sense of knowing, not only without any conceptual content but without the knowledge being attached to any particular object. I remember once hearing a Buddhist monk (he was, as a matter of face, a Scot) describe the experience of ecstasy as it was represented amongst the Buddhists of Ceylon. As the experience was remembered afterwards and described, its characteristic had been one of unparalleled intellectual clarity, a sense of immense knowledge, which yet did not leave behind it knowledge of any particular thing. No doubt this sense of knowledge, of a huge range of meaning apprehended and understood,

[1] *Mysticism East and West* (English translation, 1932), Chapter IV.

may be induced by certain drugs as well as by mental exercises. But, however induced, it seems to be a regular characteristic of experiences called mystical in a special sense. We get it, for instance, in Dante's description of his supreme vision in the last canto of the *Paradiso*. The whole universe, he says, lay clear before him in its system of intricate relations like an open book.[1] A similar experience must lie behind George Fox's description of the moment in his spiritual pilgrimage when he finally passed from his early troubles of mind into the light.

Now was I come up in spirit, through the flaming sword, into the Paradise of God. All things were new, and all the creation gave another smell unto me than before, beyond what words can utter. I knew nothing but pureness, innocency and righteousness, being removed up into the image of God by Christ Jesus; so that I was come up to the state of Adam, which he was in before he fell. The creation was opened to me; and it was shewed me how all things had their names given them, according to their nature and virtue. I was at a stand in my mind, whether I should practise physick for the good of mankind, seeing the nature and the virtue of the creatures were so opened to me by the Lord.[2]

If George Fox's experience was really parallel to the one described by the Buddhist monk and by Dante, it is plain that he misinterpreted it in retrospect. He took the sense of knowing to imply a knowledge of particular things, so that it might be applied in the practice of medicine. One may question whether he had acquired any definite knowledge of the virtues of various plants, and

---

[1] Nel suo profondo vidi che s'interna,
    Legato con amore in un volume,
    Ciò che per l'universo si squaderna—
Sustanzia ed accidenti e lor costume,
    Quasi conflati insieme per tal modo,
    Che ciò ch'io dico è un semplice lume.
La forma universal di questo nodo
    Credo ch'io vidi, perche più di largo,
    Dicendo questo, mi sento ch'io godo.
                              (*Paradiso*, xxxiii. 85–93.)

[2] *Journal* (3rd ed., 1765), p. 16.

yet not question that the tremendous sense of knowledge in general, which made him suppose that he had this particular knowledge, had been an actual experience. It was probably a sense of meaning which was attached to no narrower object than the universe as a whole, so far as George Fox had acquaintance with it.

Of course, from the point of view of someone who is not a mystic, the question may be raised what value is to be attached to such an experience. Is it really the apprehension of any Reality, or is it only a rather abnormal and curious accident in human psychology? Probably it will never be possible for those who are not mystics to answer this question with complete assurance. What seems to make it wise to regard descriptions of mystical experience with some respect, even if we are puzzled by them, is the occurrence of such experience in so many different environments and the points of resemblance which the different descriptions are found independently to present. Supposing the human race as a whole were destitute of a musical ear, and supposing there were only one or two people known who affirmed that when they heard certain combinations of sound they had a peculiar experience of apprehending a transcendent world of beauty, the experience would no doubt be put down as a psychological oddity of no real value, possibly as an insane delusion. To-day the man destitute of musical ear takes the value of music on trust, because he finds the great majority of men all round him affirming that they have an experience of a special kind, in a greater or less degree, when they hear music. The mystical experience is not so common as to make all non-mystics accept it as the veridical sense of something real of which they happen unfortunately to be destitute, but it is vouched for by a sufficient body of testimony to make it rash for non-mystics to deny the possibility of its being an apprehension of Reality in a peculiar way. They may be the more disposed to believe that it is this by the effect it has on the temper and conduct of the genuine mystic. The experience itself is inaccessible to the observation of the non-mystic, but the mode in which temper and conduct are affected by it is something of which the world generally can take knowledge, and the recorded lives of mystics seem to show the effect of the mystical experience in the stimulation and quickening of activities whose spiritual value may be plain to non-mystics.

But if we allow a value, on the one hand, to mystical experience, and yet deny, on the other hand, that it is an essential thing in the Christian life or its highest expression, we must regard its value as more or less analogous to that of a musical gift, only a much rarer endowment and one which fuses more readily with the other elements in religion. If a man has a musical gift, as well as a living religion, music will no doubt enter for him into such close association with his religion that the divine world in which he believes will get its character and meaning in part from the world of beauty opened to him by music, and the feelings aroused in him by music will often owe something to the feelings he has had in the religious apprehension of God. The religion of a musician will have a difference from the religion of man without musical sense. Yet music is not in itself religion or an essential part of religion. Similarly, the mystical experience, for those who have it, will enter into their vital apprehension of God and bring to their religion a richness of a particular kind. The Supreme Reality which a Christian mystic apprehends in his mystical experience will get a special character from Christian beliefs about God, and because these beliefs and that experience will for him run together and present themselves to him as a single unity, the beliefs will in his case have the unshakable certainty of an immediate perception. A challenge by a Rationalist to show how his belief in God is a necessary inference from data of general experience will seem to him merely absurd. He knows.

St. Paul's experience on the road to Damascus is certainly not the only case in which a man's view of the Reality behind phenomena has been suddenly changed by what appeared to be the actual voice of a Divine Person speaking to him. It is possible that a man might have an experience of this kind which made any doubt as to the reality of the Divine Person thenceforward impossible for him: no argument to disprove it could have any effect upon him and every argument to prove it would seem absurdly superfluous. So far as anyone else is impressed by it, it will be not as an argument, but as a testimony. And its force as a testimony will depend upon the impression made upon others by the man's personality in general. It would not be true to say that an experience which we cannot share can have no power to determine our belief; it may have a definite weight with us, if the personality of the man who describes it as an experience of his own commands our respect.

Yet if we came into contact with any living man to-day who assured us that he apprehended God directly, even if his personality and life had at the same time a peculiar quality, while we should be impressed, we should not, I think, feel that we could believe in God on the ground of his experience alone, without some ground in our own apprehension of things. We know, as a matter of fact, that people may have unshakable convictions which others see to be illusions, illusions whose psychological genesis they may be able to trace.

Nor is it only a simple alternative between absolute truth and complete delusion. In most cases where a man tells us that he apprehends something directly, we recognize that he does apprehend something, but it does not follow that he apprehends precisely what he thinks he does. He interprets his actual apprehension by a mass of ideas already in his mind, and the resulting belief may be an amalgam in which, while one constituent is an apprehension of reality, there may also be a large admixture of false imagination. To the man himself it may all seem indistinguishably one, but for others it will be a problem to distinguish the share of truth and the share of illusion in his belief. Thus, if we have not ourselves such a direct apprehension of God that belief in the Supreme Being in whom all conceivable kinds of perfection exist in a supreme degree is for us raised above possibility of question, we can hardly be satisfied by the assurances of any other individuals that they have such an apprehension.

In any case, such experiences are rare and cannot furnish the ground of their belief to the great majority of those who believe in God. Yet in their case too it will probably be true that they believe because of a direct perception of their own. Only it will not be the perception at one intense moment of Some One not themselves there and speaking to them; it will be, I think, not so much the perception of God as the perception of the Divine. It will be not so much in the first instance a perception of existence, as the perception of a peculiar kind of value, belonging to existing things and existing men.

Man recognizes a number of values; the Good, the Beautiful, in all their countless manifestations, command his reverence, his admiration; they have authority over his conduct and, in regard to them, he has a sense of obligation, so that if he acts in such a way as to violate them he is ashamed and condemns himself. They are matters of direct personal perception. If I do not see something as beautiful, no argument can demonstrate to me that it is beautiful. If anyone who thinks that my sense of beauty is defective because I do not recognize beauty where he sees it, all he can tell me to do is to extend my acquaintance with things of that class, in the hope that, in doing so, I shall develop a better faculty of perceiving beauty than I have now. The same thing applies to spiritual values in conduct or temper, *ēthos*. We see in a particular manner of life, life characterized by a particular *ēthos*, a quality which has value of a peculiar kind.

We may agree, I think, that there is such a thing as a typically Christian life—a life to which the lives lived by most Christians approximate only in different degrees, but which we can see eminently exemplified in certain individuals whom we know personally or from records in writing. A typically Christian life is not simply a good life: we might consider that the typical life of an ancient Stoic or of a pious Mohammedan or of a Hindu sage or of a virtuous Confucian were all in their measure good lives, but there would be about each a peculiar note which distinguished it from the others. We all of us probably have an idea, more or less distinct, of what a typically Christian life would be, though our ideas might not altogether coincide. At any rate, the personalities of these individuals in whom the Christian *ēthos* has been exhibited vividly in one or other of its varieties have something which people coming into contact with them can feel as *sui generis*, peculiar, distinctive, even if they cannot precisely describe what it is. A very large number of people throughout the ages have seen in this kind of life a worth which sets it above all other kinds of life. Many people who have not themselves been willing to try to live this life have nevertheless recognized it as the best kind of life to live: they have felt, in regard to the people who really lived it, "Those people are better than I am: if I were what I ought to be I should be like them."

Here again, as in the perception of something as beautiful, there is no possibility of proving value to the man who does not see it. If anybody honestly sees the life of the sensualist as better than the life of the saint, there is no scope for argument. I remember once being present when a writer of Christian devotional books had been asked to meet an eminent man of science who was not a believer in Christianity. The Christian writer opened conversation by an observation on the immense extent of the influence of Jesus throughout nineteen centuries: no one, he said, had had an influence comparable to his. The scientist replied: "I altogether agree with you; but I think it has been a very bad influence." The Christian had nothing to say in reply; indeed, I doubt whether there *was* anything which could be said. If you see any kind of life, any *ēthos*, as having a high degree of value, and someone else tells you that he sees very small value in it, or no value at all, the only thing you can do, as in the case of a disagreement about the beauty of something, is to ask him to acquaint himself with it further, to go on looking at it: you may be able to confront him with exemplifications of that special type, in which the characteristics of the type are seen more vividly, more purely, in the hope that in the end he may see what you see. Thus the best answer which Christians can give to those who say they cannot see value in the Christian life, is to live the life more truly and thoroughly. In the end every man must see or not see its value for himself.

There is a possible objection to this view which might be raised by anyone who holds that a particular kind of life is obligatory. It would be held by an adherent of any of the higher religions that a man who chooses a lower rather than a higher life commits definite sin. Where the superior value of the higher life is recognized and the lower life is nevertheless chosen, where the man, as we

356

say, goes against his own conscience, there is no difficulty in regarding him as a sinner. But the considerations put forward just now seem to indicate that in some cases the value of the Christian type of life or of the life which moralists, who are not Christians, would regard as the higher life, is honestly not recognized, and that some people might follow the lower life genuinely seeing it as the best life. This seems to make it depend on a mere accident of mental constitution, for which a man is not responsible, whether he sees the life of unselfishness and chastity or the life of sensual gratification as the best.

I think the answer to this objection, from the Christian standpoint, would be, that it is outside the competence of any of us to judge the degree of another man's guilt if he chooses the lower life. If we ourselves see the value of the higher life, and believe that it really is the best life for everybody, whether a man sees its value at present or not, then we are under an obligation ourselves to choose it. If anyone else admits that he is going against his conscience in choosing the lower life, he passes judgment on himself. But if anyone apparently sees the lower life as the best, when he follows it, it is for God to judge him, not for us. We may suspect indeed that he is not giving quite a true account of what is within him, that there is a voice in his heart which tells him that he is turning away from good, while he tries not to listen to it. It seems likely that, even if a man honestly does not see the value of the Christian type of life as a whole, there will be certain elements in that type—let us say, love of truth—whose value he does see, and he may well question himself whether, in choosing what, according to Christian standards, is a lower life, he is really trying to conform his life to those elements of value. If not, he will so far be responsible. But it is wisest for us probably to abstain

357

from any attempt to measure his degree of responsibility and guilt, which God alone can know.

This does not mean that anyone believing a particular kind of life to be really best for everybody is to abstain from judging kinds of life which depart from this to be bad for everybody. A view of morals has sometimes been put forward, which denies that there is any standard of conduct valid for everybody, denies, that is to say, any absolute standard. This belief, of course, if logically carried out, means that there is no such thing as right and wrong at all in conduct: the words "right" and "wrong" correspond to nothing real at all. It has been so often demonstrated that any judgment affirming one man's mode of action to be better than another's, any conception of progress or retrogression in morals from one age to another, implies some standard independent of the inclinations of a particular individual or a particular age that we need not go into the argument about that now. If we may at present take it for granted that there is a good and a bad in men's choices of conduct, it follows that anyone choosing a line of conduct because he believes it to be good has every right to declare his belief that it is really good, and that lines of conduct which depart from it are bad. What have to be carefully distinguished are the passing of judgment on modes of action, and the passing of judgment on the persons acting. It is possible to condemn emphatically a kind of conduct as wrong, and to say that a man who follows it is a bad man in the sense of a man who follows an evil course of conduct; what we can never say is how far it is his fault that he is a bad man, what degree of guilt or demerit attaches to his following that course.

But even if it were established beyond question that some kind of life was the best, would it follow that the beliefs on the ground of which particular men have lived that kind of life are necessarily true? We have still not put forward any answer to the question with which our last lecture concluded: Granting that any theory of religious symbols is unsatisfactory which does not take them to represent a Reality existing independently, why should we believe that such a Reality does exist?

Let us first consider what it means to ask for the rational ground of any belief. Obviously you do not ask for a ground for believing that of which you have immediate perception. Everything believed on a rational ground is something beyond the range of your perception, a belief in the unseen, and to that extent, as has been often pointed out, even scientific beliefs about things in the material world not immediately perceived are a matter of faith. You believe in the truth of something you do not see on the basis of what you do see. What is presupposed in your making this leap from perception to belief in the unperceived? What is presupposed is that the world has a regular pattern and that you have discovered enough what that pattern is to know, from bits of the world you perceive, or have perceived, what other bits outside the range of your perception are like. This used to be expressed by saying that all rational inference from the perceived to the unperceived presupposes the "uniformity of nature."

In great tracts of the universe we do not find order but apparently casual variety—the arrangement of stones on a shingly beach: in other tracts of the universe a regular order is at once obvious—in the sequence of day and night. Primitive man must early have come to observe that mind in man was a great agent in imposing order upon aggregates of things which did not otherwise have order: he was thus inclined wherever he found order, regular correspondence, to attribute it to the will of some conscious agent. Sooner or later, of course, man acquiesced in seeing an inanimate process of nature in those tracts

359

of things where regular order was found to be constant. In fact a regularity which meant mere repetition without any apparent adaptation to rational purpose, seemed to show inanimate nature in contradistinction to processes in which the order was one of variable adaptation to conscious purpose. Plato in the *Laws* has to meet the objection of people who felt it difficult to believe that the movements of the heavenly bodies were due to conscious purpose, as Plato believed that they were, just because the movements of the heavenly bodies were so mechanically regular.[1]

But wherever order, correspondence, was found coming in as an exception in a tract of things where man was accustomed to find haphazard disorder, it seemed a proof of mind at work. If on a shingly beach he came upon stones arranged in regular geometrical patterns, he would be certain that the arrangement was not accidental, but due to some human mind. Things like crystals showing geometrical design were only accepted as due to an inanimate natural process because they were common, and so were put into the class of things where nature showed order in design. But if only one crystal had ever been known, it would no doubt have seemed wanton to question its having been shaped by man. Thus, in Paley's stock example, the man who picks up a watch in a lonely place, having never seen a watch before, is certain by the order it exhibits that it is something put together by a rational mind. As we all know, one of the chief traditional proofs of the existence of God is based upon this connexion between orderly correspondence and mind. Just as, whenever man comes upon orderly correspondence in

[1] " 'Tis the common belief that men who busy themselves with such schemes are made infidels by their astronomy and its sister sciences, with their disclosure of a realm where events happen by stringent necessity, not by the purpose of a will bent on the achievement of good." *Laws*, Book XII. 967 (A. E. Taylor's translation).

the sequence and arrangement of things in a tract of the universe in which he is accustomed to find haphazard disorder (or at any rate, not that particular kind of order), he infers that a human mind has been at work, so, in view of the order of the universe as a whole, especially the correspondence of complicated arrangements in the physical world with human needs, ancient Greek philosophers, the Stoics especially, believed that this proved the universe to have been ordered at the outset by the Divine mind. It was argued against the Epicureans that to suppose the order of the universe due to accident was as absurd as to suppose that if you flung a multitude of letters of the alphabet out of a bag upon the ground they could by accident take the arrangement of a poem or a philosophical treatise.

This old argument has continued to be the stock teleological argument giving, it was supposed, a rational ground for believing in God till modern times. Its cogency has been very much weakened by the advances of Science since Darwin, which, it is claimed, have shown that notable correspondences, held to show conscious purpose, could be explained as the outcome of certain natural processes which required no mind to explain them except the multitude of individual animal minds in competition, or even only the unconscious struggle between different forms of vegetable life. But, on the other side, we hear it said that the teleological argument has been modified only in its presentation by modern Science, not destroyed. It remains true that the universe has an orderly pattern and order proves arrangement by mind. Yet there is certainly a difficulty here.

All belief based on rational inference, as we saw just now, means that from a bit of the universe seen the existence or the occurrence, past, present, or future, of something unseen is inferred, because these things go together according to the pattern of the universe, as we have discovered it to be. Our study of the universe, so far as it has gone, has shown us that mind imposes a regular order, according to its purposes, upon things which by themselves would not show a correspondence to those purposes. That is part of the pattern as our experience has taught us to understand it. Supposing in a tract of the universe where, according to the pattern, there is no correspondence in things left to themselves with the ideals of mind or with human purposes, we see something which shows such correspondence, we say: From our knowledge of the pattern we can affirm that here mind has been at work. No rational ground for the belief in the existence of anything unseen could be derived from reason alone, if reason means simply the laws of rational thought, reason apart from the concrete matter of experience.

Reason alone can never tell us whether anything exists. If we ask someone to give us a rational ground for his belief that something unseen exists, all he can do is to lay hold of some concrete bit of reality which we know already by direct experience, or in whose existence we believe already on rational grounds, and show us that if the world has a pattern, as reason affirms, and if our view of the pattern, as at present advised, is correct, then that bit of reality which we see or believe to exist implies the existence of another bit of reality of a particular character which we do not see. The man who finds the watch in the lonely place recognizes that, according to the pattern of the universe as he has come to read it by previous experience, the kind of order exhibited by a watch goes with a constructing mind. This is to say, all rational inference of the existence of anything unseen is inference from one part of the world-pattern to another part of the world-pattern. But when you ask for rational proof that

God exists, or that the world-pattern as a whole is due to Mind, you are asking to be shown the relation of the pattern to something other than itself, something outside it, extending beyond it, prior to it. You can argue from the watch to the human craftsman because both watch and craftsman are parts of the pattern, but you cannot argue from the order found in the pattern as a whole to a constituting Mind, unless you make that Mind itself part of the pattern it is supposed to constitute. If you say: "Order always implies Mind," your assertion is drawn from experience within the pattern. That cannot give you rational ground for an inference from the pattern as a whole to what is outside it. You can say, of course: Supposing the world-pattern as a whole is constituted by an ordering Mind, then the relation between the world and the Reality outside it is analogous to the relations found to obtain within the world-pattern; and since it is reason which tells us "The world has a pattern," it would be a gratification to us, as rational beings, to discover that the principle which holds good for the world extends beyond the world to the relation between the world and the Supreme Reality. That might be a gratification to us as rational beings, but the inference from the order of the world to the supreme ordering Mind can hardly be logically cogent, since it is based on the postulate: "The world has a pattern," which applies in reason only to the world. No cogent rational inference can be made from the world to what is outside it. If this is so, when the Rationalist asks for a rational proof of the existence of God, he is asking for something which in the nature of the case it is impossible to have. A rational proof would draw God into the world and make Him a part of the pattern He is alleged to create.

THE JUSTIFICATION OF BELIEF

In this our final lecture we have to face more directly the question which has been hovering before us all through. What ground have we for believing? How do we know that all these symbolic conceptions, adumbrating various kinds of perfection in a supreme degree, point to any real spiritual self-existent Being? It is so easy to say that all ideas of God are nothing but an illusive personification of human desires. Freud, for instance, has expounded elaborately in his own jargon how all ideas of God as Father are simply false imagination due to a craving which men had got from association and conflict with human fathers. It gave men comfort to believe in a just Father up in the sky and so they imagined a God to believe in. Of course, such theories are nothing new. It has always been an obvious way of explaining the existence of religious belief, for those who regard religious belief as a delusion. Feuerbach expounded a theory similar to Freud's a hundred years ago with greater literary effectiveness than Freud, if without Freud's array of modern anthropological discoveries or suppositions. God was simply the "projection" of human desires—the very word "projection" often used to-day you find in George Eliot's translation of Feuerbach's *Das Wesen des Christentums*.

It would be very nice, of course, if everything which

men wanted to exist did exist, but to allow your desires to shape your beliefs about what actually does exist, instead of keeping yourself strictly to what is proved by rational inquiry, is unworthy of serious thinkers, and is intellectually dishonest. Desire, we are told, ought to be quite ruled out in the search for truth, and if you suspect that you have been secretly moved to a belief by a desire that it should be true you should hold the belief invalid. All that honest inquiry does is to look at facts as they are and draw from them the inferences which reason prescribes. If it is true, as I submitted in my last lecture, that no rational inference from the pattern of the universe to the Ground of the pattern is valid, because all rational inference is confined to the relations of things within the pattern, then to make any statement at all about the Ground of the pattern, why there is a pattern at all and why it is such as it is, is vain. To project into that void the imagination of a Being into whom you crowd every kind of perfection which man values in an eminent degree is weak sentimentalism. That is very much the charge brought against religious belief by those who think it a delusion. And it may seem that it is more difficult for the believer to rebut the charge inasmuch as defence of religious belief must in some form or other take the line of urging that it gives satisfaction to a human exigence. It must take this line unless, of course, it takes the line of asserting an apprehension of God so personal and direct that the question of proof cannot even be raised.

We desire that the universe surrounding us should in some way care for values; that these should not be merely a mode of feeling which happens to have been developed by the accidents of the evolutionary process in a species of creatures crawling about on this planet; that they should represent the essential ground of things behind phenomena; that the course of the universe through time

365

should be such that Spirit, for which values subsist, should be eternal and triumphant, in spite of the apparent perishability of all material things. What is put forward as the rational ground for believing in God is some form of the argument that belief in God satisfies this exigence, this desire. Sometimes the way in which it is put is: If the world has a *meaning*, God the Supreme Spirit must be its origin and ground and goal. This seems to me indisputable, if you take the phrase "has a meaning" in the sense which it here plainly bears. We say that an action or an activity has a meaning when it is rational in the sense that it is directed to the realization of value. Reason sometimes means a proper proportion between effort and the value it is calculated to realize. Supposing a man deaf from birth saw an orchestra for the first time playing and had never had explained to him what music was, all this activity of men blowing through brass tubes and scraping strings of catgut on other strings of catgut would seem energy wholly irrational, a great volume of effort for apparently no purpose at all. For the person who hears the music the "meaning" of the activity is the value of beauty realized by it.

This sense of "reason" is something quite different from the sense in which it means a fundamental belief that the world has a pattern. In the latter sense reason has nothing to do with value except so far as the exigence in the human spirit to find a pattern in the universe makes order in itself a value. It is a satisfaction to the spirit to find order, even if the order is not seen to subserve the realization of any value beyond itself. But reason in the sense of postulating a pattern, order, does not imply any value beyond itself. The pattern is made out simply according to uniformities observed in the manifold of things. A uniformity observed is taken provisionally to be a general part of the pattern, and therefore when any constituent of the uniformity is found, reason infers that the other constituents, although unperceived, are there also. The question whether it is good that the other constituents should be there, whether their being there realizes any value appreciated by man, beauty or pleasure, does not come in at all. It is simply a question of uniformities in the past and the general inference made from them on the basis of the postulate of reason "The world has a pattern." But reason in the other sense has, as we have just seen, essentially to do with value. You cannot with any logical cogency infer that the universe is rational in the latter sense from its being rational in the former sense. You can indeed say that *if* it is rational in the latter sense, which means if the universe is such that, as a whole, it is directed to the realization of value, then it must provide a satisfaction for the exigence of spirit, and Spirit must be that for which the universe exists. This implies that Spirit must always have been there, directing material processes to its own ends, and that Spirit must always be there to the end of time, directing the material processes to whatever ends Spirit may still have in the incalculable future.

If Spirit were to become extinct by the eventual extinction of animal life on this planet, and if the material world still went according to the uniformities which have hitherto constituted its pattern, then, although the world would still be rational in one sense, it would cease to have any possible "meaning," to be rational in the other sense, there would no longer be such a thing as value. These considerations show that to argue: "If the world has a 'meaning,' Spirit must be its origin and ground and goal" is really an argument in a circle; what the argument comes to is: "If the world is such as to realize values which satisfy the exigencies of Spirit, then it must be such as to satisfy the exigencies of Spirit." If the world has a meaning, the Reality behind phenomena must be God. Probably this proposition would not be disputed by many atheists: only they would deny that the world has a meaning.

Or again the argument may be put in the form: A number of exigences are, as a matter of fact, found in the human spirit; there is a desire, which man recognizes to be the best in himself, after goodness and beauty: he recognizes that goodness has a claim upon him which constitutes an obligation: he knows the meaning of "ought" and condemns himself when he does what he ought not. These exigences are there. But in a reasonable world exigences would not arise which had not their proper satisfaction. Thirst implies the existence of water. If all these exigences existed in the spirit of man and there were no Reality at all to which they were directed, the universe would be an irrational universe. Quite so, the atheist may reply, but how do you know that the universe is not, in this sense, an irrational universe?

Or again you may hear it said: Is it thinkable that Spirit exists nowhere in the universe outside this little perishable breed of man? Do the processes going on in immense masses of matter all through stellar space go on for no purpose at all? The advances in discovering the ordered complexity of the material world made by modern Science may serve to strengthen what is almost an irrepressible reaction of the human mind contemplating such a universe, a reaction to which Francis Bacon gave utterance when he declared: "I had rather believe all the fables in the Legend and the Talmud and the Alcoran than that this universal frame is without a mind." It seems absurd because we are accustomed in human activities to see absurdity in a vast expenditure of energy and thought which realizes no value. If this universal frame of things with all its stupendous working realizes no value, or destroys in a brief space of time the values realized for a moment in human life on this planet, then the universe, judged by the principle applied to human activity, would be absurd. True: but what ground have you for denying the possibility that the universe may be absurd if judged by such a principle? In fact any attempt to prove that the universe subserves the purposes of spirit, that it exists for the production of value of any kind inevitably begs the question. You prove that the universe is rational, because if it were irrational it would not meet the demands of reason. This nobody can deny, but it does not take you anywhere. The circularity of all such arguments is concealed by the ambiguity we have already noted in the term "reason."

All belief that the world is rational, in the sense of being directed to realize value, must be an act of faith, the fundamental act of faith in all religion, unprovable by any argument not circular. It is a belief which men adopt or hold to because it gives satisfaction to demands of the spirit. This seems to admit frankly the charge that men have religious beliefs simply because they satisfy certain human desires: you believe something to be true because you want it to be true—and that, we are told, is poor and unworthy. To affirm that something is true which you have no ground for believing to be true, because you like to think it is true, is actually, we are told, immoral.

There is an ambiguity here rather like that which lies at the basis of the hedonistic theory of conduct. According to that theory, all action is said to be done for the sake of pleasure, when it is quite true that all action is done for the sake of satisfaction of some kind—the action of the most heroic self-devotion, done to satisfy a sense of duty —but to equate all satisfaction with pleasure is misleading, because "pleasure" ordinarily means a particular kind of satisfaction only. Action done for the sake of pleasure is not generally regarded as action of the greatest worth or nobility, and by calling all satisfaction "pleasure" you may seem to prove that action of the highest kind is really on a level with action of the lowest kind. Similarly, in this case, by calling all exigences of the spirit "desires" you seem to prove the unworthiness of religious belief, the term "desire" suggesting the craving for a relatively low individual gratification. The desire that the world should be rational in the sense of realizing value is not a desire of the same quality as a man's craving for his private comfort or for the flattering of his vanity. It has to be remembered that even the belief that the world is rational in the sense in which it is presupposed by Science is the satisfaction of an exigence which cannot be proved by an argument not circular.

But it may be said: The belief that the world is rational in the sense of there being a pattern is the necessary presupposition of all successful action in the world; without it men's actions could not be directed at all; but the distinctively religious beliefs, importing that the world is constituted to realize value, and so is spiritual in its basis, are not necessary for action. These are mere luxury beliefs which some men cling to for mental comfort; but men can act perfectly well without them and can direct action successfully to realize various kinds of value in life on this planet. Since they are unproven, men of the finer temper will do without them and confine themselves to that which is verifiable or probable according to the ascertained uniformities of the world-pattern. What those who raise such objections to religious belief fail to see is that no one can really base his action solely on the ascertained uniformities of the world-pattern; for all action some hypothesis regarding the unseen Ground of the world-pattern must be adopted, whether unconsciously and implicitly or consciously and expressly.

Observation of the uniformities in phenomena may give men a provisional theory of the world-pattern as it is; it can give them knowledge of things which are and have been and enable them to forecast certain things likely to come; but it can never tell them what ought to be. Science cannot speak except in the indicative mood: never in the imperative mood. When Science seems to speak in the imperative mood, it is really only saying that *if* you want to realize such and such an end these are the means you must adopt. But it cannot command you to aim at such an end. If you want to be healthy, if you want the species, or any part of it, to survive, these are the things which must be done, but if it is a question whether you ought to sacrifice your health in any cause, or whether it is good that the species, or any part of it, should survive, about that the most extensive knowledge of what simply is, has been, or will be cannot furnish the answer. Action is not only a matter of knowing what existence really is, but of bringing new reality into being, and you cannot *act* except by some decision regarding what ought to be, what is good, what has value. For action it makes a good deal of difference whether you believe that behind the world with its ascertained uniformities there is a spiritual Ground or not, and what you take the character of that spiritual Ground to be.

You cannot, as some agnostics have supposed you can, keep simply to the ground of ascertained facts and make no leap off it into unprovable hypothesis. Supposing we were spectators only of reality, and not also makers of it, it might be possible to remain purely agnostic; but the moment you act, you have to be guided by some judgment of value, you have to take some realizable end as good, as something which ought to be or which satisfies desire. And the question what is good, what ought to be, depends very much on the question: What kind of

371

universe is this, what is the Ground behind the phenomena? Reason, as inferring an unseen part of the world's
design from parts of the design already known, can give
you, as we have seen, no ground for a logically cogent
inference from the world-design as a whole to what is
behind and beyond it. Any hypothesis you adopt about
the Ground of the world is a venture beyond experience,
and yet the unarrestable advance of time pushes you, every
moment of your conscious life, willy-nilly into action of
some kind, and action necessarily presupposes some
hypothesis regarding the Ground of the Universe. You
are not securing yourself against the possibility of mistake
if you decide to act on the hypothesis that there is no
God, that the Ground of the Universe is wholly indifferent
to the values which the spirit of man recognizes. You are
acting just as much on an unproved hypothesis as the
man who adjusts his action to belief that God is. And
your action may turn out to have been defective because
your hypothesis was wrong.

Of course it may be said that, quite apart from any
hypothesis regarding the Ground of the universe or the
spiritual world, if one exists, around man on earth, there
is a large measure of agreement among all men regarding
what things are good, what are worthy ends of action. To
take the proper steps to secure your health, to control
your natural impulses according to some norm of conduct
or other, to do whatever you can to secure for your
neighbour, or for as many of your neighbours as your
circumstances allow, an adequate share in the good things
of life, to give your support to all movements for bringing
about a happier state of the world, to pursue some particular activity which is of value to society, the increase
of scientific knowledge by your specialist researches, the
production of beautiful things in art or literature—all
these kinds of action, it may be said, are recognized as

good by everybody alike, by Christians and Jews and atheists, and the recognition furnishes a sufficient guide for life without dragging in any hypothesis about the Ground of the Universe.

Now it is of course true that the norm of conduct which determines the customs of people living in any society like ours is, for a good part of life, the same for every-body: even heroic actions outside the course of everyday routine may be recognized as good alike by a Christian and an atheist. Either of them might jump into the water at the risk of his own life to save someone from drowning. But it would be a perfunctory view to which the belief in God or in a spiritual world seemed to make no difference to conduct. In the first place, although a large number of actions would be recognized as good by Christians and atheists alike, critical problems of conduct very often arise in regard to which the decision what is good will differ very much according as you believe, or do not believe, in a spiritual Ground to the Universe and according to the idea you have of that Ground. There is no grosser con-fusion of thought than to say, for instance, that it does not make any practical difference whether there is, or is not, a future life, because it is nobler to act rightly without any prospect of satisfaction beyond death than to act rightly with such a prospect. What anyone uttering such a thought fails to see is that the rightness or goodness of an action is not something attached to that particular kind of action altogether apart from its connexion with the subsequent life of the agent, but in many cases essentially depends upon the anticipation to which it is adapted. If I am going on a long journey to-morrow it may be a reasonable action for me to spend a great part of to-day in packing my trunks: you cannot argue from that that it would be a much finer action if I were *not* going on a journey, and nevertheless spent a great part of to-day in packing my trunks. It is not a question of doing the same action, labelled "right" or "good," in the one case with a prospect of happy future consequences and in the other case without; it is that the question, What *is* right action? may depend on the future which is envisaged. As I have just admitted, there are a large number of actions which would be recognized as good whether there is a future life or not; it may be plausible (though I do not think true) in regard to these to say that belief in a future life makes no difference; but there are critical decisions when it actually determines a different course of action.

The difference which belief in a spiritual Ground to the Universe makes in conduct is not merely that in a certain number of cases a different form of action would follow according as you believe or do not believe; it is that even where the same form of action would be prescribed by the Christian norm and by atheist ethics, there would be a difference in the temper and mode of feeling accompanying the action, the inner spiritual background. And our actual value-judgment in regard to actions is determined more by their inner spiritual background than by what they are externally and formally. It must, one would think, act depressingly upon a man's moral energy, if he thinks that all his standards of what is good are simply modes of feeling which happen to have been developed in man, and that the great universe in which he lives is wholly indifferent to them. A man may determine indeed to adjust his own conduct to those values—to justice and honour and lovingkindness and truth and beauty—in the midst of a universe whose processes will sooner or later annihilate them all, make all things, in the eternal night wherein masses of matter will for ever rush through space without purpose, to be as if such values had never been, a man may follow the brief light of his candle during his days on earth by a defiant resolution. Stoical we must not call such an attitude, since for Stoicism it was an essential belief that the values recognized by man were derived from the Divine Wisdom which ruled the whole universe, the Wisdom of which the light in each man was a spark. It is an attitude which may have in it something of self-conscious defiance, the head "bloody but unbow'd" of a well-known poem.

But is it really to follow the nobler hypothesis about the universe? To be loyal to human values, as if they had an absolute claim upon one, while one attributes to the encompassing universe complete indifference to such values, may seem heroic, but, supposing the universe is not indifferent to such values, supposing its Ground is really Spirit whose character the values recognized by the human spirit reflect, will it ultimately seem to have been a fine thing to adopt the drearier hypothesis about the universe simply in order that you might follow goodness in spite of it? If that is a good reason for choosing the drearier hypothesis, why not go one better and choose the hypothesis that the universe is not merely indifferent, but is actually ruled by a malignant will, a will that loves what, according to man's system of values, is evil? To follow goodness then would be still more heroic. Just as now those who believe that God is good explain all the elements of evil in the universe as permitted by God because they subserve some ultimate good, or because a universe in which their occurrence is possible realizes a greater total good than a universe in which such evils were impossible, so you might then explain all the appearances of good in the world as ordained by the governing power to realize a completer evil, the idea of values put into the human spirit simply to delude and lead to a more exquisite misery in the end.

What would make everyone recoil from such an hypothesis as unthinkable? Not, I think, that a view of

375

the world based on it was logically incoherent: I think you might invent one quite as logically coherent as the view that the Ground of the world is perfect goodness, for, after all, no one has succeeded in reconciling the goodness of God with the existence of evil in the world in a way which leaves no logical difficulty. What would make everyone recoil is, I think, partly the remains in men's subconsciousness of a very deep conviction that the world is reasonable in the sense that it *is* such as to promote value, at any rate the feeling that there is something in the nature of things to forbid such a hideous reversal of the order corresponding with value as a malignant Ground to the universe would be, and partly that to adopt a horrible hypothesis arbitrarily, when you are not forced to it by convincing evidence, simply in order to make your heroism shine out more signally on a blacker background, would seem to everyone absurd.

But if you adopt the hypothesis that the world surrounding man is indifferent to values you are in that case too adopting a dreary hypothesis without being forced to it by the evidence. You can no more prove that the world is indifferent to values than you can prove that behind it is a Power which cares for goodness: in the sense of a rational inference from a seen to an unseen part of the universe on the basis of the ascertained pattern, you cannot prove any hypothesis about that which is not a part of the pattern, but the Ground of it. You can only say: Some hypothesis regarding the Ground the necessity of action compels me to adopt: this is the one I choose to live by. If you determine to live by the faith that the Ground of the universe is Spirit, and that the values which man recognizes are the revelation of that Spirit's character, there is likely to be more buoyancy and drive in your fight for goodness and truth and beauty, in the world around you and in yourself, against all the things which militate for wrong and falsehood and ugliness. To feel that the battle for good is ultimately a losing one in an indifferent universe may make your battle, if you persist, the more admirable, but the confidence that the battle will be victorious in the long run, that you are fighting with the universe on your side, or rather that you are fighting on the side of God, may give a spiritual quality to your fight even more admirable than heroic despair. After all there will still be opportunities for heroism enough, if you seek them, in standing against the evil which seems, by all the appearances of the hour, to tower triumphant.

> To suffer woes which hope thinks infinite;
> To forgive wrongs darker than death or night;
> To defy power which seems omnipotent;
> To love and bear; to hope till hope creates
> From its own wreck the thing it contemplates;
> Neither to change, nor falter, nor repent;
> This, like thy glory, Titan, is to be
> Good, great and joyous, beautiful and free:
> This is alone Life, Joy, Empire and Victory!

It is true that the writer of those lines professed not to believe in a personal God; but Shelley's jubilant utterance was possible only because he did believe that the Ground of the Universe was spiritual in the sense of his hazy Platonism; Prometheus was to be ultimately *victorious*. We may question whether such a hope as Shelley entertained has any substance apart from belief in God. In any case, the fight for good, as Shelley saw it, was not a battle destined in the end to be a lost one in an indifferent universe. If you rule out the Christian confidence in the Power behind phenomena because it is nobler to fight without any supposition that you have the universe on the same side, then you must rule out Shelley's view of the heroic life too.

377

It is unquestionable that those human Figures who are generally recognized to be the most spiritually impressive, to begin with Jesus himself, do not show the heroism of despair, but a serenity of absolute confidence in the centre of their activity, a quiet and joy which is their commanding strength. Men have the option before them of two views of the ultimate ground of things, one that it is spiritual with a care for the values recognized by the human spirit, the other that it is some kind of physical law, or set of laws, wholly indifferent to values, whether it is in any sense like Mind or not; neither is a view of the universe capable of being demonstrated as a conclusive rational inference from phenomena; some men elect to choose the former hypothesis when they launch out into action, some elect to choose the latter. Why, it may be asked, without being shut up to it, should men choose the drearier hypothesis? One reason probably is that if you are going to take a hypothesis for action which goes beyond what can be rationally demonstrated, it seems less of a venture to suppose that behind physical law there is nothing but a blank than to suppose that there is something of so positive a character as God. To act on the hypothesis that the Ground of the Universe is God, when you have no conclusive proof that God exists, seems a more unwarrantable building on vain imagination than to act on the hypothesis of a blank when you have no conclusive proof of a blank. In the one case you fill the void with your fanciful idea of God; in the other case you simply leave a void. The negative hypothesis seems to be, as men say, the "safer" one.

I think that in this way of thought there is really a confusion between what holds good of a purely speculative problem, in which no question of action is involved, and what holds good of alternative hypotheses for action. In the case of a purely speculative problem, if no hypothesis is demonstrable, you can practise complete suspense of judgment. You can say that it is "safer" not to adopt any unproved supposition. The "danger" to be avoided—for the word "safer" of course points to some possible danger —is the danger of turning out to have been deceived. If you have withheld your belief from the unproved hypothesis you cannot turn out to have believed something untrue; you are uncommitted; you are in that respect safe.

But if you have to choose between two alternative hypotheses for action, you are no "safer" because the hypothesis you adopt is the negative one—because, that is to say, the existence of something being undemonstrated, you determine to disregard in action the possibility of its existing, to act as if it did not exist. Action commits you: suspense of judgment is no longer possible, or, rather, to suspend your judgment in theory is to commit yourself to the definitely negative judgment in practice. Thus it is just as possible for your action to turn out in the end to have been misdirected because it was based on the supposition that something did not exist which does exist, as for your action to turn out in the end to have been misdirected because it was based on the supposition that something existed which does not exist. If you have in practice to deal with a man and you have to act either on the hypothesis that he is trustworthy or on the hypothesis that he is not, you may, it is true, prove to have been deceived if you trust him and he turns out to be untrustworthy, but you may also prove to have made a mistake with unhappy consequences if you refuse to trust him and he turns out to be trustworthy. A man who has acted all his life on the hypothesis that the universe is governed by a good God may look foolish if it turns out that the universe outside man is wholly indifferent to values—though it may be asked to whom his foolishness will appear, since, on the atheistic hypothesis in its usual

379

form, the ingenuous believer will cease altogether to exist at death, and by the time that the non-existence of God is demonstrated, it is likely that he will have been in his grave for a good many ages and long forgotten by everybody—but equally a man who has acted all his life on the supposition that there is no God will look foolish if in the end God confronts him. In action there is no possibility of "safety" in the sense of security from the danger of turning out in the end to have been mistaken. And act we all of us must, pushed by the onward unarrestable movement of time: as Pascal said, whether we like it or not, *"il faut parier."*

Perhaps however when people think that to disregard in action the supposition of God's existing is "safer," it is not that they fail to recognize a possibility of mistake either way; it is that it seems a worse mistake to adopt the optimistic hypothesis and prove in the end mistaken, than to adopt the pessimistic hypothesis and prove in the end mistaken. It is, in their view, the man who has thought too well of the universe who would appear the more foolish if he turned out wrong, not the man who has not thought well enough of the universe. Should we say, though, in regard to our human relations, that it is in all cases a greater evil to have trusted someone who was untrustworthy than not to have trusted someone who was trustworthy? Would not the pain of the man who has been taken in by a rogue be less bitter than the pain which a man who had failed to trust a friend would feel, when ocular proofs that the friend had been trustworthy came to light and he recognized the true application of the saying: "Blessed are they that have not seen and yet have believed"?

It has been contended throughout this discussion that neither the hypothesis that the Power behind the Universe is a spiritual Power which cares for values nor the hypothesis that the universe is indifferent to values can be demonstrated, that both the believer and the atheist or agnostic act upon an unproved hypothesis, make a leap beyond experience. But if the statement were left at that, it would be open to two definite misconstructions. One misconstruction would be taking it to mean that the man's choice of a hypothesis to live by is purely arbitrary, in the sense that he has no reason at all for choosing it. All that has been asserted is that neither hypothesis can be demonstrated with logical necessity, as a proposition in mathematics can be demonstrated, or as a rational inference, regarding the existence of something unseen, made from something known, on the basis of a knowledge of the pattern of the universe. But because the ground on which a man acts does not reach mathematical certainty, and does not have conclusiveness of the same kind as a rational inference based on knowledge of the pattern, that does not mean that the man acts without any ground at all. If there were nothing at all in the world we know by experience and trustworthy report to point to a spiritual Reality behind phenomena, to God and to the permanence of the soul, then to adopt quite arbitrarily the hypothesis that God is and that the soul is not involved in material decay, simply because we find it pleasant to believe these things, would hardly be the proper act of a reasonable creature. But, as a matter of fact, there are many manifestations of Spirit in the world we know which do point to Spirit as being the supreme Reality behind.

The idea of the world so presented is congenial to reason in the sense in which reason desiderates a worthy end for all events, whether human actions or the existence of the universe. The relation of the universe as a whole to its Ground would then be analogous to the relation between the activity of finite spirit and its spiritual ground in the world we know, whenever we call that activity reasonable; and, although it cannot be proved that this analogy holds, it certainly makes a universe which gives man a greater satisfaction to contemplate—gives this satisfaction to man not as a lover of pleasure or comfort, of whatever kind the pleasure or comfort may be, but to man, as a reasonable being, who desires the special satisfaction of finding in the universe a correspondence to his own recognition of values.

It has to be acknowledged that great tracts of the world seem to point the other way. Outside finite spirit and its activities the course of the world does seem wholly indifferent to values. Science does not regard such an explanation as Socrates wanted given of the processes of the natural world, such an explanation as he complains of Anaxagoras for not giving, that the reason why things take the course they do is in order to realize some demonstrable *good*—as coming within its sphere of interest at all. No doubt when Science gets to the treatment of living things, there is a way in which teleological explanation comes in, but living things occupy an infinitesimal space in the universe. In the measureless time before life appeared on our small planet, through the measureless time after life on our planet has been extinguished, we see material masses whirl in space without any consciousness for which values could subsist. Those then who adopt the hypothesis that Reality, outside the momentary flash of spirit on this planet, is indifferent to values, and that the appearance of spirit must somehow be explained as due merely to an odd accident in the working of regular, but purposeless, material laws, have also facts to go upon. What then it seems to come to is this: The world we know presents us with two regions of fact—that of inanimate nature, in which the universe appears wholly indifferent to values, and that of life, which reaches its culmination in the spirit of man, and shows a progressive apprehension of value as approximation is made in animal life to that culmination, the higher values being apprehended by the human spirit alone. You may take either of these regions of fact as the basis of your hypothesis regarding ultimate Reality.

The first region, that of inanimate nature, shows an immense preponderance of material extension over the other, the manifestations of life and spirit being confined, so far as observation has yet gone, to an infinitesimal point of space and span of time. On the other hand, spirit may be regarded as having a dignity which no possible extension of material masses can countervail—Pascal's *roseau pensant*, and Coventry Patmore's declaration that he is not intimidated by the astronomical figures indicating the size of the material universe, because their effect is only to "make dirt cheap."[1] Which of those regions of fact a man takes as being the key to Reality is a matter of personal choice, in which what is deepest in him expresses itself.

And here again the attitude of a man to the universe may find a kind of analogy in the attitude of a man to some one of his fellow-men. It may be that we have to judge of someone's character, whose conduct, in great tracts of it, is a matter of routine and gives no indication of what is really in the man, how much he cares for goodness and truth, whether he feels affection for us or not. But there have been brief moments in which that which

---

[1] Not greatly moved with awe am I
To learn that we may spy
Five thousand firmaments beyond our own.
The best that's known
Of the heavenly bodies does them credit small . . .
The Universe, outside our living Earth,
Was all conceiv'd in the Creator's mirth,
Forecasting at the time Man's spirit deep,
To make dirt cheap.

(*Unknown Eros*, xviii.)

was in the man flashed out, it seemed, in some act, in some look. It is open to us to take those moments as showing us what he really is, and in some cases a trust afterwards unshakable is based upon a few crucial moments when two spirits, we believe, touched each other—moments of revelation. Or we may take the apparent indifference of his conduct in its predominant tracts as showing us what he is and judge him by those. Those who believe the Reality behind phenomena to be Spirit, to be God, hold that we see the character of that Reality in the manifestations of the human spirit, and since we see those manifestations in a scale of worth, some higher than others—a more perfect goodness and loveliness of character, a more ardent loyalty to truth, a richer genius in apprehending beauty and making beautiful things—it is as they rise in the scale, as they are brighter and purer, that they are for us more perfect manifestations of the character of the Supreme Spirit. For Christians the human spirit reaches its highest possible point in Christ, and for that reason the Christian Church believes that in Christ may be seen that for which the whole universe has come into existence.

I say advisedly in this context Christ, and not Jesus, because the Christian view does not confine the life of Christ to the life of Jesus of Nazareth, but regards it as continued in the Christian society. The full range of the Spirit could not be shown in the circumstances and the years of the earthly life of Jesus, but it may be shown, according to Christian doctrine, in the world-wide Community, as ultimately made perfect, the glorified Community which will manifest, without any obscuration by sin or earthly infirmity, all the potentialities of the spirit of man, the full riches of the life of Christ for which it is the vehicle. This may be regarded as what the apostle meant when he said that the ultimate end to which the world-process moved was the summing up of all things in Christ.[1]

I spoke just now of one misconception to be guarded against as being that the leap beyond experience was made, whether it was by the believer in God or by the disbeliever in God, from no ground of facts, and I have tried to explain how each of them bases his hypothesis on a certain part of the facts presented by the world we know, though on a different part. The other misconception may easily be suggested by the language hitherto used for short, about a man's "adopting" a hypothesis to live by. As a matter of psychological fact, it happens rarely, if ever, that a man comes to a consideration of the universe with a perfectly impartial mind and then calmly and deliberately adopts one of two or more possible hypotheses about it. In actual practice what I have called "adopting" a hypothesis could be more aptly described as adhering, after subsequent consideration, to a hypothesis which has come to rule a man's mind apart from any deliberate choice on his part. We might call it re-adopting a hypothesis. Any man who desires greatly to avoid believing things which are untrue, who wants to have some reason for his belief which he could present to another man, as a reason which all men thinking straight could find valid, will not rest simply in finding that a particular belief has laid hold of him. A man believes in God before he can say why he believes in God, but he will not go on believing in God if, being a rational man, he has brought the belief into connexion with other knowledge about the Universe and convinced himself that it is incompatible with some bit of Reality of which he is certain. If, however, after bringing his belief in God into connexion with other knowledge about the Universe, he finds the hold of the belief upon him unrelaxed, he will be able to point to

[1] ἀνακεφαλαιώσασθαι τὰ πάντα ἐν τῷ Χριστῷ. Eph. i. 10.

grounds which seem to justify his belief. He will be able "to give a reason for the faith that is in him."

It is highly improbable that anyone who had no belief in God was ever led to believe in God by any of the standard "proofs" of God's existence—the ontological, cosmological, teleological proof. They were thought of by men who already believed in God as considerations harmonizing their belief, for themselves, and for others, with a general view of the universe. It is, of course, a dogma of the Roman Church that the existence of God can be demonstrated by rational inference from visible phenomena. But no Roman Catholic could take this to mean that it can be demonstrated by arguments which are sure to be recognized by all men of normal understanding as cogent, for it is a plain fact of the world that there are many men of normal understanding who do *not* recognize the arguments put forward as cogent. Nobody who believes the dogma could take it in any other sense than that the arguments *ought to be* recognized as cogent, that if people were perfectly rational they would recognize them as cogent. If you already believe in God, then you will see everything that exists as existing because of the one Will which called the world into being, and so the cosmological argument will indicate this rational agreement between your belief and your view of the universe: you will see the order of the universe as directed to realize value in a supreme degree, and so the teleological argument will indicate rational agreement between your belief and your view of the universe. It is only, I think, in the sense of giving rational comfort to people who already believe in God that the standard arguments can be regarded as demonstrating the existence of God. What actually causes anyone to believe in God is direct perception of the Divine.

INDEX

389